"Menzies rightly reminds us that Pentecostals are people of both word and Spirit, all the more evangelical in mission because we are pentecostal in experience. That is our history and our grassroots identity, from which we are severed only at our own peril. This book's message is crucial at a time like this, when both some evangelicals and some Pentecostals seem reluctant to embrace our shared heritage and mission."

—CRAIG S. KEENER
Asbury Theological Seminary

"Here, a notable Pentecostal scribe . . . cuts a mediating path between extremes of fundamentalism and ecumenism to substantiate the essential *evangelical* nature of Pentecostalism ever since its origin. The book augments Menzies' earlier publications, firmly establishing him among leading Pentecostal theologians. . . . A Pentecostal missionary-author, you could say, after the order of Lesslie Newbigin."

—RUSSELL P. SPITTLER
Fuller Theological Seminary

"In Korea, Pentecostals have been at odds with evangelicals, particularly with regard to the work of the Spirit. Both groups are largely unaware of the close ties that unite them in their basic Christian beliefs. I am confident that *Christ-Centered* will help both parties better understand each other and how much they have in common."

—DONGSOO KIM
Pyeongtaek University

"Robert Menzies provides a convincing reminder of the relationship between evangelicalism and Pentecostalism. These overlapping Christ-centered movements, although shaped and reshaped by their cultural environments, remain the most vital force within global Christianity because of their powerful message of redemptive transformation and continuous concern for restoration of the dynamic dimension of the biblical faith in which the living God is active through the church for the renewal of society."

—PETER KUZMIC
Gordon-Conwell Theological Seminary

"Pentecostals are often described as 'people of the Spirit' because of our theology and practice of Spirit baptism. But baptism in the Holy Spirit itself is a ministry of Jesus. We are Spirit people, then, because we are Jesus people first. In this book, Robert P. Menzies argues that Pentecostalism's Christ-centered, Spirit-empowered perspective is rooted in evangelical soil, and he asks whether Pentecostals will continue reaping a gospel harvest if we try to plant on other theological grounds."

—GEORGE P. WOOD
Influence magazine

Christ-Centered

CHRIST-CENTERED

The Evangelical Nature of Pentecostal Theology

Robert P. Menzies

Foreword by George O. Wood

CASCADE *Books* • Eugene, Oregon

CHRIST-CENTERED
The Evangelical Nature of Pentecostal Theology

Copyright © 2020 Robert P. Menzies. All rights reserved. Except for brief quotations in critical publications or reviews, no part of this book may be reproduced in any manner without prior written permission from the publisher. Write: Permissions, Wipf and Stock Publishers, 199 W. 8th Ave., Suite 3, Eugene, OR 97401.

Cascade Books
An Imprint of Wipf and Stock Publishers
199 W. 8th Ave., Suite 3
Eugene, OR 97401

www.wipfandstock.com

PAPERBACK ISBN: 978-1-7252-6782-4
HARDCOVER ISBN: 978-1-7252-6783-1
EBOOK ISBN: 978-1-7252-6784-8

Cataloguing-in-Publication data:

Names: Menzies, Robert P., author. | Wood, George O., foreword writer.

Title: Christ-centered : the evangelical nature of pentecostal theology / Robert P. Menzies.

Description: Eugene, OR: Cascade Books, 2020 | Includes bibliographical references and index.

Identifiers: ISBN 978-1-7252-6782-4 (paperback) | ISBN 978-1-7252-6783-1 (hardcover) | ISBN 978-1-7252-6784-8 (ebook)

Subjects: LCSH: Pentecostalism. | Evangelicalism. | Bible—New Testament—Theology. | Jesus Christ—Biblical teaching. | Holy Spirit—Biblical teaching.

Classification: BR1644 M45 2020 (print) | BR1644 (ebook)

Manufactured in the U.S.A. OCTOBER 1, 2020

To the administration, faculty, students, and staff of Asia Pacific Theological Seminary (Baguio City, The Philippines), who exemplify what it means to be Evangelical and Pentecostal.

CONTENTS

Foreword by George O. Wood | ix
Acknowledgements | xiii
Introduction | xv

    Part I—Pentecostal Theology: Its Evangelical Origins | 1
Chapter 1—R. A. Torrey's Enduring Theological Legacy:
        The Pentecostal Movement | 3

    Part II—Pentecostal Theology: Its Evangelical Foundations | 37
Chapter 2—Baptism in the Holy Spirit: A Prophetic Empowering | 41
Chapter 3—Glossolalia: Paul's Perspective | 51
Chapter 4—Signs and Wonders: Celebrating God's Kingdom | 73

    Part III—Pentecostal Theology: Its Evangelical Trajectory | 89
Chapter 5—Jesus, Intimacy, and Language | 91
Chapter 6—Missional Spirituality: A Pentecostal Contribution
        to Spiritual Formation | 104

    Part IV—Pentecostal Theology: Its Evangelical Future | 119
Chapter 7—The Nature of Pentecostal Theology: A Response
        to Kärkkäinen and Yong | 121

Conclusion | 139
Appendix: Defining the Term, "Pentecostal" | 143
Bibliography | 149
Index of Names | 157
Index of Ancient Documents | 161

FOREWORD

IF YOU HAD TO describe Pentecostal theology and spirituality using only one Bible passage, what would it be?

Acts 2 is an obvious choice, insofar as it describes the foundational event that gives us Pentecostals our name. Zechariah 4:6 is another good choice. For decades, the Assemblies of God's *Pentecostal Evangel* carried "Not by might, nor by power, but by my spirit, saith the Lord of hosts" on its masthead. Then there is Hebrews 13:8, "Jesus Christ the same yesterday, and today, and forever," which older Pentecostals often inscribed on the walls of their sanctuaries.

All of these are good choices, of course, capturing something important about Pentecostalism. As former general superintendent of the Assemblies of God (USA), however, I can't help but think that Mark 16:15 holds pride of place. "Go ye into all the world, and preach the gospel to every creature" is inscribed on the cornerstone of the AG's national office in Springfield, Missouri. Evangelism is the first of four reasons for being listed in the AG's *Constitution and Bylaws*. The English word "gospel" translates the Greek word εὐαγγέλιον, better known to us by its Latin cognate: *evangel*, "good news." Insofar as Pentecostals are Spirit-filled Jesus people carrying on the mission Christ himself gave us, we are small-e evangelicals, i.e., "people of the gospel."

The crucial question Robert P. Menzies asks in this book is whether we are also big-E Evangelicals, a word that came to describe the eighteenth-century, trans-Atlantic revival movement associated with George Whitefield, John Wesley, and Jonathan Edwards.

FOREWORD

According to David Bebbington's famous quadrilateral, Evangelicals are characterized by "*conversionism*, the belief that lives need to be changed; *activism*, the expression of the gospel in effort; *biblicism*, a particular regard for the Bible; and what may be called *crucicentrism*, stress on the sacrifice of Christ on the cross."

Menzies' own definition, consistent with Bebbington's, emphasizes "(1) the authority of the Bible; (2) the importance of a personal relationship with Christ, who is understood to be the Lord and unique Savior of the world; and (3) that sharing the 'good news' of Jesus with non-Christians (evangelism) is thus a central aspect of the Christian life."

Defined either way, Pentecostals are clearly Evangelicals. Indeed, Menzies' core argument is simply that "the term, Pentecostal, is not only compatible with the adjective, Evangelical, but incomprehensible apart from it. Thus, to be Pentecostal is, by definition, to be Evangelical."

Unfortunately, some academics obscure the Evangelical identity of Pentecostalism, either by overemphasizing the multipolar roots of the Pentecostal movement or by lamenting the baleful influence of American neo-Evangelicalism on Pentecostals. Granted, Pentecostalism's origin story is more complex than "It started on Azusa Street." And we had (and continue to have) any number of differences theologically and practically with other Evangelicals, such as differences over what I like to call "The Four Cs": Calvinism, cessationism, complementarianism, and the character of baptism in the Holy Spirit. But those differences are differences among one family, not between two families.

Menzies also highlights a troubling move toward inclusivism among some Pentecostal theologians. What is inclusivism? It is this, in the words of one of its Pentecostal advocates: "Religions are neither accidents of history nor encroachments on divine providence but are, in various ways, instruments of the Holy Spirit working out the divine purposes in the world and that the unevangelized, if saved at all, are saved through the work of Christ by the Spirit (even if mediated through the religious beliefs and practices available to them)." What worries Menzies, and what worries me, is that inclusivism is ultimately incompatible with the church's Mark 16:15 mission. It's incompatible with the gospel.

So, mark this Pentecostal down, together with Robert P. Menzies, as a firm Evangelical. Because Christ is the same yesterday, today, and forever; because he has poured out his Spirit on all flesh to empower them to bear witness for him; and because any forward movement in the gospel comes by means of God's Spirit, not our power, let us move forward boldly, sharing the gospel with every creature!

George O. Wood

George O. Wood is chairman of the World Assemblies of God Fellowship, global co-chair of Empowered21, and former general superintendent of the Assemblies of God (USA).

ACKNOWLEDGEMENTS

A FEW YEARS AGO an Evangelical seminary professor in Hong Kong asked me with genuine concern if Pentecostals were growing hostile towards the Evangelical movement. I was puzzled by this question and asked what prompted him to ask it. I had always felt that the strong bonds that tied together the Pentecostal and Evangelical movements were widely recognized. My professor friend cited the tone and content of a number of publications associated with the Society for Pentecostal Studies as the reason for his concern. I assured him that the vast majority of grassroots Pentecostals strongly identified with Evangelical values. In a very real sense, this conversation was the beginning of this book. My friend's perceptions motivated me to write several of the lectures or articles that have become chapters in this book.

Chapter 1, "R. A. Torrey's Enduring Theological Legacy: The Pentecostal Movement," was produced for the 2018 annual meeting of the Evangelical Theological Society, which convened in Denver (November 14–16, 2018). I would like to thank Dr. James Hernando who, since I was in China at the time, presented this material in my stead at the conference. This material has not been previously published.

Chapter 2, "Baptism in the Spirit: A Prophetic Empowering," was originally presented as one of the three special lectures that I gave for the Annual Colloquium at Continental Theological Seminary in Brussels, Belgium (March 25–27, 2013).

Chapter 3, "Glossolalia: Paul's Perspective," utilizes material from chapter 7 of my book, *Speaking in Tongues: Jesus and the Apostolic Church as Models for the Church Today*. This material has been revised for this publication.

Much of the material in chapter 4, "Signs and Wonders: Celebrating God's Kingdom," was originally published in chapter 4 of my book, *The*

ACKNOWLEDGEMENTS

Language of the Spirit: Interpreting and Translating Charismatic Terms. A Chinese translation of this book, which deals with translation issues in the *Chinese Union Version* of the New Testament, is available from the Synergy Institute of Leadership (www.silhk.org; info@silhk.org). The material from *The Language of the Spirit* has been adapted and expanded for this publication.

Chapter 5, "Jesus, Intimacy, and Language," is almost entirely new material that has not been previously published. A short section which discusses Paul's descriptions of glossolalia as doxological prayer draws upon material found in my *Speaking in Tongues* (pp. 162–63).

Chapter 6, "Missional Spirituality: A Pentecostal Contribution to Spiritual Formation," was originally presented as a special lecture at Pyeongtaek University in South Korea, November 1, 2012. Some material from this oral presentation appeared in *Pentecost* (pp. 117–22) and later the entire work, in a slightly altered form, was published in the *Festschriften* for Wonsuk and Julie Ma by editor Teresa Chai, *A Theology of the Spirit in Doctrine and Demonstration: Essays in Honor of Wonsuk and Julie Ma* (pp. 39–56). This material is used here with permission.

Chapter 7, "The Nature of Pentecostal Theology," was originally published in the *Journal of Pentecostal Theology* 26 (2017) 196–213.

I am grateful to the many people associated with the various academic institutions, publishers, and journals named above for their encouragement to contribute to the current theological discussion, particularly as it impacts Pentecostals and Evangelicals. They have helped make this writing project both possible and a joy.

INTRODUCTION

THIS BOOK IS, ABOVE all, a call to remember. It is my attempt to challenge a surprising but virulent form of amnesia that appears to be infecting, with increasing vigor, significant sectors of the Christian community. Whether it be the disciples of John MacArthur or other streams of cessationist, fundamentalist Christianity on the one hand,[1] or Pentecostal scholars in the academy on the other,[2] there is a noted tendency to forget the strong links that have always bound together Pentecostal believers with their Evangelical brother and sisters. The fact is undeniable. Increasingly, many, both within the Pentecostal movement and without, have forgotten the strong Evangelical convictions that birthed the Pentecostal movement and continue to form its foundation.

This amnesia or, perhaps more accurately, this *reluctance to acknowledge* the Evangelical nature of the Pentecostal movement, is striking for two reasons. First, it is evident that the Pentecostal movement sprang from roots planted deeply in Evangelical soil. In this book, with the term *Evangelical*, I refer to those Christians who affirm: (1) the authority of the Bible; (2) the importance of a personal relationship with Christ, who is understood to be the Lord and unique Savior of the world; and (3) that sharing the "good news" of Jesus with non-Christians (evangelism) is thus a central aspect of the Christian life.[3]

---

1. For a harsh, cessationist perspective, see MacArthur, *Strange Fire*. See also the response offered by over twenty continuationist scholars in Graves, *Strangers to Fire*.

2. Daniel Isgrigg documents the current trend within the Pentecostal academy for scholars to characterize Pentecostalism's affinity for Evangelical values as a betrayal of the former's true identity (Isgrigg, "Pentecostal Evangelical Church," 8–10).

3. My summary is consistent with David Bebbington's widely cited four-point definition: "There are four qualities that have been the special marks of Evangelical religion: *conversionism*, the belief that lives need to be changed; *activism*, the expression of the

INTRODUCTION

I understand the term *Pentecostal* to refer to those Christians who believe that the book of Acts provides a model for the contemporary church and, on this basis, encourage every believer to experience a baptism in the Spirit (Acts 2:4), understood as an empowering for mission distinct from regeneration that is marked by speaking in tongues, and who affirm that "signs and wonders," including all of the gifts listed in 1 Corinthians 12:8–10, are to characterize the life of the church today.

In this way, Pentecostals might be helpfully distinguished from a number of related, but different groups within the Christian family:[4]

Neo-Pentecostal: a Christian who agrees and acts in accordance with all of the Pentecostal tenets listed above except the affirmation that speaking in tongues serves as a normative sign for Spirit baptism.

Charismatic: a Christian who believes that all of the gifts listed in 1 Corinthians 12:8–10, including prophecy, tongues, and healing, are available for the church today; but, rejects the affirmation that baptism in the Spirit (Acts 2:4) is an empowering for mission distinct from regeneration.

Non-Charismatic: a Christian who rejects the affirmation that baptism in the Spirit (Acts 2:4) is an empowering for mission distinct from regeneration and who also rejects the validity of at least one or more of the gifts of the Spirit listed in 1 Corinthians 12:8–10 for the church today.

It should be noted that all of the categories listed above are compatible with the term, "Evangelical."[5] In fact, the central thesis of this book is that Pentecostals are, by definition, Evangelicals in the broad sense of the term outlined above. Pentecostals share with their Evangelical brothers and sisters the core convictions that shape and define the global Evangelical family.[6] Indeed, the Pentecostal movement, with its emphasis on a baptism

gospel in effort; *biblicism*, a particular regard for the Bible; and what may be called *crucicentrism*, stress on the sacrifice of Christ on the cross" (Bebbington, *Evangelicalism in Modern Britain*, 2–3).

4. For more on definitions, see the Appendix, "Defining the Term, 'Pentecostal.'"

5. When one intends to speak more broadly of all of the groups that in some way feature the Spirit's work through spiritual gifts today, I feel the terms "renewalist" or "continuationist" are particularly appropriate and useful.

6. Although, by definition, I argue that Pentecostals are Evangelicals, throughout this book as a matter of convenience I will often use the term "Evangelical" to refer to non-Pentecostal Evangelicals. The context will clearly determine whether my use of the term includes Pentecostals or simply refers to the non-Pentecostal wing of the Evangelical

in the Spirit that empowers believers to bear witness for Christ, is incomprehensible without them. From the outset, it was clear that the Pentecostal movement was thoroughly Evangelical in character.[7] The founding leaders of the Pentecostal movement all shared these core Evangelical convictions. In chapter 1 we will examine in more detail the strong points of theological congruence that connected the nascent Evangelical movement, and particularly its early Fundamentalist leaders, with the Pentecostal movement that burst onto the world scene with the dramatic Azusa Street Revival in Los Angeles (1906–9).

A second reason that the "amnesia" noted above is so surprising is that the vast majority of contemporary Pentecostal denominations, churches, and believers remain solidly Evangelical. Virtually all of them affirm the doctrinal points and actively engage in the practices that are typically associated with the Evangelical movement noted above.[8] Of course, minor points of difference, emphasis, and ethos can be identified when any church or tradition is compared with another. This is true of all of the denominations that comprise the larger Evangelical family of churches. Nevertheless, the strong doctrinal unity that unites these churches should not be missed. The Pentecostal churches, which now represent the majority of the Evangelical Christian community in many countries around the globe, are no exception. When the broad definitions noted above are affirmed, it is evident that Pentecostals are Evangelicals in doctrine and practice. Those who would seek to argue otherwise either do not understand the Pentecostal movement or seek to transform it into an image of their own creation.[9]

movement.

7. Isgrigg demonstrates that the Assemblies of God (AG), the largest Pentecostal denomination in the world, from its earliest days, understood its identity as both Pentecostal and Evangelical. On the basis of his analysis of the first decade of the AG's existence (1914–27), Isgrigg rejects the notion that the AG was "'co-opted' by evangelicalism or fundamentalism;" rather, the AG constituency "saw themselves as a subset of a larger evangelical family that believed in an additional doctrine of the baptism in the Holy Spirit" (Isgrigg, "Pentecostal Evangelical Church," 11).

8. Note the doctrinal statement of the Pentecostal World Fellowship, which can be accessed at www.pentecostalworldfellowship.org. Wikipedia states, "The Pentecostal World Fellowship is a fellowship of Evangelical Pentecostal churches and denominations from across the world."

9. See, for example, Castelo, *Pentecostalism as a Christian Mystical Tradition*. Castelo argues that Pentecostals are not Evangelicals, in spite of the apparent connections in origins and ethos that these two groups share. On the contrary, Pentecostalism is best understood as a form of Christian mysticism. Castelo argues that Pentecostals, unlike Evangelicals who are children of modernism, operate with a post-modern epistemological

INTRODUCTION

We shall seek to support this thesis—that the Pentecostal movement is solidly Evangelical and cannot be understood apart from these core Evangelical convictions—in the chapters that follow. After the initial chapter which highlights the historical and theological connections between the Evangelical and Pentecostal movements, the outline of the book follows the core Evangelical convictions enumerated above. These include an emphasis on: the authority of the Bible; the importance of a personal relationship with Jesus Christ as Lord and Savior; and a commitment to sharing the gospel with the "lost" (Luke 19:10).

So, in Part II (chapters 2–4) we shall explore the emphasis on biblical authority and, more specifically, the biblical foundations of the distinctive doctrines that mark the Pentecostal movement. This section will demonstrate that Pentecostal faith and practice flow from the Bible. Pentecostal Christians are often pictured as highly emotional and experientially driven, but this caricature misses the fact that Pentecostals are fundamentally "people of the book." Although Pentecostals encourage spiritual experience, they do so with a constant eye to Scripture. The Bible, and particularly the book of Acts, fosters and shapes Pentecostal experience. The Pentecostal movement started in a Bible school and has birthed thousands of Bible schools around the world. The Bible-driven nature of the Pentecostal movement must not be missed.[10]

Additionally, it should be noted that Pentecostal theologians have made significant contributions to the Evangelical approach to and understanding

---

orientation that views experience rather than rational thought as most important for knowledge of and relationship with God. Unfortunately, Castelo does not seriously engage Pentecostal history to support his thesis. In fact, he virtually acknowledges that this description of Pentecostals as mystics is more his vision of where Pentecostals should go than an accurate historical assessment (p. xix). Castelo also fails to treat Evangelicalism seriously and simply cherry-picks representative people and quotations in order to paint his portrait of Evangelicals as sterile rationalists. Castelo proceeds to reject and reinterpret core, distinctive doctrines of the Pentecostal movement. What is left is a vague definition of Pentecostals as experientially-oriented mystics. In this way Castelo not only undermines essential features of Pentecostal theology, he also seriously misrepresents Evangelical belief and practice. In reality, grassroots Pentecostals are far more rational and biblical than Castelo admits and Evangelicals are much more experiential in their faith and devotion that Castelo's caricature allows.

10. Isgrigg's research challenges the notion that "the theology of early Pentecostals was characterized by orality and narrative," at least within the AG. "Considerable attention was given to both defining and defending doctrine from the very beginning" ("Pentecostal Evangelical Church," 12, both quotes). See also Lee, "In the Beginning There Was a Theology."

INTRODUCTION

of Scripture.[11] For previous generations of conservative scholars, Evangelical theology was largely Pauline theology. The prevailing attitude, shaped by and enshrined in the hermeneutic of the past, was that we go to Paul for theology (since his epistles are didactic in character); the Gospels and Acts simply provide the raw historical data for this theological reflection. This inevitably flattened the canon for us and, while perhaps it made talk of the unity of Scripture a bit easier, it also blinded us to the full breadth and richness of the biblical witness.

More recently Evangelical scholars, with many Pentecostals often leading the way, have emphasized the theological value and significance of biblical narratives, especially the Gospels and the book of Acts.[12] This fresh emphasis has opened new windows for Pentecostal scholars and enabled us to experience fresh winds of theological reflection. Pentecostal scholars and the Pentecostal tradition are demonstrating how Evangelical theology might be enriched by a more holistic approach, one that gives full voice to the biblical narratives and thus the entire canon of Scripture.[13] As a result, Pentecostal theology and Pentecostal churches are flourishing. This book, then, seeks to illustrate this exciting development.

Evangelicals are defined not only by their commitment to the Bible, but also by their emphasis on a personal relationship with Jesus Christ, the resurrected and living Lord. This emphasis on encountering and experiencing Christ as Lord and Savior also brings us to the center of Pentecostal spirituality. At its heart, the Pentecostal movement is not Spirit-centered, but rather Christ-centered. The work of the Spirit, as Pentecostals understand it, centers on exalting and bearing witness to the Lordship of Christ. Pentecostals echo the apostolic message: Jesus is Lord. Jesus is the one who baptizes in the Spirit. As we shall see, the core doctrines of the Pentecostal movement were often summed up in the fourfold gospel: Jesus is the Savior, Baptizer (in the Spirit), Healer, and coming King.

With our Evangelical cousins, we Pentecostals also affirm that faith in Christ involves a personal relationship with the resurrected Lord, Jesus Christ. Indeed, in Jesus we enter into an intimate, filial relationship with God. John puts it this way, we become the sons and daughters of God (John

---

11. For a good example of this influence see Craig S. Keener's fine book, *Spirit Hermeneutics*.

12. For more on this see chapter 2 of Menzies and Menzies, *Spirit and Power*.

13. For bibliographic data the interested reader might begin with Mittelstadt, *Reading Luke-Acts in the Pentecostal Tradition*.

1:12). Out of this intimate understanding of our relationship with the Father flows a new language of prayer and worship, language which expresses our sense of "sonship" with God. Jesus modeled this kind of prayer and worship (Luke 11:1–13; cf. 10:21) and Paul beautifully describes it (Rom 8:15–16; Gal 4:6–7). In chapter 5, "Jesus, Intimacy, and Language," we put forward a Pentecostal understanding and appropriation of this New Testament emphasis on the intimate relationship with God and, accordingly, the new language of prayer and worship, made possible and modeled by Jesus.

This new language of prayer and worship also calls the church to expand its understanding of God's great mission and to engage in the global quest to give every person on this planet the opportunity to hear the gospel and worship Jesus in their own mother tongue. Luther's translation of the Bible into German and his revolutionary use of German, the language of the people, rather than a special "religious" language (Latin) in hymns and worship represents an important initial step in this regard. Pentecostals take this emphasis on personal relationship with God in Christ one step further. They affirm that, as a result of their relationship with Christ, believers may also experience Spirit-inspired prayer and worship that is uttered in the language of heaven (1 Cor 13:1). This experience too has significant missiological implications.

Since Pentecostals, like Evangelicals, believe that the gospel centers on a call to enter into a personal relationship with Jesus Christ, they also highlight the importance of evangelism. Active participation in God's great mission, which prioritizes the call to repent, receive God's gracious gift of forgiveness, and become a disciple of Jesus, is not optional for Evangelicals. It is central to the Christian life. Pentecostals also stress the inextricable link between discipleship and missions. In fact, we shall argue in chapter 6, "Missional Spirituality," that Pentecostals, with their fresh reading of Luke–Acts, offer important theological insight into this missiological understanding of discipleship.

Finally, I conclude with chapter 7 by pointing the reader towards what I believe is the path that will lead Pentecostals to a bright future. In spite of calls to the contrary, I am convinced that the Pentecostal movement can fulfill its divine purpose only by holding firmly to its Evangelical heritage. This is the case because the core Evangelical convictions that have shaped Pentecostal praxis flow from the apostolic model found in the book of Acts. We must never forget this fact nor lose sight of this apostolic model. As a Chinese house church leader some years ago declared, "Acts is the pattern

INTRODUCTION

for the mission of the church. If our church does not follow the path of the early church, we will lose our way."[14]

This book, then, is a call to remember. In so doing, we will surely find our way.

---

14. My March 27, 2014 interview with Uncle Zheng of the *Zhong Hua Meng Fu* Church.

Part I

PENTECOSTAL THEOLOGY
Its Evangelical Origins

Chapter 1

R. A. TORREY'S ENDURING THEOLOGICAL LEGACY

The Pentecostal Movement

AN INFLUENTIAL AUTHOR AND editor of numerous volumes of *The Fundamentals* (1910–15) and the superintendent of both the Moody Bible Institute and the Bible Institute of Los Angeles, R. A. Torrey (1856–1928) was without question one of the most significant leaders of what is now termed the Fundamentalist movement.[1] Indeed, when it is also remembered that from 1902–6 Torrey circled the globe conducting huge, evangelistic meetings unrivaled in size at that time and that his many books and pamphlets remain wildly popular among conservative Evangelicals, R. A. Torrey might with good reason in Christian circles be called, the Father of Fundamentalism. Yet, in spite of his impressive pedigree and unparalleled influence, in this chapter I will argue that Torrey's most lasting and significant legacy is not to be found in the Fundamentalist movement. In fact, as we shall see, the Fundamentalist movement rejected significant aspects of Torrey's message and hermeneutic. Torrey's true, enduring theological legacy is to be found in a movement that was just taking shape at the time of his death in 1928, the Pentecostal movement. Although Torrey himself largely misunderstood and, at least at first sight, rejected this movement, it is nonetheless his most faithful and significant theological heir.

---

1. According to John Fea, the term, "Fundamentalist," was not used until 1920 (Fea, "Power from on High in an Age of Ecclesiastical Impotence," 24).

PART I: PENTECOSTAL THEOLOGY

My case for viewing Torrey as the Father of the Pentecostal rather than Fundamentalist movement will be presented in four parts: first, we shall review Torrey's understanding of that cardinal Pentecostal doctrine, the baptism with the Holy Spirit; second, we will examine Torrey's approach to Scripture, his hermeneutic; third, we will analyze Torrey's response to the Azusa Street Revival (1906–9), the catalyst to "the most successful social movement of the past century;"[2] and finally, we will highlight Torrey's remarkable, if often unrecognized, impact on the Pentecostal movement, particularly in its formative stages.

TORREY'S UNDERSTANDING OF BAPTISM WITH THE HOLY SPIRIT

Several years ago while I was browsing through the books housed in the Alliance Bible Seminary's library, located on Hong Kong's beautiful Cheung Chau island, I ran across R. A. Torrey's *The Person and Work of the Holy Spirit* (1910). As a Pentecostal, I was aware that Torrey and other Gilded Age Evangelicals, such as A. J. Gordon and A. B. Simpson, frequently spoke of the baptism with the Holy Spirit. However, I had never closely examined what Torrey actually said. So, when I saw the title of this volume, worn with age but still visible, it piqued my interest. I pulled the book off the shelf and began to read. The more I read, the more amazed I became. R. A. Torrey's description of baptism with the Holy Spirit sounded eerily similar to my own assessment offered in various books and periodicals. I felt as if I was reading my own words, my own thoughts put to page. Clearly, I had found a kindred spirit.

Torrey's perspective is perhaps most clearly presented in his short book, *The Baptism with the Holy Spirit* (1895), but similar descriptions appear in his later books, *The Person and Work of the Holy Spirit* (1910) and *The Holy Spirit: Who He Is, and What He Does* (1927), as well as his other writings. Torrey's views on this matter did not change over the course of his life and ministry in spite of considerable pressure to modify them or change his language. The title of Torrey's main biography, *R. A. Torrey: Apostle of Certainty*, captures well Torrey's confident, unambiguous, and direct approach.[3] Torrey is anything if not clear and his perspective is not difficult to summarize.

2. Jenkins, *Next Christendom*, 8.
3. Martin, *Apostle of Certainty*.

Torrey begins his discussion of baptism with the Holy Spirit by noting that "there are a number of designations in the Bible for this one experience."[4] Significantly, all of the terms and examples that he provides are found in Luke–Acts: "filled with the Holy Ghost" (Acts 2:4), "the promise of the Father" (Luke 24:49), "power from on high" (Luke 24:49), "the gift" (Acts 10:45), "to fall upon" (Acts 10:44), and "to receive" (Acts 10:47) "are all equivalent to 'baptized with the Holy Ghost'" (Acts 1:5; 11:16).[5]

Torrey then moves to the heart of his description of baptism with the Holy Spirit by asserting three affirmations.

A Definite Experience

First, Torrey declares that *"the baptism with the Holy Spirit is a definite experience* which one may know whether he has received or not."[6] Again, Torrey draws upon stories from Luke–Acts to support this statement (Luke 24:49; Acts 19:2–6). Yet one cannot help but see that this judgment is also supported by his own experience and that of other influential leaders of his day. Charles Finney, D. L. Moody, and R. A. Torrey all spoke of powerful experiences of the Spirit, moments when they were "baptized with the Holy Spirit," with the result that their lives and ministries were dramatically changed. Moody, keenly aware of his lack of power and challenged by the prayers and proddings of two Free Methodist ladies, was baptized with the Spirit in 1871. Moody told Torrey that this experience was so overwhelming that he "had to ask God to withhold His hand, lest he die on the very spot for joy."[7]

Although as Marsden notes, Torrey was "known to distrust excessive emotion,"[8] he did not shy away from speaking of his own experience. Torrey describes coming "to the place where I saw that I had no right to preach until I was definitely baptized with the Holy Ghost."[9] He declared to a friend that he would not enter the pulpit again "until I have been baptized with the Holy Spirit and know it." Torrey then shut himself up in his study and on his knees prayed fervently, asking God to baptize him with the Holy

---

4. Torrey, *Baptism*, 13.
5. Torrey, *Baptism*, 13–14.
6. Torrey, *Baptism*, 14 (italics his).
7. Marsden, *Fundamentalism*, 78.
8. Marsden, *Fundamentalism*, 130.
9. Torrey, *Holy Spirit*, 198.

Spirit. Several days passed and his prayers had not been answered. He was tempted to consider what might happen if Sunday came and he still had not received the promise. Yet he resolved not to preach until he had received power from on high. "But," Torrey writes, "Sunday did not come before the blessing came."[10] It happened in a manner quite different from what he expected. "It was a very quiet moment, one of the most quiet moments I ever knew.... God simply said to me, not in any audible voice, but in my heart, 'It's yours. Now go and preach'.... I went and preached, and I have been a new minister from that day to this."[11]

Torrey would later have a more emotional, dramatic encounter. He was sitting in his office when, as he tells it, "I was struck from my chair on to the floor and I found myself shouting... 'glory to God, glory to God, glory to God.'" Torrey states that he could not stop shouting. "I tried to stop, but it was just as if some other power than my own was moving my jaws." Finally, after he was able to pull himself together, he went and told his wife what had happened. It was clearly a powerful, dramatic experience. Nevertheless, Torrey insisted that this was not the moment when he was baptized with the Holy Spirit. That experience took place earlier and was the result of his "simple faith in the naked Word of God."[12]

Torrey's doctrine and his experience at this point raise a crucial question. If baptism with the Holy Spirit is a distinct, definable experience, how will we know when we have experienced it? Torrey's insistence that we must receive it through "simple faith" in God's promises, an emphasis which runs throughout his writings, seems to run counter to his affirmation that baptism with the Holy Spirit is a definite experience. There is a tension here: Do we simply accept that we have received the promise after our prayer of petition? Or do we press on until we experientially know that we have received the gift? Torrey seems to affirm the latter, but he never clearly delineates the nature of this experience. This tension between acceptance by faith and pressing through for empirical evidence (a definite experience) in Torrey's theology never seems to be resolved.

---

10. Torrey, *Holy Spirit*, 198.
11. Torrey, *Holy Spirit*, 198–99.
12. Torrey, *Holy Spirit*, 199–200.

Separate and Distinct from Regeneration

According to Torrey, baptism with the Holy Spirit is not only a definite experience, it is also "*a work of the Holy Spirit separate and distinct from His regeneration work.*"[13] Torrey did not deny the Holy Spirit's work in regeneration, he simply insisted that "to be regenerated by the Holy Spirit is one thing; to be baptized with the Holy Spirit is something different."[14] Again Torrey's affirmation here is rooted in his reading of the book of Acts. He points to Jesus' promise in Acts 1:5, "in a few days you will be baptized with the Holy Spirit," as a promise uttered to disciples who were "already regenerated."[15] In similar fashion, the Samaritan Pentecost (Acts 8:12–16) shows clearly that "one may be . . . a regenerate man, and yet not have the baptism with the Holy Spirit."[16]

With these statements, Torrey echoes the theology and experience of his mentor, D. L. Moody, and a host of other nineteenth-century Christian leaders. The groundwork for distinguishing baptism with the Holy Spirit from conversion and regeneration was actually laid earlier by Wesley's successor, John Fletcher. Donald Dayton argues that while John Wesley was reluctant to connect baptism with the Holy Spirit to sanctification for fear of undermining its connection to conversion, John Fletcher was not. Fletcher was much more willing to use Pentecostal terminology with respect to sanctification and thus to link Spirit baptism with a post-conversion moment of entire sanctification.[17] Dayton also notes that this shift of emphasis from 'Spirit baptism and conversion' in Wesley's thought to 'Spirit baptism and sanctification' in the writings of Fletcher was occasioned by a shift in the exegetical foundations. "It is a remarkable fact that, in spite of Wesley's commitment to a 'restoration' of the life of the early church, he only infrequently refers to the Book of Acts."[18] Fletcher, on the other hand, "brings the Book of Acts into a new prominence."[19] Dayton concludes, "Thus we

---

13. Torrey, *Baptism*, 16 (italics his). Torrey also describes the baptism with the Holy Spirit as a "second blessing" (*Baptism*, 18).
14. Torrey, *Baptism*, 16.
15. Torrey, *Baptism*, 16.
16. Torrey, *Baptism*, 17.
17. Dayton, *Roots*, 48–54; Dayton, "Doctrine of the Baptism of the Holy Spirit," 116.
18. Dayton, *Roots*, 52.
19. Dayton, *Roots*, 53.

may detect between Wesley and Fletcher a significant shift . . . from a basically Pauline or Johannine orientation to a Lukan one."[20]

This tendency to speak of baptism with the Holy Spirit with reference to a post-conversion experience gains momentum in Holiness circles in the later half of the nineteenth century. A number of prominent revivalists of this period, especially those influenced by the Reformed tradition, also began to emphasize Pentecostal themes and terminology. Charles G. Finney, Dwight L. Moody, A. J. Gordon, and A. B. Simpson all spoke of a baptism with the Holy Spirit distinct from conversion.[21] Nevertheless, a crucial question remained largely unanswered. What was the true purpose or result of baptism with the Holy Spirit? Although since Fletcher and increasingly in Holiness circles in the nineteenth century the term had been associated with an experience of sanctification, the biblical evidence for this interpretation was minimal at best. The more the revivalists noted above spoke of Pentecost and a baptism with the Holy Spirit, the more they were drawn to Luke's two-volume work. Increasingly, this group began to describe the baptism with the Holy Spirit as a post-conversion empowering that enabled its recipient to minister effectively as well as to overcome sin. This emphasis on "power for service" sat in uneasy tension with the Holiness focus on "purity."

Thus, when R. A. Torrey published his *Baptism with the Holy Spirit* in 1895, his presentation of Spirit baptism as a definite experience, distinct from conversion was not unique. Rather, it clearly built on an established and growing theological tradition. Yet Torrey's singular contribution to the discussion becomes evident with his next affirmation.

Always Connected with Witness and Service

Torrey was unequivocal when it came to the purpose of the baptism with the Holy Spirit. "*The baptism with the Holy Spirit,*" Torrey declared, "*is always connected with testimony and service.*"[22] While most of his contemporaries suggested that baptism with the Holy Spirit was at least partially connected to sanctification, Torrey would not be diverted from what he felt was the clear teaching of the book of Acts. "Look carefully at every passage in which the baptism with the Holy Spirit is mentioned and you

---

20. Dayton, *Roots*, 53.
21. Dayton, *Roots*, 100–108.
22. Torrey, *Baptism*, 17 (italics his).

will see it is connected with and is for the purpose of testimony and service (for example, Acts 1:5, 8; 2:4; 4:31, 33)."[23] Furthermore, Torrey noted that while "there is a work of the Holy Spirit of such a character that the believer is 'made . . . free from the laws of sin and death' (Rom 8:2)," he emphatically declared, "But this is not the baptism with the Spirit; neither is it the *eradication* of a sinful nature . . . it is something that must be momentarily maintained."[24] Repeatedly, Torrey drives home his point, "The baptism with the Holy Spirit is not for the purpose of cleansing from sin, but for the purpose of empowering for service."[25]

The specificity and clarity of Torrey's vision sets him apart from all of his contemporaries.[26] As we have noted, many others spoke of baptism with the Holy Spirit as a definite experience, distinct from conversion. But, almost without exception, these colleagues connected this experience in some manner with sanctification. This is true of Charles G. Finney, A. J. Gordon, and A. B. Simpson.[27] The one possible exception is D. L. Moody, but Moody did not present his own views on the matter in a clear, reasoned, and systematic manner. Indeed, Dayton notes that Moody was "reluctant to speak openly of [his own] experience,"[28] although Moody did frequently encourage Torrey to preach and teach on this topic.[29] This latter point suggests that Moody stood in general agreement with Torrey's more narrow, focused understanding of baptism with the Holy Spirit.

Torrey did qualify his *"power for service"*[30] understanding of Spirit baptism in one way. He acknowledged that "this power will not manifest itself in precisely the same way in each individual."[31] Here Torrey departs from his normal exegetical foundation, Luke–Acts, and shifts to Paul's discussion of gifts of the Spirit in 1 Corinthians 12. Torrey points to Paul's

23. Torrey, *Baptism*, 17–18.

24. Torrey, *Baptism*, 19.

25. Torrey, *Baptism*, 18, and also again on p. 19.

26. Gilbertson, *Baptism of the Holy Spirit*, 197: with reference to the impact or sign of Spirit Baptism, Gilbertson writes, "Others [in contrast to Moody and Torrey]. . .tended to focus on the believer's newfound ability to lead a holy life."

27. Gilbertson, *Baptism of the Holy Spirit*, 145–92; Gresham, *Charles G. Finney's Doctrine*, 86.

28. Dayton, "Doctrine of the Baptism of the Holy Spirit," 121.

29. Martin, *Apostle of Certainty*, 116, and Marsden, *Fundamentalism*, 79.

30. Torrey, *Baptism*, 20: "The baptism with the Holy Spirit imparts power, power for service."

31. Torrey, *Baptism*, 20.

emphasis on the diversity of gifts (1 Cor 12:4, 8–11) and notes that the Holy Spirit "will impart to us the power that will qualify us for the field He has chosen [for us]."[32] In Torrey's view, not all are called to be preachers, evangelists, or missionaries. However, all are called to bear witness for Christ and serve in various ways. If we are to fulfill God's purposes for our lives and serve effectively, we need to be baptized with the Holy Spirit. For "while the power that the baptism with the Holy Spirit brings manifests itself in different ways in different individuals, *there will always be power.*"[33]

Torrey's emphasis on Spirit baptism as the source of diverse gifts led him to reject speaking in tongues as its normative sign. Torrey writes:

> In my early study of the baptism with the Holy Spirit, I noticed that in the Scripture, in many instances, those who were so baptized 'spoke in tongues.' The question came often to my mind, 'If one is baptized with the Holy Spirit, will he not speak with tongues?' But I saw no one so speaking and I often wondered, 'Is there anyone today who actually is baptized with the Holy Spirit?' This twelfth chapter of I Corinthians cleared me up on that, especially when I found Paul asking of those who had been baptized with the Holy Spirit, 'Do all speak with tongues?' (I Cor. 12:30).[34]

Torrey penned these words in 1895, well before the miraculous events that accompanied the Azusa Street Revival (1906–9). During these remarkable meetings thousands reported that they were baptized with the Holy Spirit and spoke in tongues. One can only wonder if Torrey might have responded differently had he had, at this stage in his life, personal contact with these modern-day Pentecostals.

TORREY'S HERMENEUTIC

I have argued that Torrey's understanding of baptism with the Holy Spirit was, on the one hand, based on a developing theological tradition. In the Gilded Age to describe Spirit baptism as a definite experience, distinct

---

32. Torrey, *Baptism*, 24.

33. Torrey, *Baptism*, 24 (italics mine). So also pp. 25–26: "The baptism with the Holy Spirit is the Spirit of God coming upon the believer, taking possession of his faculties, imparting to him gifts not naturally his own but which qualify him for the service to which God has called him."

34. Torrey, *Baptism*, 20–21. Moody also advised, "You shouldn't be looking for any token...just keep asking and waiting for power" (Moody, "Question Drawer," 204–5).

from conversion was not particularly striking or novel. Here, Torrey stood in a growing line of Holiness preachers and revivalists. Yet, on the other hand, Torrey did offer something quite unique. With his firm and focused description of Spirit baptism as "power for service," Torrey broke from the crowd that consistently interpreted this experience, generally utilizing Wesleyan or Holiness categories, as integral to sanctification. While a few did highlight power for service as one result of baptism with the Holy Spirit, they inevitably also coupled this with sanctification or holiness. In this regard, Torrey was exceptional.[35]

As is often the case with innovations, particularly in theological circles, Torrey's perspective received a cool reception from many of his colleagues. While, as we have seen, some felt comfortable describing Spirit baptism as a "second blessing," many others believed that it referred to an incorporation of the believer into the body of Christ, the moment of regeneration. Another group consigned baptism with the Spirit to the apostolic age.

On one occasion Moody asked Torrey to speak with a group of teachers at Moody's Northfield Bible Conference.[36] These men opposed Torrey's understanding of Spirit baptism. Moody and Torrey spoke with the men for hours. However, as Torrey put it, "they did not altogether see eye to eye with us." As the men finally began to leave, Moody signaled for Torrey to remain. Torrey described the scene:

> Mr. Moody sat there with his chin on his breast, as he so often sat when he was in deep thought; then he looked up and said: 'Oh, why will they split hairs? Why don't they see that this is just the one thing that they themselves need? They are . . . wonderful teachers, and I am so glad to have them here; but why will they not see that this baptism with the Holy Ghost is just the one touch that they themselves need?'[37]

Undoubtedly many of the objections voiced by this group of Northfield teachers were echoed by others in succeeding years. Indeed, they can still be heard today. Nevertheless, in spite of significant opposition and

---

35. Moody might also be considered exceptional in this regard. However, while Moody emphasized "power for service," he used the term, "baptism of the Holy Spirit," sparingly. Richard Gilbertson suggests that "he preferred to avoid this more controversial term" (Gilbertson, *The Baptism of the Holy Spirit*, 158).

36. In 1879 Moody established the Northfield Conference Grounds in his hometown, Northfield, MA. This campus hosted regular Bible conferences.

37. R.A. Torrey, *Why God Used D. L. Moody* (digital version), loc. 1383–92 (both quotes). See also Martin, *Apostle of Certainty*, 117–18.

controversy, throughout his life Torrey remained steadfast in his convictions concerning the baptism with the Holy Spirit. What enabled him to speak with such confidence and conviction? How was he able to forge a new theological path? The answer is to be found in Torrey's unwavering commitment to Scripture, and more particularly, in his hermeneutic. I would like to highlight four aspects of Torrey's hermeneutic that enabled him to speak with confidence and make his unique contribution.

A Focus on Luke–Acts

A key reason for Torrey's ability to clearly and confidently describe the baptism with the Holy Spirit's nature, purpose, and availability is his focus on Luke's two-volume work. Torrey's adherence to the key Lukan texts for his analysis of Spirit baptism is striking and quite unique.[38] As Dayton points out, in the eighteenth century the Wesleyan emphasis on a "second blessing" associated with sanctification gained momentum as John Fletcher, unlike John Wesley, increasingly began to draw upon Luke–Acts and use Pentecostal language to describe this experience.[39] This connection between a "second blessing" and Luke's Pentecostal texts proved problematic though, since these texts did not resonate well with the sanctification theme. As a result, the vast majority of the nineteenth-century Holiness and revivalist ministers who spoke of Spirit baptism and the work of the Spirit, did so by evoking Pauline (and, at times, Johannine) texts as they sought to develop aspects of the sanctification theme.

This privileging of Paul was and has been for some time characteristic of Protestant theology, particularly that of the conservative and Reformed variety. The great truths of the Reformation were largely gleaned from Paul's epistles. The terminology, "justification by faith," echoes Paul. So, following the lead of Luther, Calvin, and the other reformers, the Protestant churches have largely emphasized the Pauline epistles as their core texts.[40]

38. Simpson, for example, linked the Pentecostal gift to the new covenant promises of Jer 31:31–34 and Ezek 36:25–28; while Rom 7–8 and Gal 3:2,14 were commonly used by Keswick teachers to describe the gift (Gilbertson, *Baptism of the Holy Spirit*, 73–77, 195, 212).

39. Dayton, "Doctrine of the Baptism of the Holy Spirit," 116.

40. Kenneth J. Archer notes that Dispensationalists also de-emphasized the Gospels and elevated the epistles because, in their view, while the epistles were written for the church, the Gospels were written for life in the future millennial kingdom (Archer, *Pentecostal Hermeneutic*, 57).

This penchant to elevate Paul to a large extent has been passed on to the children of these Gilded Age conservatives, modern-day Evangelicals. Elsewhere I have outlined how Evangelicals, in a knee-jerk reaction to liberal scholarship that challenged the historical reliability of Luke's writings, rejected the notion that Luke was a theologian.[41] Evangelicals maintained that Luke and the other Gospel writers were *not* theologians; they were historians. In Evangelical circles any discussion of the theological purpose of Luke and his narrative was muted. The Gospels and Acts were viewed as historical records, not accounts reflecting self-conscious theological concerns. This approach essentially created a canon within the canon and, by giving Paul pride of place as the "theologian" of the New Testament, had a significant Paulinizing effect on Evangelical theology. Evangelicals are just now beginning to come to terms with the theological significance of the biblical narratives.

Torrey, by focusing almost exclusively on Luke–Acts, was able to avoid the ambiguity and confusion caused by the tension between the Lukan Pentecostal texts and the Pauline emphasis on the Spirit's role in sanctification outlined above. With respect to baptism with the Holy Spirit, Torrey did the opposite of what many Evangelicals do today. He defined the experience in light of the Lukan texts and read 1 Corinthians 12, including 1 Corinthians 12:13, in light of this Lukan perspective.[42] The result was a very clear and focused understanding of the baptism with the Holy Spirit, one that harmonized beautifully with an emphasis on the Holy Spirit's role in the ongoing process of sanctification in the life of every believer. Torrey was able to see that these two dimensions of the Spirit's work, the former clearly articulated by Luke and the latter by Paul, need not be confused. The result, I would suggest, was a faithful and clear articulation of an important biblical truth. This accounts for the remarkable interest in Torrey's messages on the baptism with the Holy Spirit during his lifetime as well as the contemporary appeal of his writings, which remain hugely popular.[43]

---

41. See Menzies and Menzies, *Spirit and Power*, 37–45.

42. See Torrey, *Holy Spirit*, 117–19; *What the Bible Teaches*, 322; and *Baptism*, 120–26. For a Pentecostal perspective on Paul's pneumatology and how it relates to that of Luke, see Menzies, "Subsequence," 342–63.

43. Moody constantly asked Torrey to preach on the baptism with the Holy Spirit. So much so that Torrey once queried, "Mr. Moody, don't you think I have any sermons but those two?" The two sermons referenced here are "Ten Reasons Why I Believe the Bible to Be the Word of God" and "The Baptism with the Holy Ghost." See Torrey, *Why God Used D. L. Moody*, loc. 1396–405.

PART I: PENTECOSTAL THEOLOGY

Continuity in Salvation-History

As a result of his interest in Luke–Acts, Torrey also affirmed that the power and gifts of the Spirit are available to contemporary Christians. Torrey was adamant on this point. On the strength of Acts 2:39, Torrey declared, "The baptism with the Holy Spirit is the birthright of every believer."[44] Spirit baptism, according to Torrey, is not only available, it is essential for effective service. So, he states the logical corollary, "If I may be baptized with the Holy Spirit, I *must* be."[45] Furthermore, with words that mirror his own experience, Torrey urges, "Any man who is in Christian work who has not received the baptism with the Holy Spirit ought to stop his work right where he is and not go on with it until he has been 'clothed with power from on high.'"[46]

Clearly, Torrey was not a cessationist. He points to Jesus' anointing with the Spirit at the Jordan River as a model for believers today. "If it was in the power of the Holy Spirit that Jesus Christ, the only begotten Son of God, lived, worked, and triumphed, how much more are we dependent upon Him."[47] Indeed, "The same Spirit by which Jesus was anointed for service is at our disposal for us to be anointed for service . . . Whatever He realized through the Holy Spirit is there for us to realize also."[48] Again, the key texts Torrey cites with regard to Jesus' anointing for service are from Luke–Acts: Luke 3:21–22; 4:1, 14, 18 (citing Isa 61:1); and Acts 10:38.[49] The structure of Luke–Acts, particularly the parallels between Jesus' sermon at Nazareth and Peter's sermon at Pentecost (cf. Luke 4:16–21; Acts 2:16–21), supports Torrey's conclusions,[50] although this observation is not explicitly developed by Torrey.

---

44. Torrey, *Person and Work of the Holy Spirit*, 151.

45. Torrey, *Baptism*, 35 (italics his).

46. Torrey, *Baptism*, 31. While Torrey emphasized that the baptism with the Holy Spirit was a definite experience, he also saw that this experience had a repetitive or ongoing character: "It is not enough that one be filled with the Holy Spirit once. We need a new filling of the Holy Spirit for each new emergency of Christian service" (Torrey, *What the Bible Teaches*, 331, and *Baptism*, 67–70).

47. Torrey, *What the Bible Teaches*, 343. Torrey also declares that Jesus "worked his miracles in the power of the Holy Spirit" (p. 342).

48. Torrey, *What the Bible Teaches*, 343.

49. Torrey, *What the Bible Teaches*, 340–41. See also Torrey, *Holy Spirit*, 139–41.

50. Menzies, *Pentecost*, 52–55.

In light of Jesus' command to wait for "power from on high" (Luke 24:49; cf. Acts 1:4–5) and the practice of the early church to immediately pray for new believers to be baptized with the Spirit (Acts 8:12–17; 19:1–6),[51] Torrey insists that,

> every child of God is under the most solemn obligation to see to it that he definitely receives the Holy Spirit, not merely as a regenerating power and as an indwelling presence, but as a definite enduement of power, before he undertakes service of any kind for God.[52]

All of this points to the fact that Torrey saw considerable continuity between, on the one hand, the ministry of Jesus and the early church as recorded in Luke–Acts and, on the other hand, that of believers today. This emphasis on continuity, which flows naturally from a careful reading of Acts 2:17–22,[53] encouraged Torrey not only to highlight the availability of baptism with the Holy Spirit, it also challenged him to practice and espouse divine healing and living by faith.[54]

Our Promises and Stories

One of the most striking features of Torrey's hermeneutic is the way that he reads the New Testament, and especially the book of Acts, with a strong sense of expectation, anticipating that the text contains promises and precepts for the contemporary reader. Torrey's rhetorical and literary style has been critiqued by some as dry and void of any trace of emotion. Grant Wacker offers a colorful, but blunt description, "Always impeccably attired, Torrey earned a reputation for humorless, tediously exegetical sermons—a reputation well deserved if the unrelieved gravity of his forty-odd books is any indication."[55] George Marsden is no less caustic when he offers William McLoughlin's assessment of Torrey, "On the street he usually wore a high hat, and he always talked as though he had one on."[56] It may be true that

---

51. Torrey, *Holy Spirit*, 137 (for Luke 24:49) and p. 141 (for Acts 8:12–17; 19:1–6).

52. Torrey, *Holy Spirit*, 141.

53. Menzies, "Acts 2:17–21: A Paradigm for Pentecostal Mission," 200–218. See also chapter 6.

54. Waldvogel, "Reformed Evangelical Contribution," 9. For Torrey on living by faith see Gloege, *Guaranteed Pure*, 82–84. We shall examine Torrey's views on divine healing in more detail below.

55. Wacker, "Spirit of the Age," 51.

56. Marsden, *Fundamentalism*, 47, citing McLoughlin, *Modern Revivalism*, 371.

PART I: PENTECOSTAL THEOLOGY

Torrey was "almost immune to emotional persuasion" and only "swayed by the logical element of cold reason."[57] Nevertheless, I find Torrey's sermons and writings gripping, full of insight and edification. This is undoubtedly due, in part, to his logical, straightforward, and clear presentation of the significance of biblical texts. Kenneth Archer suggests that Torrey, like many others of his day, including most Pentecostals, utilized "the Bible Reading Method" to formulate doctrine. This method "encouraged readers to trace out topics in Scripture and then synthesize the biblical data into a doctrine."[58] While this description is accurate to a degree—certainly Torrey liked to formulate propositions and arrange in orderly fashion the biblical texts upon which these propositions were based—Torrey's method differed from many of his contemporaries in several significant ways. We have already noted the way that his discussion of baptism with the Holy Spirit centered on Luke–Acts and highlighted important connections between Luke's Gospel and the book of Acts. In this way, it might be argued that Torrey anticipated insights that would be later associated with redaction criticism. Additionally, by highlighting the strong continuity that linked the ministry of Jesus and the early church together with contemporary Christians, Torrey broke from the traditional Reformed perspective.

Yet the aspect of Torrey's hermeneutic that I find most compelling, even if it is not entirely novel, is the strong sense of expectation that permeates his writings, an approach to the text that highlights its relevance for the contemporary reader.[59] This latter quality, this sense of identification with the text, mirrors Pentecostal approaches to Scripture. Torrey, like the early Pentecostals, read the Bible, and particularly the narrative of Acts with its account of the Pentecostal outpouring of the Holy Spirit (Acts 2), as providing models for contemporary Christian life and ministry. He understood that the Bible was full of rich promises and wise instruction. He also understood that the stories of the Bible are indeed our stories, written for our edification and encouragement. So, Torrey helps us read the Bible with eager expectation. We simply need to read with eyes alert and open. And as we do, the promises and stories become our promises and stories: promises

57. Marsden, *Fundamentalism*, 47. Both quotations are found in Marsden, but the second quote is cited as coming from Harkness, *Reuben Archer Torrey*, 10.

58. Archer, *Pentecostal Hermeneutic*, 82.

59. Gloege speaks of "Torrey's contractual understanding of the Bible" and states that "Torrey could construe most any passage as a promise to him personally." He adds, "Torrey's Bible was not primarily a book of science, theology, ethics, or poetry but a living text" (*Guaranteed Pure*, 79 and 80 respectively).

of the Holy Spirit's power, stories of God enabling ordinary disciples to do extraordinary things for his glory.

Torrey on Speaking in Tongues

We have noted that Torrey ultimately rejected speaking in tongues as the normative sign of Spirit baptism.[60] This is striking because, in view of the theological convictions and hermeneutical approach outlined above, we would have expected Torrey to accept this position.[61] Charles Parham affirmed tongues as the sign of Spirit baptism only a few years later.[62] His student, William Seymour, became the match that ignited the Azusa Street Revival.[63] At the very least, we would have expected Torrey to be supportive of or sympathetic to the emerging Pentecostal movement, particularly as it became prominent in Los Angeles when Torrey was residing there.[64] As neighbors, given their theological proximity, one might have expected a warm relationship. As we shall see, this was not the case.

Torrey's response at this point is perplexing and deserves analysis. At the outset, we should note that Torrey's rejection of tongues as a normative sign appears to stand in tension with his theology and hermeneutic at several points. First, we have already seen how Torrey presents Jesus and the early church as models for the church today. Given the way that he anchors his understanding of baptism with the Spirit in the book of Acts, it would seem natural for him to connect tongues with this experience like the Pentecostals who followed after him.

Second, Torrey's emphasis on Spirit baptism as "*a definite experience which one may know whether he has received or not,*"[65] seems to virtually demand this kind of affirmation. Torrey's views may have softened a bit on this point over the years. In his last work on the Holy Spirit, *The Holy*

---

60. Torrey, *Baptism*, 20–21.

61. So also Gloege observes, "The practice of speaking in tongues was Pentecostalism's most emblematic and controversial feature, but even this, at least in its original form, was simply Torrey's underlying belief in Spirit Baptism taken to its logical end" (*Guaranteed Pure*, 132).

62. Synan, *Century*, 42–45.

63. Synan, *Century*, 46–61.

64. Torrey moved to Los Angeles in January of 1912 (Martin, *Apostle of Certainty*, 226). Although this was perhaps a few years after the high point of the Azusa Street Revival, Los Angeles continued to be a center of Pentecostal ministry.

65. Torrey, *Baptism*, 14 (italics his).

Spirit: Who He Is, and What He Does (1927), he speaks of two ways through which believers may know they have been baptized with the Spirit: "First, by the plain statements of God's Word, and Second, by experience."[66] Torrey qualifies this statement by asserting that "knowing by God's Word is a surer way of knowing than knowing by experience."[67] A few pages later Torrey poses the question, "Will there be no manifestation of the Baptism with the Holy Spirit when we are thus baptized?"[68] His answer is affirmative, but vague, "What was the manifestation in every case recorded in the Bible? *Some new power in service*."[69] He also implies that this "new power" might not be immediately evident. The sequence is "God's promise," "our faith," and then "experience."[70] All of this reveals a tension in Torrey's position that is never adequately resolved. He maintains that Spirit baptism is a definite experience, one that is verifiable, and yet no clear or specific description of this experience is forthcoming. Indeed, in his later years he appears to soften his earlier claims of an immediate, verifiable experience. How will we know that we have been baptized in the Spirit? The question is never adequately answered.[71]

Perhaps this unresolved question helps explain a curious change in theology and practice. During the early years at Moody Bible Institute and the Northfield Bible Conferences, Moody and Torrey routinely called for the gathered assembly to pray for the baptism with the Holy Spirit.[72] One eyewitness account describes how Moody and Torrey "lined up the [Bible Institute] students, walked behind them, and laid hands on each one, saying as they did so, 'Receive ye the Holy Ghost.'"[73] This practice, and the theology that supported it, were quickly discarded after Torrey's departure. Those who received, acted upon, and passed on Torrey's teaching on Spirit baptism, but now with the addition of tongues as the evidential sign, were the Pentecostals.

66. Torrey, *Holy Spirit*, 192.
67. Torrey, *Holy Spirit*, 193.
68. Torrey, *Holy Spirit*, 195.
69. Torrey, *Holy Spirit*, 196 (emphasis his, Torrey capitalizes these words).
70. Torrey, *Holy Spirit*, 197.
71. I have argued elsewhere that Luke's narrative (see esp. Luke 11:9–13; Acts 19:1–7) anticipates this question. See Menzies, *Speaking in Tongues*, 15–41.
72. Torrey, *Why God Used D. L. Moody*, loc. 1396–405; and *Holy Spirit*, 200–201.
73. Horton, *Reflections of An Early American Pentecostal*, 12 (as described by Horton's grandmother). Gloege shares another first-hand account of "an all-night prayer vigil designed to help students attain the Baptism of the Holy Spirit" (*Guaranteed Pure*, 93–94).

Finally, Torrey acknowledges that he was initially drawn to the Pentecostal proposition that speaking in tongues is the result and confirming sign of baptism with the Holy Spirit.[74] However, his own lack of experience with speaking in tongues, both personally and in the lives of those he knew, led him to question this doctrine. As a result, we find that he deviates from his normal practice of privileging Luke–Acts, and in an uncharacteristic hermeneutical move, interprets the significance of the Acts narrative in light of a questionable reading of 1 Corinthians 12:30.[75]

Summary

We have highlighted how Torrey's hermeneutic was, in many respects, unique. He privileged Luke–Acts and linked Luke's Gospel with the book of Acts in his descriptions of baptism with the Holy Spirit. He saw significant continuity between the experience of the early church and that of contemporary Christians, particularly in their reception of the Spirit's power for ministry gifts and miracles. Finally, Torrey read the Bible, and especially Acts, as a treasure trove of promises and stories that offered untold riches for those willing to receive them by faith. This approach to reading the Bible would resonate well in the numerous Pentecostal churches that were soon to be established. This was especially the case in the non-Holiness, more Reformed wing (with reference to sanctification) of the movement, which today is perhaps best represented by the Assemblies of God.[76]

Nevertheless, in spite of the close affinities that tied Torrey's theology and hermeneutic together with the emerging Pentecostal movement, Torrey rejected one of its cardinal doctrines (tongues as a normative sign) and the movement as a whole. This is particularly surprising in that just prior to the catalyst of the Pentecostal movement, the Azusa Street Revival, Torrey spoke with great passion of the coming of a great revival. On his deathbed in 1899, Moody voiced his regret that he would not be alive to see the great

---

74. Torrey, *Baptism*, 21: "The question came often to my mind, 'If one is baptized with the Holy Spirit, will he not speak with tongues?' But I saw no one so speaking and I often wondered, 'Is there anyone today who actually is baptized with the Holy Spirit?'"

75. For Pentecostal responses to Torrey's reading of 1 Cor 12:30 see Horton, "Review of R.A. Torrey, *The Person and Work of the Holy Spirit*," 29–30; Smeeton, "Charismatic Theology of R.A. Torrey," 21; Menzies, *Speaking in Tongues*, 89–106.

76. With sixty-nine million members worldwide, the Assemblies of God is the world's largest Pentecostal denomination (ag.org, accessed on July 20, 2018).

revival that was coming.⁷⁷ In Torrey's sermon at Moody's funeral, "a prophetic ring characterized his words."⁷⁸ Torrey based his message on Joshua 1:2, "Moses my servant is dead . . . . Now . . . get ready to cross the Jordan River into the land I am about to give to [you]," and declared, "[Moody's] death, with the triumphal scenes that surround it, are part of God's way of answering the prayers that have been going on for so long in our land for a revival."⁷⁹ In the wake of Moody's funeral, a series of prayer meetings for revival were established by Torrey and the MBI leaders. In November of 1900, just weeks before the beginning of the Pentecostal revival, which was initiated on January 1, 1901 at Parham's Bible school in Topeka, Kansas with an outpouring of the Spirit marked by speaking in tongues, Torrey exclaimed, "I have been expecting a great revival to break out throughout the country."⁸⁰ Yet, when the fire of Pentecost fell in Topeka, Los Angeles, and around the world, Torrey could not accept it as the revival he was seeking. Why was this case? What caused Torrey to reject a movement that was certainly emboldened and perhaps established as a result of his teaching?⁸¹ In the following section we shall seek to answer this question.

TORREY'S RESPONSE TO THE PENTECOSTAL MOVEMENT

Torrey has been described as a theological "pugilist."⁸² Although this assessment may not give enough consideration to the unique challenges that he faced, I think here particularly of the rise of modernism and theological liberalism, Torrey's response to the emerging Pentecostal movement was not overly gracious. Torrey offered his assessment in a regular column, "Questions and Answers," that he wrote for *The King's Business*, a publication associated with the Bible Institute of Los Angeles. In the July 1913 edition of *The King's Business* Torrey responded to the question, "Is the present 'Tongues Movement' of God?"⁸³ The way the question is framed masks the

77. Martin, *Apostle of Certainty*, 129.

78. Martin, *Apostle of Certainty*, 129.

79. Martin, *Apostle of Certainty*, 130.

80. Martin, *Apostle of Certainty*, 132.

81. The nature of Torrey's influence upon both Charles Parham and William Durham are topics of importance for future historical research.

82. Wacker, "Spirit of the Age," 51.

83. Torrey, "Questions and Answers," *The King's Business* (July 1913), 360–62. This

strong points of agreement that united Torrey with the Pentecostal movement and highlights the one area of disagreement. Predictably, Torrey's response was negative.

His terse answer to the question, "It is not," in good Torreyite fashion is supported by seven affirmations. His first affirmation restates his position that baptism with the Holy Spirit provides power for service through a diverse range of gifts (1 Cor 12:4–11) and that the rhetorical question of 1 Corinthians 12:30, "Do all speak in tongues?," which anticipates a negative answer, states the matter clearly. Thus, he concludes that the Pentecostal teaching on tongues "contradicts the plain teaching of God's Word."[84] Torrey's second and third affirmations make the charge that Pentecostals portray tongues as the "most important of all manifestations of the Spirit's presence and power," while in reality the gift of tongues is one of the least profitable gifts, and that believers are encouraged to seek after the "greater gifts," which refers to gifts such as prophecy and clearly not tongues.[85] With his fourth point of contention, Torrey chides Pentecostals for allowing uninterpreted tongues and disorder to reign in corporate gatherings. He charges:

> Now in the gatherings of the 'Tongues' people, oftentimes many speak in tongues in a single gathering; oftentimes several speak at the same time, and they constantly speak even when there is no one present to interpret. In these matters they disobey God in the most unmistakable way.[86]

One wonders if Torrey himself witnessed this sort of behavior or whether he heard of it secondhand. Although admittedly a lot of "wild fire" did occur,[87] Pentecostal services were generally conducted in an orderly way that, while allowing for spontaneity, did seek to follow established biblical patterns.[88] Yet this Pentecostal 'order' might not have been understood by those unaccustomed to 'the leading of the Spirit' and times of prayer permeated with glossolalic praise and intercession. As I have argued elsewhere, Paul's instructions concerning the use of tongues in the assembly (1 Cor 12–14) were polemical in nature and address an aberrant situation.

article later appeared under the same title as a tract.

84. Torrey, *King's Business* (July 1913), 360.
85. Torrey, *King's Business* (July 1913), 360 (both quotes).
86. Torrey, *King's Business* (July 1913), 361.
87. For vivid descriptions see Wacker, *Heaven Below*, 99–103.
88. Wacker, *Heaven Below*, 103–11.

Additionally, the context and purpose of the glossolalic prayer impacts whether it is appropriate, edifying, and in need of interpretation.[89] It appears unlikely that Torrey, with his limited exposure to Pentecostal worship, was well-positioned to address these issues in a wise and knowledgeable way.

Torrey, with his fifth, sixth, and seventh points, spirals out of control and appears to give in to his "pugilistic" instincts. His *ad hominem* attacks include charges of "the grossest immoralities,"[90] demonic behavior,[91] and duping "clear-minded men and women" like heretical groups of the past.[92] This leads Torrey to conclude that "God has set the stamp of His disapproval in a most unmistakable way" upon the Pentecostal movement. Indeed, "everyone who believes and obeys the Word of God should leave [it] severely alone except to expose … the gross errors and evils connected with it."[93]

Stanley Frodsham, a leader in the Assemblies of God,[94] offered a gracious and thoughtful response to Torrey's attack that is still worth reading.[95] His response drew heavily upon his own experience in the movement. He dismissed several of Torrey's claims as inaccurate and was able to speak with authority because he was personally present at one of the meetings criticized and he had widespread knowledge of the Pentecostal movement, having visited Pentecostal churches throughout the United States and in many other countries around the world. However, I found Frodsham's later article, written in 1928 after the Pentecostal movement was officially "disfellowshiped" by the World Christian Fundamentals Association (WCFA) in a meeting that Torrey had helped organize, even more powerful. The language of the WCFA was harsh:

89. Menzies, *Speaking in Tongues*, 107–55.

90. Torrey, *King's Business* (July 1913), 361 (point five). Gerald W. King writes: "Torrey accused the movement of gross immorality, most particularly in the lapse of its leaders–one (Parham) whose sin he could not specify in print (sodomy) and another from Ohio (Lupton) whose sin he could (adultery). In recent meetings conducted in Los Angeles by a woman (Maria Woodworth-Etter), hypnotic methods felled men and women, who lay indecently supine for hours" (King, *Disfellowshiped*, 74).

91. Torrey, *King's Business* (July 1913), 362 (point six, but incorrectly listed again as point five).

92. Torrey, *King's Business* (July 1913), 362 (listed as point six, but actually point seven).

93. Torrey, *King's Business* (July 1913), 362.

94. Frodsham was elected the General Secretary of the Assemblies of God in 1916 and also served as the denomination's Missionary Treasurer. He became the Editor of the *Pentecostal Evangel* in 1920.

95. Frodsham, "Why We Know the Present Pentecostal Movement Is of God," 4–5.

> Whereas, the present wave of Modern Pentecostalism, often referred to as the "tongues movement," and the present wave of fanatical and unscriptural healing which is sweeping over the country today, has become a menace in many churches and a real injury to the sane testimony of Fundamental Christians, Be it resolved, that this convention go on record as unreservedly opposed to Modern Pentecostalism, including the speaking with unknown tongues, and the fanatical healing known as general healing in the atonement, and the perpetuation of the miraculous sign-healing of Jesus and His apostles, wherein they claim the only reason the church cannot perform these miracles is because of unbelief.[96]

Yet Frodsham's response was remarkable for its graciousness. He wrote,

> Although the Fundamentalists have by this action disfellowshiped a great company of us who believe in all the fundamentals of the faith as much as they do, we will, by the grace of God, continue to love and fellowship [sic] every child of God, especially those who stand as we do in teaching that the whole Bible is verbally inspired . . . the miraculous virgin birth of our Lord . . . His absolute deity . . . His perfect humanity . . . His vicarious death . . . His bodily resurrection . . . His coming again in glory.[97]

Frodsham then cited Acts 2 and Mark 16, key Pentecostal texts, and noted that these too are part of the Bible. Yet Frodsham continued, "But while we believe in these things that God has set forth in His Word, we do not condemn any who do not see as we do." Additionally, after speaking of healing flowing from the atoning work of Christ, he acknowledges, "It is only fair, however, to say that a number of Fundamentalists like Dr. R. A. Torrey do recognize that 'the gospel of Christ has in it salvation for the body as well as the soul.'"[98] Finally, Frodsham concludes with these charitable words:

> Although we Pentecostal people have to be without the camp, we cannot afford to be bitter against those who do not see as we do. Our instructions from the Throne are set forth clearly in Holy Writ, 'This is His commandment, that we should believe on the name of His Son Jesus Christ, and love one another as He gave us

---

96. Cited in Frodsham, "Disfellowshiped!," 7.
97. Frodsham, "Disfellowshiped!," 7.
98. Frodsham, "Disfellowshiped!," 7 (both quotes).

commandment.' So our business is to love these Fundamentalists and to unitedly pray, 'Lord, bless them all.'[99]

Frodsham's response reminds us that the Pentecostals were doctrinally united at almost every point with their Fundamentalist brothers and sisters. They too "believed in all the fundamentals of the faith."[100] Torrey's writings and ministry call us to recognize that this theological unity, at least for some, went beyond a commitment to the fundamentals and included a common vision for Spirit baptism, divine healing, and living by faith.

Torrey had been praying for revival and one came. Although from his vantage point, particularly in 1913, it would have been impossible to predict the true nature, scope, and significance of the movement that it would generate. Indeed, it is estimated that by 2050 the Pentecostal movement, if understood more broadly to include neo-Pentecostals and charismatics, "should surpass the one billion mark."[101] And so the revival came—a revival that would sweep the globe and impact virtually every nation, a revival that would transform the face of global Christianity, a revival that in no small measure could attribute its genesis to Torrey's influence—and yet Torrey himself missed it. How could it be?

In retrospect, it seems clear that three factors clouded Torrey's vision so that he was unable to see his own fingerprints on the nascent movement and unwilling to look beyond minor points of disagreement.[102]

Cultural Distance

"Respectability was his birthright."[103] This is how Timothy Gloege describes R. A. Torrey's childhood and upbringing, and appropriately so. Torrey was born into a wealthy family. His father, a wealthy banker and manufacturer, illustrates why the last decades of the nineteenth century (roughly 1870–1900) have been called, the Gilded Age. It was a period of rapid industrialization, great wealth, and tremendous economic inequality, a period in which the lives of those in the wealthy class were marked by

---

99. Frodsham, "Disfellowshiped!," 7.

100. Frodsham, "Disfellowshiped!," 7.

101. Jenkins, *Next Christendom*, 8.

102. After all, Torrey, at least in theory, recognized the validity of contemporary tongues. He simply rejected the notion that tongues might serve as the normative sign of Spirit baptism, a view to which he himself was initially drawn.

103. Gloege, *Guaranteed Pure*, 69.

great affluence and grand excess. Torrey grew up on "a lavish two-hundred-acre estate in Geneva, New York."[104] Although his life would not always be so comfortable—family fortunes would take a turn for the worse, and as a mature adult Torrey would have to make his own way—Torrey was raised in privilege. Torrey's 'gilded' background enabled him to study at a number of prestigious universities. He graduated from Yale University in 1875 and Yale Divinity School in 1878. After a short stint as a Congregationalist pastor in Ohio, he spent roughly a year studying theology at universities in Leipzig and Erlangen (1882–83). This privileged background makes his decision to embark on a ministry among the inner-city poor of Minneapolis, when he returned to the United States, all the more impressive. But it also perhaps helps explain his inability to sympathetically identify with the largely lower-class, "rough and ready" congregations that populated the Pentecostal churches of his day. Pentecostals "came from the wrong side of the tracks"[105] and this was a long way from his estate in Geneva or the halls of academia in Erlangen.

In addition to his well-heeled upbringing and elite education, Torrey was well known for being rather pompous. McLoughlin's line is worth repeating, "on the street [Torrey] usually wore a high hat, and he always talked as though he had one on."[106] His biographer, Roger Martin, describes Torrey in this way:

> He wore a finely tailored Prince Albert coat with white shirt, starched collar and cuffs, and white bow tie. His shoes were polished. There was hardly a wrinkle in his clothing. He gave the impression of immaculate cleanness and neatness, and had a stunning look of culture and dignity.[107]

These trappings of Victorian culture were accompanied by a serious demeanor, steeped in logic and seemingly devoid of emotion. One friend indicated that "he did not remember [Torrey] ever getting a laugh from any

---

104. Gloege, "Gilded Age," 202.

105 Grant Wacker, "Travail," 513. Wacker acknowledges that economic, class, and gender differences played a role in the conflict between Fundamentalists (he uses the term, "Radical Evangelicals") and Pentecostals, but he suggests the differences were more perceived than real.

106. Marsden, *Fundamentalism*, 47 (both quotes).

107. Martin, *Apostle of Certainty*, 91.

congregation."[108] Torrey characterized his own preaching style as "scholarly," like "a lawyer before a jury."[109]

With this portrait of Torrey in mind, I have tried to picture how he might have responded had he entered the Apostolic Faith Mission on Azusa Street in Los Angeles during the summer of 1906. The leaders of the revival rented an old frame building that once served as a Methodist church but had more recently fallen into disrepair and was used as a warehouse. They "cleared space enough in the surrounding dirt and debris to lay some planks on top of empty nail kegs, with seats enough for possibly thirty people."[110] In this simple setting, an eyewitness observer describes what typically transpired:

> Brother Seymour generally sat behind two empty shoe boxes, one on top of the other. He usually kept his head inside the top one during the meeting, in prayer. There was no pride there. The services ran almost continuously. Seeking souls could be found under the power almost any hour, night and day. The place was never closed nor empty. The people came to meet God. He was always there .... The meeting did not depend on the human leader. God's presence became more and more wonderful. In that old building, with its low rafters and bare floors, God took strong men and women to pieces, and put them together again, for His glory .... Pride and self-assertion, self-importance and self-esteem, could not survive there ....
>
> No subjects or sermons were announced ahead of time, and no special speakers for such an hour. No one knew what might be coming, what God would do. All was spontaneous, ordered of the Spirit ....
>
> Someone might be speaking. Suddenly the Spirit would fall upon the congregation .... Men would fall all over the house, like the slain in battle, or rush for the altar en masse, to seek God. The scene often resembled a forest of fallen trees. Such a scene cannot be imitated.[111]

It is hard to imagine Torrey, with his Victorian bearing and aristocratic manner, fitting easily into this setting. One can only speculate, but it is hard

---

108. "Interview with Dr. Ernest W. Wordsworth," Torrey File, Moody Bible Institute Archives, cited in Marsden, *Fundamentalism*, 47.

109. Marsden, *Fundamentalism*, 47.

110. Bartleman, *Azusa Street*, 47.

111. Bartleman, *Azusa Street*, 58–60.

not to feel that the cultural distance was simply too great. It rendered him incapable of recognizing at Azusa Street the revival that he had been seeking, the move of the Spirit for which he had prepared the way.

Peer Pressure

Torrey was a man of principle and not one to waver once his mind was settled.[112] This quality is surely rooted in his commitment to the Bible as the word of God. His views on Spirit baptism, healing, and living by faith changed little over the years.[113] Yet it is also true that Torrey was not immune to the power of peer pressure and the sentiments of his colleagues. His decision to depart from Moody Bible Institute and launch out on a world-wide evangelistic tour in 1902 may have been encouraged by the growing opposition he faced from colleagues upset with his radical views, particularly his position on divine healing.[114] It is also apparent that when the Pentecostal movement, with its frenetic, spontaneous services, boisterous worship, and emotional responses, burst onto the scene, it was "a wedge that forced evangelicals who wanted to maintain their middle-class respectability to choose affiliation."[115] Would they side with the rational, dispensational conservatives or would they join with the modernist liberals? For men like Torrey, already established in respectable, conservative institutions, it would have been difficult even to contemplate siding with those from "the other side of the tracks." The need to draw a clear line of separation must have been especially acute for Torrey since his theology and teaching in so many respects anticipated the Pentecostal movement.[116] Surely Gloege's assessment is on mark, "With Pentecostalism following close behind Torrey's meetings, he felt a need to distinguish himself from the movement and to critique—often in harsh terms—what he believed were its excesses."[117]

---

112. King, *Disfellowshiped*, 140.

113. Gloege, "Gilded Age," 218.

114. Gloege, *Guaranteed Pure*, 8–9.

115. Gloege, "Gilded Age," 218. Marsden notes that "revivalist evangelicals. . .were embarrassed by the emergence of these cousins in Christ" (*Fundamentalism*, 94).

116. Wacker notes that Holiness leaders strongly denounced Pentecostal excesses and sought to distance themselves from the Pentecostal Movement precisely because they were so close in many other respects (Wacker, "Travail," 524).

117. Gloege, "Gilded Age," 218.

PART I: PENTECOSTAL THEOLOGY

Negative Personal Encounters

Throughout his life, Torrey was a firm believer in divine healing. His book, *Divine Healing: Does God Perform Miracles Today?*, was published in 1924 and reflects his mature views on the subject.[118] Torrey insisted that divine healing is available today, but criticized those who featured healing in 'healing crusades.' Torrey felt the focus should be placed squarely on the gospel and healing as an extension of this.[119] Indeed, Torrey claimed that many had been healed in "private meetings" at the conclusion of his evangelistic crusades.[120] Torrey also stressed that while healing comes from Christ's atoning death on the cross, this does not mean that we should or will always experience this healing now.[121] Finally, Torrey insisted that utilizing doctors or medicine might be appropriate, although in some instances it might not (i.e., when we are called to rely on God alone).[122]

These positions, particularly his approval of the use of medical means, represent perspectives that Torrey appears to have embraced only after suffering through several difficult experiences. Many Radical Evangelicals in Torrey's day felt that resorting to doctors and medicine reflected a lack of faith that would undermine prayer for healing.[123] As we shall see, the younger Torrey appears to have shared this point of view.

Torrey's "brief foray into a faith healing ministry was cut short" when he publicly prayed for the healing of a nineteen-year-old lady suffering from leukemia. Initially, it appeared the lady had been healed. However, when she died the following day, pandemonium broke out. The girl's mother believed that God would raise her from the dead and retrieved the body from the morgue. The mother maintained that six days of prayers had achieved a "partial resurrection," while the medical examiner declared that the young lady had been pronounced dead prematurely while in a coma. Sadly, the mother blamed her own "lack of faith" for her daughter's death. Newspapers widely reported the details of this sad event. Gloege notes, "After this

---

118. Torrey, *Divine Healing*.
119. Torrey, *Divine Healing*, 35–39.
120. King, *Disfellowshiped*, 98–99.
121. Torrey, *Divine Healing*, 47–48.
122. Torrey, *Divine Healing*, 52.
123. Gloege, *Guaranteed Pure*, 100: with reference to a veritable "phalanx of modern faith-healing advocates" that emerged in the late 1800s, Gloege writes, "nearly everyone initially agreed that faith healing should replace, rather than augment, doctors and medicine."

incident, Torrey limited his practice of faith healing to the more-controlled setting of his immediate family, deciding that his public ministry was better devoted to evangelism."[124]

Yet the really devastating blow came with the death of Torrey's eight-year-old daughter, Elizabeth. When Elizabeth contracted diphtheria, Torrey decided to rely on prayer alone and declined "the use of the well-proven antitoxin."[125] Initially all seemed well, but when Elizabeth's breathing became labored, Torrey called for a doctor who administered the medicine. Tragically, it was too late and Elizabeth died. Torrey was distraught. He felt that his lack of faith, demonstrated in his call to the doctor, was the reason Elizabeth had died. He later described it "as a stunning blow," and asked, "Why did God permit it?"[126] Torrey's answer: "Because He loved us" and "We needed it." Torrey explained,

> This chastisement . . . led to deep heart searchings and discovery of failure and thereby led to confession of sin. It led also to new consecration and love for souls and devotion to God. It brought answers to prayers . . . It was one of the things that led to my leaving Chicago a few years later to enter on a world-wide ministry.[127]

A short time later Torrey's fourteen-year-old daughter, Blanche, showed similar signs of illness. This time Torrey relied entirely on prayer. Torrey not only prayed himself, but he also sent a letter to the well-known but extremely controversial figure, John Alexander Dowie, asking him to pray for his daughter's healing as well. In this letter Torrey repented of his previous lack of faith, revealing the more radical side of his views on faith healing. Thankfully, Blanche recovered and Torrey sent a second letter to Dowie, rejoicing that their prayers had been answered. In spite of this happy outcome, the letters Torrey sent to Dowie ignited a firestorm of controversy that would cause him considerable grief. Dowie published Torrey's letters

---

124. Gloege, *Guaranteed Pure*, 81. For Gloege's account of this incident, see *Guaranteed Pure*, 80–81, and also "Gilded Age," 213.

125. Gloege, *Guaranteed Pure*, 108.

126. From Torrey's sermon, "Keynote of the Bible (God Is Love)," in Torrey, *Sermons*, 143.

127. Torrey, *Sermons*, 144. Torrey also describes the incredible comfort he found in the midst of this trial. The morning after Elizabeth's death he walked the streets crying out her name. "And just then this fountain that I had in my heart broke forth with such power as I think I had never experienced before, and it was the most joyful moment that I have ever knownin my life! Oh, how wonderful is the joy of the Holy Ghost!" (Torrey, *Holy Spirit*, 95).

PART I: PENTECOSTAL THEOLOGY

as a means of defending his own rapidly deteriorating reputation. A string of acrimonious articles published by Torrey, Dowie, and others followed.[128] As a result, Torrey's reputation suffered greatly.

Moody was troubled by the thought that radical views on healing might be associated with the Bible Institute. He sent Torrey away for several months to minister to troops in Tennessee who were mobilizing for the Spanish-American War and also brought in James M. Gray to provide a more sober-minded perspective on healing. In October 1898 when Torrey returned to Chicago from his time of ministering to the troops, he was dismissed from his teaching duties at the YMCA. For years Torrey had taught a weekly Bible class for the YMCA, but now they terminated that arrangement.[129] Although Torrey continued to serve at the Bible Institute, concerns regarding his Pentecostal leanings were clearly coming to the fore. Moody's death (December 22, 1899) "in the midst of this crisis . . . signaled the end of the era."[130] The Institute rapidly traded Torrey's "miracle-tinged faith," which had generally received Moody's support, for Gray's "safe for middle-class consumption" form of Evangelicalism.[131] As Torrey's comments cited above suggest, the whirlwind of controversy surrounding these events likely encouraged his decision to leave Moody Bible Institute and embark on his world-wide evangelistic tour (1902–6). In the midst of these pressures, one can appreciate how difficult it would have been for Torrey to openly identify with the kindred spirits he might have found in Pentecostal churches. Additionally, although Dowie predated Pentecostalism, many of his friends and followers flooded into the movement. Torrey's painful relationship with Dowie surely must have soured him on pursuing any further links.

---

128. See Dowie's *Leaves of Healing* 6.20 (March 10, 1900), 639–48, esp. 642–43 and 645, where he reproduces Torrey's letters, which originally appeared in *Leaves of Healing* 5.24 (April 8, 1899), 460; for Dowie's comments on Moody's opposition and death, see *Leaves of Healing* 6 (Feb. 3, 1900), 470; for his comments on the authenticity of Torrey's letters, see *Leaves of Healing* 6 (April 21, 1900), 826–27. Note also R. A. Torrey's lengthy letter repudiating Dowie published in *The Ram's Horn* (March 17, 1900), 11, and the article, "Henderson on Faith Cure," *The Chicago Tribune* (Oct. 16, 1899), 8, that is critical of Dowie and which links his Zion Community to the Evangelical churches.

129. Gloege provides a detailed and well-documented account of these events in *Guaranteed Pure*, 108–9. On the conflict with the YMCA, see also Findlay, *Dwight L. Moody*, 404–5.

130. Gloege, *Guaranteed Pure*, 8.

131. Gloege, *Guaranteed Pure*, 8–9.

TORREY'S IMPACT ON THE PENTECOSTAL MOVEMENT

In spite of Torrey's harsh repudiation of the "Tongues Movement," Pentecostals loved him nonetheless. British Pentecostal statesman, Donald Gee, stated that it was Torrey "who first gave the teaching of Baptism of the Holy Ghost a new, and certainly more scriptural and doctrinally correct, emphasis on the line of 'power from on high', especially for service and witness (Acts i. 8)." Gee also noted that Torrey's "logical presentation of truth did much to establish the doctrine," adding that "his preaching [in Berlin] of the Baptism of the Spirit sowed seeds that undoubtedly flourished a few years later when the Pentecostal Movement broke out in Germany."[132] Of course Torrey's impact was not limited to Germany. He was a catalyst for Pentecostal-like revival in England, Wales, and beyond. Testimonies from Torrey's preaching around the globe permeate the early Pentecostal periodicals.[133]

In addition to Torrey's preaching, early Pentecostals loved to reference Torrey's writings. Pentecostal apologist Carl Brumback cites Torrey's definition of the baptism with the Holy Spirit, adding that it "represents the basic view of the Pentecostal movement toward the experience."[134] Many Pentecostal schools used Torrey's *What the Bible Teaches* (1898) as a textbook.[135] One of Torrey's declarations contained in this book, "The baptism with the Holy Spirit is an operation of the Holy Spirit distinct from, subsequent to, and additional to His regenerating work,"[136] is "the most frequent quotation by a non-Pentecostal to be found in Pentecostal literature."[137] Additionally, Horace Ward describes Torrey's book, *The Holy Spirit: Who*

---

132. Gee, *Pentecostal Movement*, 4–5 (all of the quotes from Gee). Torrey's influence is chronicled by Hollenweger and led Marsden to speak of Torrey as "a kind of John the Baptist figure for later international Penecostalism" (see Hollenweger, *Pentecostals*, 221–23 and Marsden, *Fundamentalism*, 94 respectively).

133. See the following for Torrey's impact in various nations: A. Boddy, "Scenes in Denmark," *Confidence* (Oct. 10, 1910), 229 (Denmark); *Confidence* (Dec., 1914), 229 (Berlin); Minnie Abrams, "How the Recent Revival Was Brought About in India," *The Latter Rain Evangel* (July, 1909), 8 (Australia); E. N. Bell, "Questions and Answers," *The Pentecostal Evangel* (April 21, 1923), 9 (China); J. Narver Gortner, "Sins of Omissions," *The Pentecostal Evangel* (April 4, 1925), 3 (Australia); David Leigh, "Thousands Turning to Christ in China," *The Pentecostal Evangel* (Feb. 26, 1927), 1 (England).

134. Brumback, *What Meaneth This?*, 183–84, as cited in Smeeton, "Charismatic Theology of R.A. Torrey," 22.

135. King, *Disfellowshiped*, 164.

136. Torrey, *What the Bible Teaches*, 322.

137. Bruner, *Theology of the Holy Spirit*, 46.

He Is, and What He Does (1927), as "the most acceptable non-Pentecostal treatise on Pentecostal doctrine."[138] Clearly, this book too was widely read in Pentecostal circles. It should also be noted that the man that many would deem the theological catalyst of the Pentecostal movement, Charles Parham, read Torrey's writings.[139] A survey of the early Pentecostal literature confirms Frederick Bruner's conclusion, "Torrey was, after Wesley and Finney, the most influential figure in the pre-history of Pentecostalism."[140] Indeed, given his close proximity in time and doctrine to Parham, Durham, and the Azusa Street Revival, it might be argued with some force that Torrey's role should be considered primary.

Torrey's influence extended beyond his preaching and writing into the classroom. As Stanley Horton notes, "a number of the early leaders of the Pentecostal Movement studied under or were influenced by Dr. Torrey."[141] Frank Bartleman, Francisco Olazabal, and Marie Burgess were all students at Moody Bible Institute during Torrey's tenure there.[142] Thus, through his preaching, teaching, and numerous books, Torrey exerted a tremendous, indeed formative influence, on emerging Pentecostal leaders and the movement as a whole. His impact can hardly be overstated.

Nevertheless, Torrey's influence on the Pentecostal movement has not been adequately acknowledged. On the one hand, Pentecostals have too often lumped Torrey together with other Keswick preachers making it appear as if they all taught essentially the same thing.[143] I believe more

---

138. Ward, "Anti-Pentecostal Argument," 108.

139. Gloege, *Guaranteed Pure*, 131.

140. Bruner, *Theology of the Holy Spirit*, 45. A search of the online holdings of the Flower Heritage Pentecostal Center (www.ifhpc.org) is instructive: Torrey's name, which was linked to numerous testimonies, cited favorably in a variety of articles, and listed as the author of many books advertised by the publications, appeared in 126 entries from 1908 through 1939. This confirms Bruner's judgement, "Pentecostalism found in Torrey's theology of the Spirit a special affinity" (*Theology of the Holy Spirit*, 45).

141. Horton, "Review of R.A. Torrey, *The Person and Work of the Holy Spirit*," 29. So also Smeeton, "Charismatic Theology of R.A. Torrey," 22.

142. Gloege, *Guaranteed Pure*, 133–34.

143. Gilbertson helpfully notes that "in contrast to D.L. Moody and particularly R.A. Torrey, Keswick teachers devoted much more attention to the Spirit's work in sanctification" (*Baptism of the Holy Spirit*, 180). Charles Nienkirchen notes, for example, that A. B. Simpson "de-emphasized the baptism of the Holy Spirit as a source of power for service" and instead highlighted "its role in bringing 'union with Christ' and 'cleansing from sin'" (Nienkirchen, "A.B. Simpson: Forerunner and Critic of the Pentecostal Movement," 143). This judgment is supported by Gilbertson's detailed analysis (*Baptism of the Holy Spirit*, 207–19).

nuance is required. Although all Keswick preachers associated Spirit baptism with power, unlike Torrey, virtually all of the others connected this power with sanctification (as well as power for service) in significant ways. On the other hand, Torrey's Fundamentalist students and colleagues have attempted to erase or de-emphasize the strong Pentecostal currents that flowed through his theology. This point is illustrated well by an "awkward exchange between James Gray and Torrey's daughter Edith in 1931." Moody Bible Institute wanted to alter a section of Torrey's correspondence course on the baptism with the Holy Spirit, but due to copyright restrictions they needed the Torrey family's permission to do so. "Torrey's teachings were too close to 'extreme Pentecostalists,' like Aimee Semple McPherson, Gray explained."[144] Most Fundamentalists, with their Dispensationalist orientation, had rejected this approach. Edith was horrified by Gray's request and firmly rejected it, asking that he never mention the matter again.[145] This judgment is also supported by Torrey's wife. When some of Torrey's students attempted to distance his teaching on Spirit baptism from that of Pentecostalism by claiming that Torrey simply had been careless with his use of terms, Mrs. Torrey emphatically denied these "reports, claiming that his views on the subject had never changed despite his rejection of glossolalia as uniform initial evidence."[146]

CONCLUSION

We have noted that R. A. Torrey, with good reason, might be called, the Father of Fundamentalism. Yet we have documented how his views, particularly with reference to the baptism with the Holy Spirit, anticipate and significantly influence the nascent Pentecostal movement. Torrey's understanding of Spirit baptism as a definite experience, distinct from regeneration, that empowers witness and service, to a large degree shapes the doctrinal formulations of later Pentecostal denominations, including the Assemblies of God. We have also emphasized that Torrey's hermeneutic

---

144. Gloege, *Guaranteed Pure*, 227.

145. Gloege, *Guaranteed Pure*, 227. Gloege cites the correspondence for this exchange on 260n2.

146. Waldvogel, "Reformed Evangelical Contribution," 19n32. See there the correspondence and sources Waldvogel cites. So also King states, "To his credit, Torrey's position changed little if at all over the years since *The Baptism with the Holy Spirit* had come out in 1895" (*Disfellowshiped*, 140).

PART I: PENTECOSTAL THEOLOGY

was, in many respects, unique. He privileged Luke–Acts and highlighted the continuity that linked the early church with believers today. Additionally, Torrey read the Bible, and especially Acts, as a treasure trove of promises—promises which include the baptism with the Holy Spirit and that are available to every believer today. Thus, Torrey also blazed an interpretative trail that many Pentecostals would follow. While it is true that Torrey rejected the Pentecostal position that "tongues" serve as the normative sign of Spirit Baptism, it is also evident that this doctrine simply reflects Torrey's reading of Acts taken to its logical end. It is a natural extension of Torrey's hermeneutic. We have thus explored reasons for Torrey's inability to affirm or express sympathy for this position, which include cultural factors, peer pressure, and his negative encounters with proto-Pentecostal John Alexander Dowie. Finally, we have described the remarkable and significant influence that Torrey has exerted on the Pentecostal movement, shaping its doctrine, hermeneutic, and practice at a number of points.

When one considers the impressive resume of shared values and impact that link Torrey together with the Pentecostal movement, it is difficult to find their equivalent in the Fundamentalist (or non-Pentecostal Evangelical) world. This is particularly the case when we remember that Pentecostals affirmed (and still affirm) all of the key doctrines delineated in *The Fundamentals*, and that the Fundamentalists rejected (and still reject) many of Torrey's teachings, including his approach to divine healing and living by faith as well as his understanding of Spirit baptism, that the Pentecostals embraced. An honest review of the evidence leads to the following conclusion: R. A. Torrey's enduring theological legacy is to be found in the sons and daughters of the Azusa Street Revival rather than in the stepchildren of post-Torrey Fundamentalist institutions.

This conclusion challenges traditional notions held both by Pentecostals and Fundamentalists alike. We Pentecostals often portray our own roots as if we had almost nothing to do with the dry, rationalistic, Fundamentalists. These historical reconstructions often pit the inspiration of the Spirit against serious study of the Bible and assert that the early Pentecostals had a largely community-driven, subjective hermeneutic.[147] In the

---

147. For example, see Archer, *Pentecostal Hermeneutic* and Smith, "Closing of the Book," 49–71. Torrey does not easily fit into Archer's categories, which tend to pit rationalistic Fundamentalists against experiential Pentecostals. Archer claims that "Fundamentalists read the Bible as a past inspired revelatory document, but Pentecostals read the Bible as a presently inspired story" (*Pentecostal Hermeneutic*, 69), yet for Torrey clearly the Bible was a presently inspired story. Smith states, "my goal has been to sketch

golden age, we are told, experience reigned supreme and was given primacy over a rational reading of Scripture.[148] Torrey's hermeneutic demonstrates that Pentecostals were not so unique as is often thought in this regard. He too read the Bible as a living text. Torrey's approach also reminds us that a logical, rational approach to Scripture can be combined with a deep desire to hear the voice of the Spirit and to respond obediently. Additionally, Torrey's significant influence on the Pentecostal movement, particularly in its formative stages, calls us to see the important points of agreement that unite us together with our Fundamentalist brothers and sisters, and to acknowledge that a logical, reasoned approach to Scripture actually forms the bedrock of the Pentecostal movement.

This study also encourages Fundamentalists to take another look at Torrey and his teaching, particularly his understanding of Spirit baptism. Torrey cannot easily be pushed aside as a marginal thinker or as someone who was simply misunderstood. Torrey was a theological giant, the architect of *The Fundamentals*, and he was in many respects also a Pentecostal. Perhaps by honestly reexamining Torrey's work we can all find much more common ground than we have previously imagined possible. I firmly believe that Torrey, the theological pugilist, would encourage this effort and call us to see that, in the power of the Spirit, we have "a fighting chance" to achieve great things for the kingdom of God.

---

the relationship between textual and oral/prophetic communities as one traditionally accompanied by exclusion and oppression of the latter by the former" ("Closing of the Book," 70). Again, Smith's construct, which pits Fundamentalists (a textual community) against the early Pentecostals (an oral/prophetic community), does not account for Fundamentalists like Torrey.

148. Sociologist Margaret M. Poloma exemplifies the tendency by charismatic scholars to pit the cognitive and doctrinal aspects of the faith against the affective and experiential, and to elevate the latter over the former. So, Poloma asks whether the Assemblies of God might "morph into modern, plain-vanilla evangelicalism that emphasized cognitive 'knowing' over the affective experiences that characterized Pentecostal 'knowing'?" (Poloma and Green, *Assemblies of God*, 61). See also Castelo, *Pentecostalism as a Christian Mystical Tradition*, in this regard.

Part II

PENTECOSTAL THEOLOGY
Its Evangelical Foundations

My father was a church historian. He loved to speak of the value of studying church history, and often described the rich truths and important perspectives that flowed from his study. When it came to the emergence of the modern Pentecostal movement, my father was quite clear. He emphasized that the unusual experiences that marked the Azusa Street Revival and later Pentecostal gatherings were not unique. Indeed, he pointed to over twenty charismatic movements that have appeared throughout the church's history, most of which experienced similar phenomena. Prophecy, healing, exorcism, speaking in tongues—these experiences are not new or novel, nor were they one hundred years ago. These kinds of charismatic experiences have punctuated the life of the church in diverse places and among different groups at various times over the past two thousand years. No, the modern Pentecostal movement in this regard is not unique.

"What is unique about the modern Pentecostal revival," my Father would say with a gleam in his eye, "is that it has survived." It has survived and become an integral part of mainstream, Evangelical Christianity. You see, if we study these twenty-plus charismatic movements of the past, we find that none of them ended well. This is a sobering fact. The Montanists are an excellent example of a charismatic group that probably started well, but ended badly. The list of other such movements is painfully long. Most of these movements started well, but all of them remained on the periphery of the life of the church. In time, due to an overemphasis on charismatic gifts and a lack of grounding in Scripture, these groups went astray. A charismatic leader or self-proclaimed prophet would arise and lead the group into self-destructive fanaticism and heresy. However, as my Father would say, here is where the modern Pentecostal movement is different. Here we find its *uniqueness*. The Pentecostal movement has survived long enough to become a part of mainstream Christianity. It survived and it did not remain on the periphery. Indeed, as our last chapter chronicles, the Pentecostal movement began with a strong sense that it was a part of the larger Evangelical church. Over time, relationships with the broader church deepened and matured. The result was, in my view, a wonderful cross-pollination. The Pentecostals influenced their Evangelical neighbors, and in turn they too were impacted by their Evangelical brothers and sisters. One positive aspect of this Evangelical influence was an affirmation of what was present from the beginning—a strong commitment to the Bible as the standard, the measuring stick, for doctrine, practice, and spiritual experiences.

So, while the experiences (prophecy, healing, tongues, etc.) of the modern Pentecostal movement are not new, the fact that it has become an integral part of mainstream, orthodox Christianity—indeed, a vital part of the global Evangelical church—is unique. Herein lies the Pentecostal movement's significance and incredible promise: for the first time in the history of the church a charismatic movement has become mainstream and significantly impacted the church universal. This is no doubt the case because the early Pentecostal leaders were committed to judging their theology and practice, their spiritual experiences, according to the word of God. The warm relationships that developed over time with their Evangelical brothers and sisters clearly facilitated this healthy and essential posture. If the early leaders of the Pentecostal movement had departed from a firm commitment to judge their message and experience against the standard of the Bible, history tells us that the movement would have become marginalized from the larger body of Christ and spiraled downward into irrelevancy due to heresy and excess. Thankfully, this was not the course of the modern Pentecostal movement.

One early example of the way that biblical authority was affirmed by Pentecostal leaders is found in the manner in which William Seymour, the primary leader of the Azusa Street Revival, dealt with the issue of *glossographia*. Some Pentecostal believers, at both Charles F. Parham's Bethel Bible School and the Azusa Street Revival, claimed that when they were inspired by the Spirit, they could not only speak in "other tongues," but that they could also miraculously write in languages that were previously unknown to them. Seymour's wise and biblically-grounded response is worth noting:

> We do not read anything in the Word about writing in unknown languages, so we do not encourage that in our meetings. Let us measure everything by the Word, that all fanaticism may be kept out of the work. We have found it questionable whether any real good has come out of such writing.[149]

I would acknowledge that Pentecostals have not always been so wise. Examples of "wild fire," extremes and excess, can certainly be found in our colorful history. Nevertheless, for the most part, the Pentecostal Movement has followed the wise course advocated by William Seymour and attempted to measure its message and ministry against the standard of the Bible.[150]

In the following section, "Evangelical Foundations," I want to illustrate, in successive chapters (chapters 2–4), how this is true of the three most distinctive doctrines of the Pentecostal Movement: our understanding of baptism in the Spirit; our affirmation of speaking in tongues as an edifying form of Spirit-inspired prayer and praise; and our approach to "signs and wonders." My goal is to show how these convictions are all strongly grounded in careful analysis of the Bible. Some may, for various reasons, ultimately disagree with my conclusions, but I do not believe an objective reader can read these chapters and come away without an appreciation for their force and merit. They certainly cannot deny that the arguments put forth are firmly grounded in Scripture. This, then, is our Evangelical foundation.

At times I have been challenged by well-meaning friends or even publishers with the question, why do you write with an Evangelical audience

---

149. *Apostolic Faith* 1.10 (September, 1907). I am indebted to Yi Zhi Gang, a student at the Asia Pacific Theological Seminary, for pointing me to this quotation. See his fine unpublished paper, "Glossographia: A Lens for Examining the Role of Glossolalia in Mission."

150. Although some Pentecostals in the academy appear to be moving away from a focus on historical meaning (e.g., Amos Yong, *Spirit of Love*, 111; Kenneth Archer, *Pentecostal Hermeneutic*, 208; and the Cleveland School, cf. Archer, "Cleveland School"), this does not reflect the viewpoint of the vast majority of Pentecostal believers, churches, and institutions. For more on this issue, see my chapter "Jumping Off the Post-Modern Bandwagon" in Menzies and Menzies, *Spirit and Power*. The danger of a focus on experience that loses sight of the historical meaning of the biblical text is illustrated in the trajectory of Pietism, which influenced Immanuel Kant and Friedrich Schleiermacher (see Noll, *Scandal of the Evangelical Mind*, 48). For a balanced and contemporary defense of historical meaning, see Keener, *Spirit Hermeneutics*, 99–151.

in view? Isn't that audience a bit too narrow? My response is unequivocal: I write for an Evangelical audience because we speak the same language, the language of the Bible. My positions and arguments are rooted in Scripture. If my readers do not share with me a common commitment to the authority of the Bible, then I have no way of speaking to them with clarity and conviction. Additionally, they also have no way of engaging me in fruitful discussion or helping me better understand my subject. Simply put, we are unable to encourage one another because we do not speak the same language. I trust as you read the following chapters you will recognize that we do indeed speak the same language, and that we can encourage one another in our common pursuit to better understand the word of God and more faithfully apply it in our lives.

Chapter 2

BAPTISM IN THE HOLY SPIRIT
A Prophetic Empowering

SOME YEARS AGO A Chinese house church leader commented, "When Western Christians read the book of Acts, they see in it *inspiring stories*; when Chinese believers read the book of Acts, we see in it our *own lives*." My Chinese friend's point was clear: their experience of opposition and persecution impacts how they read Luke's narrative. Chinese believers tend to read Luke–Acts with a sense of urgency and desperation, a sense of hunger generated by their need. So, they easily identify with the struggles of Peter and John, of Stephen and Paul. And so also they readily accept the promise of the Spirit's enabling to persevere and bear bold witness for Jesus in the face of opposition. Implicit in my friend's comment is also the belief that Christians who live in stable and affluent countries, Christians who live in contexts where the church has a long and storied history, may have a difficult time reading the book of Acts in this way. He was suggesting that many of these Christians may find it hard to identify with the struggles and needs of the early disciples, and thus they do not read with the same sense of solidarity or with the same sense of urgency.

I believe that this conversation touches on perhaps the greatest contribution the Pentecostal movement is making to the larger church world: The Pentecostal movement is calling the church universal to take a fresh look at Luke's two-volume work. And in the process, it is encouraging the church to consider once again its own understanding and its own need of the Holy Spirit's power. It is precisely here, in Luke–Acts, where we find the central and distinctive message of the Pentecostal movement. From the earliest days of the modern Pentecostal revival, Pentecostals have proclaimed that all Christians may, and indeed should, experience a baptism in the Holy Spirit "distinct from and subsequent to the experience of new birth."[1] This understanding of Spirit baptism flows naturally from the conviction that the Spirit came upon the disciples at Pentecost (Acts 2), not as the source of new covenant existence or new spiritual life (regeneration); but rather, as the source of power for effective witness. Pentecostals, like R. A. Torrey, resist the temptation to interpret the Pentecostal "baptism in the Holy Spirit" in Pauline terms as the source of regeneration and the climax of conversion (cf. 1 Cor 12:13).[2] Instead, Pentecostals take Luke's description seriously: "But you will receive power when the Holy Spirit comes on you; and you will be my witnesses . . . to the ends of the earth" (Acts 1:8).[3] This understanding of Spirit baptism has given the modern Pentecostal movement its identity, its unifying experience, and its missiological focus.

The rapid growth of Pentecostal churches around the world, particularly in the Two-Thirds World, makes it difficult for the global church to ignore this movement and its theology. Indeed, Pentecostal churches around the world have been growing with such rapidity that "some historians refer

---

1. *Minutes of the 44th Session of the General Council of the Assemblies of God* (Portland, OR; August 6-11, 1991), 129.

2. In his influential book, *Baptism in the Holy Spirit*, James Dunn argued that the authors of the NT uniformly present the gift of the Spirit as "the most fundamental aspect of the event or process of becoming a Christian, the climax of conversion-initiation" (quote from Dunn, "Response to Pentecostal Scholarship," 2, where he summarizes his thesis developed in *Baptism in the Holy Spirit*). More recently, Max Turner has offered an updated but similar view. According to Turner, throughout the New Testament the Spirit as the Spirit of prophecy provides wisdom "essential for fully authentic human existence before God" (Turner, *Holy Spirit and Spiritual Gifts*, 15). Thus, for Turner as for Dunn, the gift of the Spirit is a key element of conversion-initiation and essential to authentic Christian existence. These views largely define non-Pentecostal perspectives.

3. Pentecostals maintain that Luke's perspective on the work of the Spirit is complementary to that of Paul and that we need to do justice to both biblical authors. While Paul tells us that every Christian receives the Spirit when they repent and come to faith, Luke speaks of another dimension of the Spirit's work. Luke tells us that every believer (cf. Acts 2:17-18; Luke 11:13) may receive a prophetic anointing (i.e., baptism in the Holy Spirit) that enables its recipients to bear bold witness for Jesus. Although for Luke "baptism in the Spirit" describes the initial experience of this prophetic power, his narrative also encourages his readers to experience this power in an ongoing way. Thus, the same disciples that were "baptized" in the Spirit on the day of Pentecost (Luke uses a variety of terms to describe the Pentecostal outpouring of the Spirit), are also "filled with the Spirit" when they encounter persecution a short time later (Acts 4:31).

to the 20th century as the 'Pentecostal Century.'"[4] So, let us heed the call and turn once again to the pages of Luke–Acts. More specifically, let us seek to understand what Luke means when he speaks of people being "baptized in the Holy Spirit" (Luke 3:16; Acts 1:5; 11:16). I hope to facilitate this goal by analyzing three important texts from Luke's Gospel—texts that, I will argue, affirm the Pentecostal approach by defining the Pentecostal gift or "baptism in the Spirit" as an empowering for mission distinct from conversion.

JOHN THE BAPTIST'S PROPHECY

John the Baptist's prophecy concerning the one who will baptize in Spirit and fire, recorded in Luke 3:16–17, is particularly important for our study:

> John answered them all, "I baptize you with water. But one more powerful than I will come, the thongs of whose sandals I am not worthy to untie. He will baptize you with the Holy Spirit and fire. His winnowing fork is in his hand to clear his threshing floor and to gather the wheat into his barn, but he will burn up the chaff with unquenchable fire." (Luke 3:16–17)[5]

The interpretation of this prophecy—specifically, the functions it attributes to the Spirit—is crucial, for Luke clearly sees this prophecy at least partially fulfilled at Pentecost in the disciples' baptism in the Spirit (Acts 1:4–5). James Dunn speaks for many when he states that the prophecy presents the Spirit as "purgative and refining for those who had repented, destructive . . . for those who remained impenitent."[6] However, I believe this interpretation must be rejected in light of the Jewish background, the immediate context with its winnowing metaphor, and the larger context of Luke–Acts.

The Jewish background is particularly instructive. There are no pre-Christian references to a messianic bestowal of the Spirit that purifies and transforms *the individual*. However, there are a wealth of passages that describe the Messiah as charismatically endowed with the Spirit of God so that he may rule and judge (e.g. 1 En. 49:3; 62:2). Isaiah 4:4 refers to the Spirit of God as the means by which the nation of Israel (not individuals!)

---

4. Synan, *Century*, 2.

5. All English Scripture citations are taken from the NIV (1996) unless otherwise noted.

6. Dunn, *Baptism in the Holy Spirit*, 13.

shall be sifted with the righteous being separated from the wicked and the nation thus cleansed. Several texts tie these two concepts together. Perhaps most striking is Psalms of Solomon 17:26–37, a passage which describes how the Messiah, "powerful in the Holy Spirit" (17:37), shall purify Israel by ejecting all aliens and sinners from the nation. Isaiah 11:2–4 declares that the Spirit-empowered Messiah will slay the wicked "with the breath [*ruach*] of his lips."[7] Against this background it is not difficult to envision the Spirit of God as an instrument employed by the Messiah to sift and cleanse the nation.[8] Indeed, these texts suggest that when John referred in metaphorical language to the messianic deluge of the Spirit, he had in mind Spirit-inspired oracles of judgment uttered by the Messiah (cf. Isa 11:4), blasts of the Spirit that would separate the wheat from the chaff.

Luke, writing in light of Pentecost, sees the fuller picture and applies the prophecy to the Spirit-inspired witness of the early church (Acts 1:4–5). Through their witness, the wheat is separated from the chaff (Luke 3:17). This interpretation is reinforced by the winnowing metaphor, which portrays the wind as the source of sifting. Since the term translated "wind" in Greek (πνεῦμα) and Hebrew (*ruach*) is also used to refer to "the Spirit," the symbolism is particularly striking. This Spirit-inspired witness and its impact is foreshadowed by Simeon's prophecy in Luke 2:34. Simeon, with reference to Jesus, declares: "This child is destined to cause the falling and rising of many in Israel."

In short, John described the Spirit's work, not as cleansing repentant individuals, but rather as a blast of the "breath" of God that would sift the nation. Luke sees this prophecy, at least with reference to the sifting work of the Spirit, fulfilled in the Spirit-inspired mission of the church. The essential point for our purpose is that here Luke presents Spirit baptism, not as the source of cleansing for the individual, but rather as the animating force behind the church's witness.[9]

THE SENDING OF THE SEVENTY (LUKE 10:1–16)

Let us now turn to a text unique to Luke's Gospel, Luke's account of the Sending of the Seventy (Luke 10:1–16). All three synoptic Gospels record

---

7. This passage is echoed in 1 En. 62:2 and 1QSb 5:24–25.

8. So also Best, "Spirit-Baptism," 237.

9. For a more detailed version of my argument, see Menzies, *Empowered for Witness*, 123–31.

Jesus' words of instruction to the Twelve as he sends them out on their mission. However, only Luke records a second, larger sending of disciples (Luke 10:1-16). In Luke 10:1 we read, "After this the Lord appointed seventy-two [some mss. read, 'seventy'] others and sent them two by two ahead of him to every town and place where he was about to go." A series of detailed instructions follow. Finally, Jesus reminds them of their authority, "He who listens to you listens to me; he who rejects you rejects me; but he who rejects me rejects him who sent me" (10:16).

A central question centers on the number of disciples that Jesus sent out and its significance. The manuscript evidence is, at this point, divided. Some manuscripts read "seventy," while others list the number as "seventy-two." Bruce Metzger, in his article on this question, noted that the external manuscript evidence is evenly divided and internal considerations are also inconclusive. Metzger thus concluded that the number "cannot be determined with confidence."[10] More recent scholarship has largely agreed with Metzger, with a majority opting cautiously for the authenticity of "seventy-two" as the more difficult reading.[11] Although we cannot determine the number with confidence, it will be important to keep the divided nature of the manuscript evidence in mind as we wrestle with the significance of this text.

Most scholars agree that the number (for convenience, we will call it "seventy") has symbolic significance. Certainly Jesus' selection of twelve disciples was no accident. The number twelve clearly symbolizes the reconstitution of Israel (Gen 35:23-26), the people of God. This suggests that the number seventy is rooted in the Old Testament narrative and has symbolic significance as well. A number of proposals have been put forward,[12] but I would argue that the background for the reference to the "seventy" is to be found in Numbers 11:24-30. This passage describes how the Lord "took of the Spirit that was on [Moses] and put the Spirit on the seventy elders"

---

10. Metzger, "Seventy or Seventy-Two Disciples?," 299–306 (quote, p. 306). See also the response of Jellicoe, "St Luke and the 'Seventy(-Two)'," 319–21.

11. A "more difficult reading" refers to a unique version of a text preserved in early manuscripts that is hard to explain as a scribal correction, omission, or addition. Thus, this "difficult" reading is often viewed as authentic. All of the following scholars favor the "seventy-two" reading as original: Bock, *Luke 9.51—24.53*, 994; Marshall, *Luke*, 415; Green, *Luke*, 409; Tannehill, *Narrative Unity*, 233; Evans, *Luke*, 172. One exception to this general rule is John Nolland, who favors the "seventy" reading (Nolland, *Luke 9.21—18.34*, 546).

12. For the various options see Metzger, "Seventy or Seventy-Two Disciples?," 303–4, and Bock, *Luke 9.51—24.53*, 1015.

(Num 11:25). This resulted in the seventy elders, who had gathered around the Tent, prophesying for a short duration. However, two other elders, Eldad and Medad, did not go to the Tent; rather, they remained in the camp. But the Spirit also fell on them and they too began to prophesy and continued to do so. Joshua, hearing this news, rushed to Moses and urged him to stop them. Moses replied, "Are you jealous for my sake? I wish that all the Lord's people were prophets and that the Lord would put his Spirit on them!" (Num 11:29).

The Numbers 11 proposal has a number of significant advantages over other explanations: (1) it accounts for the two textual traditions underlying Luke 10:1 (How many actually prophesied in Numbers 11?); (2) it finds explicit fulfillment in the narrative of Acts; (3) it ties into one of the great themes of Luke-Acts, the work of the Holy Spirit; and (4) numerous allusions to Moses and his actions in Luke's travel narrative support our suggestion that the symbolism for Luke's reference to the Seventy should be found in Numbers 11.[13]

With this background in mind, the significance of the symbolism is found in the expansion of the number of disciples "sent out" into mission from the Twelve to the Seventy. The reference to the Seventy evokes memories of Moses' wish that "all the Lord's people were prophets," and, in this way, points ahead to Pentecost (Acts 2), where this wish is initially and dramatically fulfilled. This wish continues to be fulfilled throughout Acts as Luke describes the coming of the empowering Spirit of prophecy to other new centers of missionary activity, such as those gathered together in Samaria (Acts 8:14–17), Cornelius' house (Acts 10:44–48), and Ephesus (Acts 19:1–7). The reference to the Seventy, then, does not simply anticipate the mission of the church to the Gentiles; rather, it foreshadows the outpouring of the Spirit on all the servants of the Lord and their universal participation in the mission of God (Acts 2:17–18; cf. 4:31).[14]

In Luke's view, every member of the church is called and empowered to take up Israel's prophetic vocation and be "a light to the nations" by bearing bold witness for Jesus (Acts 1:4–8; cf. Isa 49:6).[15] Far from being unique

---

13. For more detailed support of this position, see Menzies, *Language of the Spirit*, 73–82.

14. Nickle, *Preaching the Gospel of Luke*, 117: "The 'Seventy' is the church in its entirety, including Luke's own community, announcing the in-breaking of God's royal rule throughout the length and breadth of God's creation."

15. For a dissenting perspective, see Max Turner's two articles, "Does Luke Believe Reception of the 'Spirit of Prophecy' Makes All 'Prophets'?," 3–24, and "Every Believer

and unrepeatable or limited to a select few, Luke emphasizes that the prophetic enabling experienced by the disciples at Pentecost is available to all of God's people. At Pentecost, Moses' wish now begins to be realized. Luke 10:1 anticipates the fulfillment of this reality.

In short, Luke presents the Sending of the Seventy, with its call to "heal the sick" and proclaim "the Kingdom of God" (Luke 10:9; cf. Acts 8:12), as a model for the later "sending" of all of Jesus' disciples that begins at Pentecost.[16] The missiological nature of this "sending" and the anointing (or baptism in the Spirit, cf. Acts 1:5) that makes it possible cannot be minimized. This passage, then, offers strong support for the Pentecostal position.[17]

POWER FROM ON HIGH (LUKE 24:45-49)

In the last chapter of Luke's Gospel, there is a striking emphasis on the necessity of Jesus' death and resurrection. This theme begins with the message directed to the women at Jesus' tomb by two angels. The angels declare to the frightened women, "Why do you look for the living among the dead? He is not here; he has risen! Remember how he told you, while he was still with you in Galilee: 'The Son of Man must [δεῖ] be delivered into the hands of sinful men, be crucified and on the third day be raised again'" (Luke 24:5-7).

This theme continues with Jesus' conversation with the two disciples on the road to Emmaus. The two disciples, who do not recognize the risen Lord, describe all that has happened to Jesus. They describe Jesus' ministry as "powerful in word and deed," and speak of his crucifixion, the empty tomb, and the startling report of the angels that Jesus was alive. Then, Jesus breaks in with these words, "How foolish you are, and how slow of heart to

---

as a Witness in Acts?," 57–71. Turner argues that only a select group is empowered for prophetic witness. Yet I would suggest that his discussion fails to adequately account for this text.

16. Luke intended for his readers to read Jesus' instructions to the Seventy (Luke 10:1–16), which includes eight directives, as a model for their own lives. The one exception is the command to travel lightly, without "a purse or bag or sandals" (Luke 10:4), which Jesus specifically rescinds in Luke 22:36. All of the other commands shape the missionary practice of the early church as it is recorded in Acts. For a detailed discussion of this thesis, see Menzies, "Sending of the Seventy and Luke's Purpose," 87–113.

17. Contra Max Turner, who asserts, "Luke does not in fact portray the whole church as actively involved in witness" (Turner, *Power from on High*, 432).

believe all that the prophets have spoken! Did not the Christ have [δεῖ] to suffer these things and then enter his glory?" (Luke 24:25–26). In the next verse, we begin to learn why these events were so necessary: "And beginning with Moses and all the Prophets, he explained to them what was said in all the Scriptures concerning himself" (Luke 24:27).

Finally, this theme reaches its climax with Jesus' appearance to the disciples who had gathered in Jerusalem. Jesus declares to them all, "This is what I told you while I was still with you: Everything must [δεῖ] be fulfilled that is written about me in the Law of Moses, the Prophets and the Psalms" (Luke 24:44). Then Jesus "opened their minds so they could understand the Scriptures" (Luke 24:45). But here we are told that Jesus not only revealed to the disciples the meaning of Old Testament passages that speak of the Messiah's death and resurrection (Luke 24:46); we are also told that Jesus taught them from the Scriptures of the mission of the church (Luke 24:47). Indeed, Jesus declares, "repentance and forgiveness of sins will be preached in [the Christ's] name to all nations, beginning at Jerusalem. You are witnesses of these things" (Luke 14:47–48).

It is interesting to consider what texts Jesus explained to the disciples. Surely, this was the greatest Bible study ever conducted. What texts did Jesus open their minds to? Although none of us were there, Luke gives us plenty of clues concerning the identity of the key texts discussed. For example, what Old Testament passages speak of the Messiah's death and resurrection? Certainly one text that Jesus "opened their minds" to in this regard was Isaiah 53. Later in the narrative of Acts, a portion of Isaiah 53 is quoted by Luke as he tells the story of Philip's dramatic encounter with the Ethiopian Eunuch. "Tell me," the Eunuch asks, "who is the prophet talking about, himself or someone else?" (Acts 8:34). Beginning with this very text, Philip "told him the good news about Jesus" (Acts 8:35).

We also have some important clues concerning the texts that Jesus used to teach about the mission of the church. One key text was certainly Isaiah 49:6.[18] In their sermon in the synagogue at Pisidian Antioch, Paul and Barnabas specifically cite this text (Acts 13:47). It also forms the backdrop to Jesus' promise in Acts 1:8, "But you will receive power when the Holy Spirit comes on you; and you will be my witnesses in Jerusalem, and in all Judea and Samaria, and to the ends of the earth."[19] The phrase, "the

---

18. See Tiede, "Exaltation of Jesus and the Restoration of Israel in Acts 1," 285–86.

19. Other allusions to Isa 49:6 may be found in Luke 2:32; Acts 26:23; and perhaps Acts 28:28.

ends of the earth," is echoed in Isaiah 49:6. This important verse, which undoubtedly helped shaped the early church's identity, reads: "He [the Lord] says, 'It is too small a thing for you to be my servant, to restore the tribes of Jacob, and bring back those of Israel I have kept. I will also make you a light for the Gentiles, that you may bring my salvation to the ends of the earth'" (Isa 49:6).

Against this backdrop, Jesus' words in Acts 1:8 take on fresh meaning. In response to the disciples' rather limited and ethnocentric question, "Lord, are you at this time going to restore the kingdom to Israel?" (Acts 1:6), Jesus declares that they should not worry about the restoration of Israel. He is doing that. But the Lord's plan for them is larger than they can imagine. He will use them—not only to restore Israel—but to fulfill Israel's prophetic calling. They are to be "a light to the nations."[20]

The reason for this emphasis on the necessity of Jesus' death and resurrection is now laid bare. It is all a part of God's wonderful, unstoppable, and incredible plan—a plan that was foretold in the Scriptures (i.e., the Old Testament). Amazingly, this plan includes us (Luke 10:1; Acts 2:17-18). We, too, have been called to declare his "name to all nations" (Luke 24:47). We, too, are witnesses of these events . . . witnesses to "the ends of the earth" (Acts 1:8). And so the promise comes: "I am going to send you what my Father has promised; but stay in the city until you have been clothed with power from on high" (Luke 24:48-49). Torrey had it right: this is what the power of Pentecost is all about.

---

20. In "Spirit and Salvation in Luke-Acts," 103-16, Turner places great weight on the veiled references to Isaiah 32:15 in Luke 24:49 and Luke 1:35, much more weight it would appear than on Luke's direct statements (e.g., Luke 11:13; 24:47-49; Acts 1:8, 2:17-18). These allusions encourage Turner to suggest that in Luke's view the Spirit is the agent of the Christian community's "righteousness, peace, and life" (p. 110). I find Isaiah 49:6, which has a missiological focus, to be a much more convincing backdrop for Luke 24:49 and Acts 1:4-8. In any event, none of this should obscure the force of Luke's explicit statements. These allusions also lead Turner to see Jesus' miraculous birth by the Spirit (Luke 1:35) as a parallel to the believer's experience of the Spirit at Pentecost (p. 113n31). Yet certainly Luke has crafted his narrative in such a way as to present Jesus' experience of the Spirit at the Jordan (and his OT commentary on this event at the synagogue in Nazareth)—which Turner himself acknowledges to be an empowering for mission—as the true parallel to the disciples' experience on Pentecost (again, interpreted as a fulfillment of OT prophecy by Peter).

PART II: PENTECOSTAL THEOLOGY

CONCLUSION

At the end of the last century, those considering themselves to be Pentecostal or charismatic numbered over five hundred million.[21] A movement that started on January 1, 1901, in the space of a hundred years, had emerged as "the largest aggregate of Christians on the planet outside the Roman Catholic Church."[22] Yet, in spite of this phenomenal growth, many still do not see Pentecostals as having much to offer by way of theology. It is a movement of emotion and experience, we are told. These voices urge us to look elsewhere for sound doctrine. In this chapter I have sought to challenge this faulty assumption. Pentecostals have tremendously important theological contributions to make to the larger church world.

First and foremost, Pentecostals are calling the church to take a fresh look at Luke–Acts. Only by hearing Luke's distinctive voice can we develop a truly holistic doctrine of the Holy Spirit. Only by reading Luke–Acts on its own terms can we understand the significance of the promised baptism in the Holy Spirit (Acts 1:5). For far too long Protestant theology has highlighted Paul's important insights into the work of the Spirit, but largely ignored Luke's contribution. In this regard, Pentecostals are calling for a new reformation.

One of the great strengths of this fresh reading of Luke–Acts is that it highlights the missiological nature of discipleship and the church. Luke reminds us that the Holy Spirit is all about inspiring praise and witness for Jesus, and his vision knows no boundaries. Regardless of one's race, gender, or class, all are called to participate in God's great redemptive mission. And all have been promised power to fulfill this calling (Acts 1:8). Pentecostals are calling the church to recover its primitive power and its apostolic calling. The church is nothing less than a community of prophets who are called to bear bold witness for Jesus.

---

21. Barratt and Johnson, "Annual Statistical Table on Global Mission: 2001," 25.
22. Wacker, *Heaven Below*, 8.

Chapter 3

GLOSSOLALIA
Paul's Perspective

GLOSSOLALIA HAS BEEN CRUCIALLY important for Pentecostals the world over for many reasons, but I would suggest that two are of particular importance. First, speaking in tongues highlights and validates the unique way that Pentecostals read the book of Acts: Acts is not simply a historical document; rather, Acts presents a model for the life of the contemporary church. Thus, tongues serve as a sign that "their experience" is "our experience" and that all of the gifts of the Spirit (including the "sign gifts") are valid for the church today. Secondly, speaking in tongues calls the church to recognize and remember its true identity: the church is nothing less than a community of end-time prophets called and empowered to bear bold witness for Jesus. In short, the Pentecostal approach to tongues symbolizes significant aspects of the movement: its unique hermeneutic—that Acts and the apostolic church represent a model for the church today—and its central pneumatological emphasis—the prophetic and missionary nature of the Pentecostal gift. For Pentecostals, then, tongues serve as a sign that the calling and power of the apostolic church are valid for contemporary believers.

In the chapter that follows I would like to explore this important topic, "speaking in tongues," by examining Paul's perspective on this spiritual gift. Elsewhere I have argued that it is important to understand the polemical nature of Paul's words in 1 Corinthians 12–14 and the underlying concerns that shape them.[1] When we approach this important passage from this fuller perspective, we find that Paul is more appreciative of the sign-value of

---

1. See chapter 6 in Menzies, *Speaking in Tongues*.

tongues than is often recognized. His perspective fits together harmoniously with and complements the Spirit-inspired witness provided by Luke and by the author of the Long Ending of Mark (Mark 16:9–20). Additionally, when we read this passage with sensitivity to Paul's ultimate concerns, we also discover that Paul clearly highlights the edifying nature of glossolalia for the individual believer, affirms its availability to every believer, and recognizes its value, in special instances, for the entire church gathered together in corporate worship.[2] We may summarize by saying that the New Testament, and Paul is a major contributor here, highlights three ways in which speaking in tongues serves to encourage and edify individual Christians and the Christian community: (1) Tongues serve as a dramatic, observable sign of God's powerful presence in our midst and his call upon our lives; (2) Tongues are a powerful means by which the Spirit energizes our prayer and praise; and finally (3) Tongues, in a manner similar to prophecy, can be the means by which the Holy Spirit speaks to the larger body through the inspired utterances of individual believers. In my previous writings I have highlighted the way in which glossolalia functions as a sign and, at times, in corporate settings as a form of proclamation.[3] In this chapter I will explain how, in Paul's view, speaking in tongues functions as an aid to our prayer life and assists us in our worship of God.

TONGUES AS GLOSSOLALIA

Paul begins his discussion of spiritual gifts in 1 Corinthians 12–14 with a striking statement. He reminds the Corinthians of their pagan past: "You know that when you were pagans, somehow or other you were influenced and led astray to mute idols" (1 Cor 12:2). Paul here echoes the Old Testament's repudiation of the folly of worshiping objects made by human hands. Psalm 115:5, which drips with irony, illustrates the theme well, "They have mouths, but cannot speak, eyes, but they cannot see."

Paul then shifts the focus from the pagan past to the Christian present. The reference to "mute idols" stands in stark contrast to the Corinthian Christians' present experience of God. The God who has so beautifully and concretely revealed himself in Christ continues to speak through the Holy Spirit. Paul reminds the Corinthians that God is truly speaking in

---

2. For detailed, supporting arguments for these conclusions, see Menzies, *Speaking in Tongues*, especially chapters 5–7.

3. Menzies, *Speaking in Tongues*, esp. 107–23, 146–55.

and through them when the Holy Spirit inspires praise to Jesus in their midst. Paul declares, "no one can say, 'Jesus is Lord,' except by the Holy Spirit" (1 Cor 12:3).

Paul's instruction on the gifts of the Spirit that follows (1 Cor 12–14) is, in reality, a continuation of this theme. The God who speaks and acts through the inspiration of the Holy Spirit is the transcendent God who longs for relationship, who "is not far from each one of us," and who has revealed himself supremely in Jesus (Acts 17:24–31). This God, the one true God, speaks.

One of the ways that God speaks is through prayers inspired by the Holy Spirit. As we have noted, these prayers sometimes take the form of glossolalia. Paul refers to this kind of prayer when he describes the ability to speak in "different kinds of tongues" (γένη γλωσσῶν; 1 Cor 12:10) as one of the "gifts" (χαρισμάτων; 1 Cor 12:4) of the Spirit. Paul frequently uses the phrase, λαλέω γλώσσαις ("to speak in tongues"), when he refers to this gift.[4]

It should be noted that this phrase, λαλέω γλώσσαις ("to speak in tongues"), typically refers to unintelligible utterances inspired by the Holy Spirit. This is certainly the case for Paul.[5] According to Paul, tongues must be interpreted if they are to be understood (1 Cor 14:6–19, 28; cf. 12:10, 30). The one who speaks in tongues "does not speak to men but to God" and "utters mysteries" by the Spirit (1 Cor 14:2). Paul also declares, "If I pray in a tongue, my spirit prays, but my mind is unfruitful" (1 Cor 14:14). Furthermore, according to Paul, these unintelligible "tongues" typically do not take the form of unknown human languages (xenolalia). This is evident from Paul's usage throughout this passage, 1 Corinthians 12–14. Paul does not countenance the possibility that someone with an acquired knowledge of the "tongue" spoken might be present and able to interpret. On the contrary, Paul insists that one can interpret these tongues only if one has a special gift of the Spirit to do so (1 Cor 12:10). For this reason a number of commentators have suggested that Paul considered the gift of tongues to be the miraculous ability to speak the languages of the angels (1 Cor 13:1).[6] In 1 Corinthians 13:1 the phrase, "the tongues of men and angels," most likely refers to two kinds of spontaneous, Spirit-inspired speech. Here Paul appears to link the former with prophecy and the latter with "speaking in

---

4. 1 Cor 12:30; 13:1; 14:2, 4, 6, 13, 18, 23, 27, 39.
5. The only instance of xenolalia in the NT is found in Acts 2.
6. See, for example, Stibbe, *Know Your Spiritual Gifts*, 156.

tongues" or glossolalia. All of this indicates that when Paul refers to the gift of tongues or speaking in tongues, typically he does not have xenolalia in mind. Quite the contrary, with these phrases Paul refers to spontaneous utterances inspired by the Holy Spirit that are unintelligible to both the speaker and the hearer.

At this point, many may be tempted to ask, then why speak in tongues? What is the value of speaking words that no one understands? That is the question that I wish to address in the pages that follow. Let us begin our answer by examining Paul's attitude toward tongues in 1 Corinthians 12–14.

PAUL'S ATTITUDE TOWARD TONGUES

Even a casual reading of 1 Corinthians 12–14 reveals an obvious fact: all was not well in the church at Corinth. The Christians at Corinth exhibited a serious lack of understanding concerning the purpose and use of spiritual gifts. This in turn had a significantly negative impact on their corporate gatherings. Their misuse of spiritual gifts was creating divisions within the church and unnecessarily alienating others outside the church.

The problems at Corinth, at least with reference to their corporate worship, centered on their misunderstanding and abuse of the gift of tongues. The Corinthians exhibited a remarkable lack of concern for intelligibility in their meetings (1 Cor 14:23–25). So, Paul reminds them that one who speaks in tongues "utters mysteries" (1 Cor 14:2) and does not edify others (1 Cor 14:4). And he asks, "unless you speak intelligible words with your tongue, how will anyone know what you are saying?" (1 Cor 14:9). Finally, Paul urges them to "stop thinking like children" (1 Cor 14:20). He insists that tongues should not eclipse proclamation or instruction (1 Cor 14:23–25). Paul then concludes with a command: "If anyone speaks in a tongue ... someone must interpret" (1 Cor 14:27).

The Corinthians' abuse of tongues, however, flowed from an even more disturbing source. At least one faction at Corinth viewed speaking in tongues as a means of establishing their superior status. Speaking in tongues offered them a means by which they might display their authority and power over others in the church. Paul seeks to correct this immature and destructive mindset. He does so by highlighting the rich variety of God's gracious gifts (1 Cor 12:4–6). Paul declares that everyone has a role to play in corporate worship (1 Cor 12:11–27) and that edification is the overriding goal (1 Cor 12:7). Ultimately, Paul's argument reaches rhetorical heights with his call to exercise love: "If I speak in tongues... but have not love, I am only a resounding gong or a clanging cymbal" (1 Cor 13:1).

All of this is clear, but it is not the full picture. Unfortunately, many Christians today miss this point. They simply gloss over the surface, read Paul's polemical language, and dismiss tongues as an exotic aberration, an immature and emotional response that is at best outdated and often damaging and divisive. These negative perceptions have been reinforced by various psychological studies from a previous generation that merely parroted already established presuppositions. Although the spurious methodologies and dubious conclusions of these early studies have been discredited by more recent and credible research,[7] the negative stereotypes these studies fostered die hard.

It is important to read Paul's polemic against the abuse of tongues in 1 Corinthians 12–14 with two additional strands of biblical evidence in mind. First, we must recognize that Paul criticizes the abuse of tongues, not the gift itself. This explains why Paul shows such remarkable restraint in his teaching on gifts of the Spirit in general and speaking in tongues in particular. In view of the problems in Corinth, Paul's words at the very beginning of this letter to the church are truly astonishing. Paul writes:

> I always thank God for you because of his grace given you in Christ Jesus. For in him you have been enriched in every way—in all your speaking and in all your knowledge—because our testimony about Christ was confirmed in you. Therefore you do not lack any spiritual gift as you eagerly wait for our Lord Jesus Christ to be revealed. (1 Cor 1:4–7)

Thus, at the outset of his epistle, Paul unequivocally affirms the divine origin and the potentially rich impact of the very gifts that were causing the greatest problems in the church. That this is not merely some rhetorical strategy to win over the Corinthians becomes clear when we take a close look at Paul's instruction in 1 Corinthians 12–14. Although Paul clearly seeks to correct erroneous views and practice, Paul will not deny the validity of tongues nor will he denigrate the gift's value. Actually, Paul is quite positive concerning tongues when the gift is used for the right reasons and in the appropriate setting. Paul affirms that the private manifestation of tongues is edifying to the speaker (1 Cor 14:5) and, in an autobiographical note, he

---

7. Max Turner states, "Contrary to earlier claims, there is no evidence that 'tongues speech' is correlated with low intellect, education, social position or pathological psychology" (*Holy Spirit and Spiritual Gifts*, 305). See also the numerous studies he cites.

thanks God for the frequent manifestation of tongues in his private prayer-life (1 Cor 14:18). Fearful that his instructions to the Corinthians concerning the proper use of tongues "in the assembly" might be misunderstood, he explicitly commands them not to forbid speaking in tongues (1 Cor 14:39). And, with reference to the private manifestation of tongues, Paul declares: "I would like every one of you to speak in tongues" (1 Cor 14:5).

Let us now return to the question posed earlier, why should we speak words that no one understands? How does speaking in tongues enrich us "in every way?" The answer lies in Paul's description of speaking in tongues as a special form of prayer, a special form of communion with God. Here it is helpful to keep in mind the second strand of biblical data that helps us maintain a more balanced reading of Paul: numerous New Testament passages outside of 1 Corinthians, most of which were also written by Paul, add further perspective on this gift. These texts, in concert with Paul's teaching in 1 Corinthians 12–14, enable us to describe the nature of the gift of tongues in some detail. When we examine this biblical material, we find that the New Testament and Paul in particular present speaking in tongues as Spirit-inspired prayer that issues forth as either praise to God or intercession for others.

TONGUES AS PRAISE

Paul describes speaking in tongues as a gift that functions in two distinct settings: the private and the communal. The Corinthian abuse of tongues took place during their meetings when they worshiped together. So, Paul challenges their improper attitudes and expression of tongues in these corporate settings. I have examined Paul's teaching on the proper use of tongues in the corporate setting elsewhere.[8] Here, however, I want to examine what Paul's directives tell us about the private expression of this gift.

As we have noted, Paul is quite positive about the private expression of tongues. He explicitly states that tongues are edifying, that tongues "build up" the one speaking (1 Cor 14:4). Paul's words here also help us begin to understand how this edification takes place. Paul declares that "anyone who speaks in a tongue does not speak to men but to God" (1 Cor 14:2). Indeed, the person speaking in tongues "utters mysteries" by the Spirit (1 Cor 14:2). While Paul can use the term "mystery" (μυστήριον) to refer to specific aspects of God's redemptive plan (e.g., the inclusion of the Gentiles; Eph 3:6),

---

8. Menzies, *Speaking in Tongues*, chapter 7.

he uses the term in various ways. Here, the term simply "carries . . . the sense of that which lies outside the understanding, both for the speaker and the hearer."[9] As Gordon Fee notes, this understanding of the term flows naturally from the fact that the speaker is addressing God. The content of specific mysteries pertaining to God's plan revealed by the Spirit would "scarcely need to be spoken back to God."[10] Paul's point is thus relatively simple: the person who speaks in tongues speaks words known only to God.

Two other important implications follow. Paul declares that these words, known only to God, are inspired by the Holy Spirit and they are addressed to God. Although the description of tongues as addressed "not . . . to men but to God" (1 Cor 14:2) may highlight their unintelligibility (only God understands them) rather than their specific content (only praise addressed to God), there can be little doubt that Paul anticipates that the private expression of tongues will often take the form of praise directed to God. This understanding of tongues as doxological prayer is anticipated at the outset of Paul's discussion of spiritual gifts. While the idols are mute, the true God inspires praise to Jesus through the Holy Spirit (1 Cor 12:3). Of course this inspired praise is often expressed with intelligible words, whether they be sung or proclaimed. Nevertheless, Paul here makes it clear that at times this praise will be expressed in words that are not understood (i.e., glossolalia).

1 Corinthians 14:14-17. This doxological understanding of tongues surfaces again later in Paul's argument. In 1 Corinthians 14:14-17 Paul's primary objective is to persuade the Corinthians to emphasize intelligible discourse in their corporate meetings. So he declares,

> If I pray in a tongue, my spirit prays, but my mind is unfruitful. So what shall I do? I will pray with my spirit, but I will also pray with my mind; I will sing with my spirit, but I will also sing with my mind. (1 Cor 14:14-15)

The contrasts that Paul makes between praying and singing with "my spirit" and with "my mind" are instructive. First, it is evident that when Paul here speaks of praying with "my spirit," the activity of the Holy Spirit praying with or through his spirit is implied.[11] The larger context of 1 Cor-

---

9. Fee, *Corinthians*, 656.

10. Fee, *Corinthians*, 656.

11. In 1 Corinthians 14:15 the Greek is ambiguous and can be translated "pray with my spirit" or "pray in the Spirit;" so also with the verb, "sing." Either way, the inspiration of the Holy Spirit is either implied or explicitly stated.

inthians 12–14 demands this (1 Cor 12:7–11; 14:2, 16). Additionally, the contrast Paul offers with the terms "my spirit" and "my mind" highlights the important point noted above. When the Spirit produces glossolalic praise by praying with and through our spirit, our minds are not fully engaged; or, to put it simply, we do not understand what the Spirit is saying through us. Nevertheless, in spite of this lack of understanding, Paul affirms that as the Spirit prays through us, we are edified.

The fact that we are edified and enriched by this non-cognitive communion with God should not surprise us. The mystics and the contemplative tradition have highlighted this truth for centuries. I recall several years ago attending an early-morning prayer meeting at a theological institution. The leader of the session called for a long period of silence. In fact, almost all of our prayer time was spent in absolute silence. After the time of prayer ended, I spoke with the man who had led the session. I noted that I appreciated the period of silence, but wondered if they ever expressed their prayers with joyful shouts and loud declarations of praise as well. He thought for a moment and then responded, "No, we follow the mystics and the contemplative tradition." He added, "The mystics felt that through silence we are able to experience God directly, in an unmediated way that transcends our rational faculties." I smiled and then he began to smile too. He knew I was a Pentecostal and he anticipated my response. I replied, "That is exactly how we Pentecostals describe our experience of speaking in tongues. When we speak in tongues, we experience God directly, in a way that transcends our cognitive processes. However, there is a difference. When we speak in tongues, it's rarely quiet. It's usually loud and joyful."

I would add that we Pentecostals together with Paul do understand that there is an important, cognitive dimension to our faith and worship. This mystical experience of tongues is grounded in the gospel and biblical teaching. As a result, it is an experience that above all brings praise and glory to Jesus. If speaking in tongues for Paul and Pentecostals is a mystical experience, it is nonetheless an experience centered on Christ. Ulrich Luz, in his essay, "Paul as Mystic," states the matter well. He argues that the gift of the Spirit is the experiential basis of Paul's Christ-mysticism, which centers on "the conformity of the believer with the Lord Jesus in his passion and in his resurrection glory."[12] Luz notes that "the fear and panic at 'enthusiasm'

---

12. Luz, "Paul as Mystic," 140.

and any *theologia gloriae* which marks out many Protestant theologians is unknown to Paul, for it is not a question of his own glory, but Christ's."[13]

The Christ-centered nature of this charismatic experience becomes even more apparent as we examine further Paul's understanding of glossolalia as doxological prayer. Before we proceed, however, let us first summarize our argument up to this point. Paul affirms that glossolalia is speech inspired by the Holy Spirit. While the specific meaning of the words uttered is unknown to us, it is known to God. Indeed, these words typically take the form of praise directed to God. This doxological function of tongues is anticipated in 1 Corinthians 12:2–3 and explicitly stated in 1 Corinthians 14:14–17.

In 1 Corinthians 14:14–15 Paul refers to praying and singing with his spirit, which undoubtedly takes place through the inspiration of the Holy Spirit. As we have seen, the context, "For if I pray in a tongue . . . " (vs. 14), and the "spirit" and "mind" contrast, indicatesthat this Spirit-inspired type of praying (προσεύξομαι τῷ πνεύματι) and singing (ψαλῶ τῷ πνεύματι) is, in reality, praying in tongues and singing in tongues.

Paul describes the nature of this praying and singing in tongues further in 1 Corinthians 14:16–17. In verse 16 he refers to this praying and singing in tongues as praise directed to God ("If you are praising God with your spirit").[14] Then, in the next verse, Paul describes this Spirit-inspired glossolalia as a means of giving thanks, "You may be giving thanks well enough" (1 Cor 14:17). Although Paul does not elaborate here further since his chief concern lies elsewhere, these verses indicate that Paul understands praying and singing in tongues (literally, I will pray [προσεύξομαι τῷ πνεύματι] and sing [ψαλῶ τῷ πνεύματι] in the Spirit) as a charismatic form of thanksgiving and praise.

Ephesians 6:18. This understanding of tongues as doxological prayer is affirmed in several other Pauline passages. In Ephesians 6:18, immediately after encouraging his readers "to take the sword of the Spirit" (v. 17), Paul urges them to "pray in the Spirit [προσευχόμενοι . . . ἐν πνεύματι] on all occasions with all kinds of prayers and requests." James Dunn's paraphrase of this verse is helpful, "in every specific situation hold yourselves open to the prayer of the Spirit."[15] The wording here is almost identical with

---

13. Luz, "Paul as Mystic," 141.

14. Again, the Greek text is ambiguous here. 1 Cor 14:16 can be rendered, "If you are praising God with your spirit" or "If you are praising God in the Spirit."

15. Dunn, *Jesus and the Spirit*, 239.

1 Corinthians 14:15. Both verses speak of "praying in the Spirit" (προσεύχομαι ἐν/τῷ πνεύματι). This suggests that in Ephesians 6:18 Paul's exhortation to engage in charismatic prayer includes the notion of praying in tongues even if it is not restricted exclusively to it. The fact that Paul urges the Ephesians to pray "on all occasions" or "at all times," an exhortation that is repeated in the second half of the verse ("With this in mind, be alert and always keep on praying for all the saints" [Eph 6:18]), suggests that Paul here is speaking broadly of spontaneous, Spirit-inspired prayer. In Paul's mind, this kind of prayer likely included glossolalic prayer as well as intelligible forms of praise, intercession, and petition. This wider perspective is probably also implied with the phrase "with all kinds of prayers and requests" (Eph 6:18). The thought of intercession is clearly foremost in Paul's mind in the latter part of the verse, but the initial exhortation is broad and would appear to include praise and thanksgiving as well.

Jude 20. The exhortation to "pray in the Spirit" also appears in a non-Pauline passage, Jude 20. In Jude 20 we read, "But you, dear friends, build yourselves up in your most holy faith and pray in the Holy Spirit [ἐν πνεύματι ἁγίῳ προσευχόμενοι]." Jude was written by the brother of Jesus (and James) in the late 50s or early 60s AD. Jude wrote to combat false teachers who had misappropriated Paul's teaching on grace by taking it to unhealthy extremes.[16] These false teachers claimed to have the Holy Spirit, but Jude insists that they merely "follow their natural instincts and do not have the Spirit" (Jude 19).[17] In Jude 20 the false teachers' lack of the Spirit is contrasted with the Spirit-inspired quality of the prayers of the brothers and sisters in the church. The language that Jude uses here, "pray in the Holy Spirit," parallels closely Paul's usage in 1 Corinthians 14:15-16 and Ephesians 6:18. Thus, as Towner and Harvey observe, "there is a strong consensus that here Jude means prayer in a Spirit-given tongue (glossolalia)."[18]

Praying in the Spirit here is described as a means of building yourself up "in your most holy faith." How does this edification take place? The context of Jude and the way in which this charismatic prayer is described

---

16. Green, *Jude*, 17-18.

17. According to Harvey and Towner, the term "dreamers" (Jude 8) suggests that the false teachers laid claim to prophetic and visionary revelation (Harvey and Towner, *Jude*, 196).

18. Harvey and Towner, *Jude*, 225. So also Dunn, *Jesus and the Spirit*, 245-46, and Bauckham, *Jude*, 113: both describe the prayer as "charismatic prayer" which includes glossolalia.

elsewhere in the New Testament suggest that there are at least three ways that Spirit-inspired glossolalia "builds up" the one who prays.

First, as we see so clearly in Acts, praying in tongues strengthens the believers' sense of connection with the apostolic faith. More specifically, in this instance, glossolalia serves as a dramatic, tangible sign (both for the individual and the community), over against the false teachers, that they are indeed the true people of God.

Additionally, I would add that the Spirit builds us up in our most holy faith by interceding through us and for us (Rom 8:26–27). In the midst of our weakness, the Spirit prays for us. This is a theme that we will develop below.

Finally, as the Spirit prays through the believers, there is also a strong sense of communion with Christ. This is expressed beautifully in the *Abba* prayer of Romans 8:15–16 and Galatians 4:6, and implied in 1 Corinthians (cf. 12:3; 14:2, 14–17). Paul declares that "the Spirit himself testifies with our spirit that we are God's children" (Rom 8:16). Although the *Abba* prayer probably describes charismatic prayer more broadly, it undoubtedly includes glossolalic prayer.[19] Furthermore, it paints a powerful picture of what happens as the Spirit prays through us. We are caught up in the love of Christ and filled with joy as we begin to glimpse in part the wonder of our adoption as God's children. Somehow the Holy Spirit reveals a bit of the majesty and wonder of God's grace to us as he prays through us. No wonder that we are caught up in spiritual rapture and that human words fail to adequately express what we feel.[20] No wonder that as the Spirit prays through us and declares "the wonders of God" (Acts 2:11; cf. 1 Cor 14:16–17) that he reverts to his vernacular, the language of heaven.

This last point serves to remind us of the beauty and transforming power of worship. As we give praise and thanks to God, our perspective is changed. Our weakness and struggles seem to fade away as we are ushered into the presence of a mighty and powerful God. Certainly every encounter with God, every experience of worship that is centered on Christ is energized by the Holy Spirit. Nevertheless, Paul and the early church understood

---

19. That is to say, on occasion the *Abba* prayer may be expressed through speaking in tongues.

20. As we have noted, both Moody and Torrey spoke of experiences of spiritual rapture: Torrey, struck from his chair, repeatedly shouted, "glory to God," and later noted, "it was just as if some other power than my own was moving my jaws" (*Holy Spirit*, 199–200); Moody's experience was so overwhelming, he "had to ask God to withhold His hand, lest he die on the very spot for joy" (Marsden, *Fundamentalism*, 78).

that our worship is often energized in a special way by the Holy Spirit. These spontaneous moments of spiritual rapture are described with the phrase "in the Spirit."[21] These wonderful experiences often include glossolalic praise.

1 Thessalonians 5:19. In 1 Thessalonians 5:16–22 Paul alludes to this kind of charismatic experience. He offers the church at Thessalonica a series of exhortations. He urges them on with these words: "Be joyful always; pray continually; give thanks in all circumstances, for this is God's will for you in Christ Jesus" (1 Thess 5:16–18). These exhortations apply primarily to individual believers and are expressed daily in the midst of the diverse challenges and situations that each person faces. Then, I would argue, Paul shifts his attention to the Thessalonians' community life. He issues a series of commands that are designed to enhance their corporate worship, which in turn will enable individual Christians to embrace the personal exhortations he has just delivered. Paul's instructions for their "life together" are as follows: "Do not put out the Spirit's fire; do not treat prophecies with contempt. Test everything. Hold on to the good. Avoid every kind of evil" (1 Thess 5:19–22).

The structure of Paul's words at this point is instructive. Notice how Paul juxtaposes, "do not put out the Spirit's fire," with "do not treat prophecies with contempt." Paul's wording at this point is reminiscent of his coupling of tongues and prophecy in 1 Corinthians 14:39, where he declares, "be eager to prophesy, and do not forbid speaking in tongues." Indeed, this verse forms a striking parallel to 1 Thessalonians 5:19–20. Of course the close association between prophecy and tongues is characteristic of the book of Acts as well. Tongues and prophecy are explicitly linked in Acts 19:6, and by implication in Acts 2:16–18 and Acts 10:43–46. All of this suggests that when Paul encourages his readers to "not put out the Spirit's fire," he has speaking in tongues specifically in mind.[22]

This conclusion in turn suggests that speaking in tongues, like prophecy, may assist us in our quest to "be joyful always" and aid us as we seek to "pray continually" and "give thanks in all circumstances" (1 Thess 5:16–18). The larger context of Paul's epistles indicates that this is very much in line with Paul's teaching elsewhere (cf. 1 Cor 14:15–17; Eph 5:18–20; 6:18). When we see that tongues is, above all, Spirit-inspired doxological prayer,

---

21. So also Bauckham, *Jude*, 113, who cites numerous NT texts including Luke 2:27; 4:1; Acts 19:21; and 1 Cor 12:3 among others.

22. So also Sweet, "Glossolalia," 153.

the connections Paul draws between speaking in tongues and joyful prayer and thanksgiving are entirely understandable.

Ephesians 5:18 and Colossians 3:16. In addition to 1 Corinthians 12:2-3; 14:14-17; Ephesians 6:18; Jude 20; and 1 Thessalonians 5:19, two other passages present speaking in tongues as a form of doxological prayer.[23] In Ephesians 5:18 Paul admonishes his readers not to get drunk on wine; instead, he declares, "be filled with the Spirit." In the verses that follow (Eph 5:18-21), Paul uses a series of participles to describe what this imperative means. To be filled with the Spirit, then, involves: (1) "speaking" to one another with psalms, hymns, and spiritual songs (v. 19a); (2) "singing" and "making music" in your heart to the Lord (v. 19b); (3) "giving thanks" always to God the Father in the name of our Lord Jesus Christ for everything (v. 20); and (4) "submitting" to one another out of reverence for Christ (v. 21).

The initial phrase in Ephesians 5:19 cited above is especially important for our study. Paul exhorts the Ephesian believers to "speak to one another with psalms, hymns and spiritual songs [ᾠδαῖς πνευματικαῖς]" (Eph 5:19). We find another close parallel to this passage in Colossians 3:16. There Paul encourages his readers with these words: "Let the word of Christ dwell in you richly as you teach and admonish one another with all wisdom, and as you sing psalms, hymns and spiritual songs [ᾠδαῖς πνευματικαῖς] with gratitude in your hearts to God" (Col 3:16). The Greek phrase translated, "psalms, hymns, and spiritual songs," in both texts is virtually identical.

As James Dunn notes, these texts, in concert with 1 Corinthians 14:15, demonstrate that "Paul recognizes a kind of charismatic hymnody—both a singing in tongues . . . and a singing with intelligible words."[24] There are indeed several indications that point to the fact that Paul views this charismatic hymnody as inclusive of speaking in tongues. First, as we have noted, the contrast in 1 Corinthians 14:15 between singing "with my spirit" and singing "with my mind" clearly distinguishes between singing in tongues on the one hand, and singing with intelligible words on the other. So, here, in this text, Paul unambiguously refers to singing in tongues as a form of charismatic thanksgiving and praise (cf. 1 Cor 14:16-17). Secondly, there is a spontaneity and obvious charismatic quality that is implied in both the contrast between being drunk with wine and being filled with the Spirit

---

23. Acts 2:11 and 10:46 (and implicitly 19:6) could also be added to this list, but we will not discuss these texts here.

24. Dunn, *Jesus and the Spirit*, 238.

(Eph 5:18) and the vocabulary employed in Colossians 3:16 ("word of God," "in all wisdom," and "with grace").[25] Finally, the adjective that qualifies the third type of singing named in both lists, "spiritual" (πνευματικαῖς), suggests that Paul here, like in 1 Corinthians 14:15, is again speaking about different kinds of charismatic singing: intelligible (psalms and hymns) and unintelligible or glossolalic songs (spiritual songs).[26] Since the term "spiritual" (πνευματικαῖς) derives from the word, "Spirit" (πνεῦμα), the term "spiritual song" is essentially a reference to singing "in the Spirit." We have already noted that in the early church this phrase, "in the Spirit," becomes virtually a technical term for charismatic inspiration and typically includes glossolalia.

These references to singing in tongues highlight once again the fact that Paul understands speaking in tongues as doxological prayer, a Spirit-inspired form of praise and thanksgiving. In Colossians 3:16 Paul suggests that the "spiritual songs" should be sung "with gratitude" and directed to God. These "spiritual songs" are also understood to be a source of encouragement for the entire community (cf. "admonish one another"). We probably should also understand the phrases that qualify what it means to be "filled with the Spirit" in Ephesians 5:18–21 as interrelated. Thus, "speaking" to one another in spiritual songs is not unrelated to "singing" to the Lord, "giving thanks" to God, and "submitting" to one another. Together these activities all enhance corporate praise and the life of the community. In short, here we have references to corporate "singing in tongues" that are edifying to the body of believers and glorifying to God. This is, of course, what we would expect when we begin to understand that singing in tongues, like speaking in tongues, represents a spontaneous, Spirit-inspired expression of love and devotion to the triune God, the God who has supremely and wonderfully revealed himself in Jesus.

TONGUES AS INTERCESSION

Paul not only presents speaking and singing in tongues as a form of praise and thanksgiving to God, he also describes tongues as a means of intercessory prayer. This is perhaps nowhere more clearly expressed than in Romans 8:26. In Romans 8 Paul seeks to encourage his readers by helping

---

25. This point is made by Dunn, *Jesus and the Spirit*, 238.

26. If "spiritual" qualifies all three categories of songs, then all three would refer to charismatic singing and embrace both intelligible and glossolalic expressions.

them understand that our present experience of the Holy Spirit is a foretaste of the glorious future salvation that we await. Although we struggle with the fact that now we only experience this glorious "life of the future" in part (8:23), we can be encouraged by the fact that the Holy Spirit is presently at work in our lives, transforming us into the people that God has called us to be (8:9–13) and enabling us to share rich fellowship with God in Christ (8:14–17). In fact, our present experience of the Spirit is so rich, it serves as a testimony to us that God will consummate his redemptive plan; and when he does, we will experience the full richness of his blessings, including the transformation of our bodies and intimate fellowship with him (8:23, 39).

Paul refers to our present experience of the Holy Spirit in Romans 8:16. He declares that we are moved to cry, "*Abba*, Father," because "the Spirit himself testifies with our spirit that we are God's children" (8:16). This leads Paul to declare: "I consider that our present sufferings are not worth comparing with the glory that will be revealed in us" (8:18). This suffering, this longing for God's full redemption, is experienced by all of creation. So, Paul observes, "We know that the whole creation has been groaning as in the pains of childbirth right up to the present time" (8:22). However, Paul emphasizes that this struggle is one that is felt on the personal level as well as the cosmic, "Not only so, but we ourselves, who have the firstfruits of the Spirit, groan inwardly as we wait eagerly for our adoption as sons, the redemption of our bodies" (8:23).

In this gripping description of the tension that we face as Christians—as people who experience inwardly and see outwardly on a daily basis the transforming power of the Holy Spirit at work in the midst of sin, death, and decay—Paul reminds us once again that we are not alone (cf. Rom 8:16, 23). He declares that we do not face the inevitable struggles that mark this "already/not yet" tension on our own. No, "the Spirit helps us in our weakness" (8:26). Paul continues,

> We do not know what we ought to pray for, but the Spirit himself intercedes for us with groans that words cannot express. And he who searches our hearts knows the mind of the Spirit, because the Spirit intercedes for the saints in accordance with God's will. (Rom 8:26–27)

This is a stirring picture: Although we often do not know what or even how to pray, the Spirit prays through us, and in the process inspires words that sound like inarticulate groans. The Spirit's prayers, although unintelligible to us, are filled with meaning, for they represent God's own intercession on behalf of his people. Romans 8:27 echoes the earlier reference to intercession in verse 26 and might be paraphrased in this way, "He, that is the Spirit, who searches our hearts, knows what is spiritual, and thus he intercedes for the saints according to God's plan."

Two lines of argumentation suggest that Paul here has glossolalia primarily, though perhaps not exclusively, in view.[27] The first set of arguments are linked to the immediate context; the second, to the larger context of Paul's epistle to the Romans.

The immediate context highlights the fact that these "groans," like the *Abba* cry of Romans 8:15, are: actual utterances inspired by the Spirit; that these utterances flow from an intimate encounter with God rather than a rational apprehension of specific truths; and these utterances are especially powerful and meaningful because the speaker recognizes that in some amazing way "God is speaking in and through me."

It goes without saying that when Paul declares that by the Spirit "we cry, 'Abba, Father'" (Rom 8:15), he has in mind actual utterances. If the believers at Rome had no experience of this sort of cry, then Paul's words would make little sense and have no value. The same must be said of the Spirit-inspired "groans" of Romans 8:26. Paul is clearly referring here to charismatic manifestations, spontaneous utterances inspired by the Holy Spirit that his readers have actually experienced. In other words, Paul is appealing to experiences that he and the Christians at Rome share.[28] The fact that Paul can make such appeals should remind us that this kind of charismatic experience was not rare but rather the norm for the early church. A survey of the New Testament documents establishes this fact.[29]

We should also note that these utterances were undoubtedly articulated and typically loud. Dunn notes that the verb Paul uses when he describes the *Abba* cry, κράζειν ("to cry out," Rom 8:15; Gal 4:6), "is a very

---

27. Frank D. Macchia notes a string of ancient and modern scholars who interpret the "groans" of Romans 8:26 as a reference to glossolalia (Macchia, "Sighs Too Deep for Words," 59).

28. So also Fee, *God's Empowering Presence*, 577–78, 584 and Käsemann, who also highlights this fact and states that "the place of these sighs must rather be. . .the church's assembly for worship" (Käsemann, *Perspectives on Paul*, 129).

29. There are thirty-five explicit references to speaking in tongues in the NT: twenty-eight are found in 1 Corinthians, twenty-three of these in 1 Cor 14. The other occurrences are found in Acts and the Gospel of Mark. See 1 Cor 12–14; Acts 2:4–11; 10:46, 19:6; as well as Mark 16:17. For more general references to charismatic activity that probably include speaking in tongues see: Rom 8:15–16, 26–27; 2 Cor 5:4; Eph 5:19, 6:18; Col 3:16; 1 Thess 5:19; and Jude 20.

strong one." It generally means "to cry out loudly," and thus is used for the "screams and shrieks of demoniacs" (e.g., Mark 5:5; 9:26; Luke 9:39). Dunn concludes that the context of Romans 8:15 and Galatians 4:6 suggests κράζειν in these verses is "a cry of some intensity, probably a loud cry, and perhaps . . . an ecstatic cry."[30]

The same can be said of the "groans" of Romans 8:26. Similar Greek terms (forms of the verb, στενάζω, or the noun, στεναγμός) are used to describe the groaning of creation in Romans 8:22, the groans of believers who have "the firstfruits of the Spirit" in Romans 8:23, and the groans prompted by the intercession of the Spirit in Romans 8:26. The fact that Paul can speak of "the whole creation . . . groaning as in the pains of childbirth" (Rom 8:22) should make it abundantly clear that these are not silent sighs or quiet murmurings. No, Paul is describing with these words loud utterances, utterances known and shared by the congregation, utterances inspired by the Spirit that have marked their worship and their prayers.

Paul suggests that these utterances are not only vocalized and loud, but that they issue from a deep, intimate encounter with God. Paul declares, "The Spirit himself testifies with our spirit that we are God's children" (Rom 8:16). What relational bond can be stronger than that of parents to their child? This incredible sense of relationship, of confidence before God, is the source of the *Abba* cry. And it is not simply understood; rather, it is felt. Just as a small infant knows intuitively that she is loved by her parents, so also we know that we are "heirs of God and co-heirs with Christ" (Rom 8:17). We know this because we experience the reality, the fruit of this relationship, through the work of the Holy Spirit in our hearts. When we do, as Paul and the Romans testify, occasionally this remarkable realization will erupt in joyful, Spirit-inspired speech.

Paul also envisions another kind of realization that will produce charismatic speech. This is the realization of our utter weakness that he describes so vividly in Romans 8:18–27. We long for the completion of the process that began with our repentance and faith in Christ. We long for the transformation that is hinted at by the presence and leading of the Holy Spirit in our lives. We long to see Christ face to face. And yet we know that we cannot even begin to express the longings and desires that the Spirit has birthed within us. We know that we are incapable of fathoming the depths of God's love, the majesty of his holiness, or the wonder of his redemptive plan. We do not even know how to pray for our own needs, let alone those

---

30. Dunn, *Jesus and the Spirit*, 240.

of our friends. Yet, just as we are overwhelmed by the realization of our utter weakness, the Spirit begins to pray through us. Even though we do not know how to pray, the Spirit intercedes for us and through us, utilizing words that have no meaning to us. Nevertheless, even as we speak in this inarticulate manner, even though our speech reflects our yearning and sounds like "groans" (cf. 2 Cor 5:1–4), we sense that something remarkable is taking place. We sense that God is speaking through us. It is this incredible awareness—this recognition that somehow God is present in our weakness and accomplishing through us that which we cannot comprehend but sense to be precisely what we need—that makes the groans of Romans 8:26 so edifying and so special. So, it is to a charismatic manifestation marking our weakness that Paul appeals. Here he and the Christians at Rome stand on common ground.

All of this indicates that Paul has in mind spontaneous, Spirit-inspired utterances (i.e., charismatic speech) when he speaks of our "groans" prompted by the Spirit. I would suggest, however, that we can say more. We have already noted that Paul's descriptions of the *Abba* cry and our inarticulate groans draw upon common, shared experiences. His words carry little meaning unless they describe experiences known and recognized by the believers at Rome. The one charismatic experience that fits Paul's description of inarticulate groans, that is cited in numerous New Testament documents, and that thus was clearly well-known and established in the early church, is speaking in tongues.[31]

Many scholars have rejected this interpretation, arguing that since Paul in Romans 8 speaks of an experience of the Spirit that is common to every Christian, "glossolalia can at most be in the background."[32] Yet this judgment misses the fact that for Paul speaking in tongues can be experienced by every believer.[33] Furthermore, it is predicated on the erroneous assumption that speaking in tongues was a rather rare and exotic experience for the early church. We have established that there is ample evidence to challenge this view.[34]

Other scholars have also questioned whether Paul has tongues in mind here because the term, στεναγμοῖς ἀλαλήτοις or "groans that words

---

31. So also Käsemann, *Romans*, 241.

32. Sweet, "Glossolalia," 152.

33. On the significance of 1 Cor 12:30; 14:5, 18, and 39, see Menzies, *Speaking in Tongues*, chapter 5.

34. Menzies, *Speaking in Tongues*, chapters 1, 4, 5, 7.

cannot express" (Rom 8:26), does not seem to mesh well with Paul's understanding of tongues as a language, albeit a heavenly language, one that we do not understand.[35] The judgment that Paul views speaking in tongues as an actual language is grounded in two facts: this is the normal sense of the term, γλῶσσα ("tongue"); and Paul's reference to a gift of interpretation (1 Cor 12:10, 30) seems to demand it. While I agree that Paul does view speaking in tongues as a language (probably angelic, certainly heavenly rather than human), I have trouble seeing this judgment as standing in conflict with Paul's reference to tongues as "groans" in 1 Corinthians 8:26. Surely to suggest otherwise is a classic example of over-exegesis. Paul here is not speaking as a linguist; rather, he speaks as one who shares this dramatic, powerful experience with the Christians at Rome. The similarities between speaking in tongues and "groans" were for Paul and his readers (as they are for those familiar with tongues today) so vivid and clear that they do not require explanation.

Still others point to the fact that Paul does not specifically mention speaking in tongues in his gift list in Romans 12:6-8. This would suggest, in their view, that Paul's Roman readers were not so familiar with tongues and would not have understood this allusion.[36] Yet this argument from silence is particularly weak. It may well be that Paul does not explicitly refer to tongues in Romans 12 or the rest of his epistle because this gift was well-known to these believers and not abused or the source of a problem. There is, however, one other possibility that we must consider.

One other line of evidence lends support to our contention that Paul has glossolalia in mind when he speaks of the Spirit interceding for us and through us with inarticulate groans (Rom 8:26). Although Paul does not have firsthand knowledge of the church in Rome, he seems to be aware of at least the potential for trouble. His exhortations to the weak and to the strong in Romans 14:1–15:6 and his warnings in Romans 16:17–20 suggest that disagreements were ready to boil over. A number of passages indicate that, "a group in Rome shared at least some of the attitudes and values of the Corinthian gnostics."[37] More specifically, this group probably advocated an over-realized eschatology that shared many points of contact with

---

35. See, for example, Wedderburn, "Romans 8.26—Towards a Theology of Glossolalia," 373.

36. So also Dunn, *Jesus and the Spirit*, 241, who concludes that while the reference to inarticulate groans in Romans 8:26 does not exclude glossolalia, it is not confined to it.

37. Dunn, *Jesus and the Spirit*, 268. He cites Rom 6:1 and 1 Cor 5–6; Rom 13:13 and 1 Cor 11:17-22; Rom 14:1–15:6 and 1 Cor 8, 10:23-33; Rom 16:17-18 and 1 Cor 1-4.

the problematic views that caused so much trouble in Corinth (cf. 1 Cor 15:12).[38] The group at Corinth taught that they had already experienced a "spiritual" resurrection and were thus fully "mature." It is, indeed, quite likely that a group in Rome advocated these views as well. Additionally, the Corinthian group viewed speaking in tongues as a sign of their exalted, spiritual status. It is not without reason, then, that we suggest that the faction at Rome, like the one at Corinth, viewed speaking in tongues in this inappropriate manner as well.

If this was the case, then we can see why Paul would remind the church at Rome that speaking in tongues, far from being a sign that they had already received the fullness of "salvation," was rather a sign of their weakness and expressed their yearning for the fullness of redemption, which we still await. This sign of yearning for our future, full redemption beautifully parallels and adds balance to the *Abba* cry, which is a sign of our present, though partial, experience of God's glorious inheritance. In short, Paul's language in Romans 8:26, where he pictures speaking in tongues as Spirit-inspired groans, may well have highlighted a much needed and important theological truth. Ernst Käsemann puts it well, "what enthusiasts regard as proof of their glorification [Paul] sees as sign of a lack."[39]

This truth, I would add, not only speaks to the church at Rome, but also to our contemporary situation. Contemporary Pentecostals and charismatics also need to recognize that speaking in tongues is not a sign of our "maturity" or our "strength." Although we do with good reason celebrate the present-ness of God's kingdom, we must acknowledge that it has not yet fully "arrived." And neither have we. Quite the contrary, our groaning serves to remind us of our utter dependence on and need for God. Speaking in tongues is a symptom of our weakness, a manifestation of our yearning for that which we have been promised but have not yet received. Yet here is the beauty of this incredible experience. In the midst of our weakness, the Spirit himself intercedes through us on our behalf. In so doing, the Spirit reveals to us a bit of the life of the future. He also reveals his desire to use those of us who are willing to acknowledge our need and, in our desperation, eagerly come to him with open hearts.

---

38. Dunn asserts that Paul uses guarded language in Romans 6:4–5 when he speaks about the resurrection and in this way highlights that "our participation in Christ's resurrection is still outstanding and future" (*Jesus and the Spirit*, 268).

39. Käsemann, *Romans*, 241.

CONCLUSION

All of this adds up to a very positive resume for the gift of tongues, if not for the church at Corinth. At Corinth we must not confuse the problem of application with the gift itself. And we must also be sensitive to and learn from Paul's allusions to speaking in tongues outside of 1 Corinthians. Although the gift of tongues, like so many of God's rich blessings, can be abused, it is nevertheless a beautiful gift from God full of rich blessing (cf. Luke 11:13). This too Paul clearly affirms.

We have seen that Paul understands speaking in tongues typically to be spontaneous, Spirit-inspired prayer. This special type of unintelligible, charismatic prayer often takes the form of praise and thanksgiving directed to God; however, these utterances may also give voice to intercessory prayer, as the Spirit prays for us and through us. Paul understands that this kind of charismatic prayer will normally take place in private settings, not during corporate worship. This appears to be his own practice and this is what he advocates for the church at Corinth. However, it should be noted that Paul's exhortations concerning singing in the Spirit (Eph 5:19; Col 3:16) call for a corporate expression of glossolalia. The more restrictive approach to this practice which Paul articulates in 1 Corinthians 14:15-17 clearly does not represent his normal practice. Paul's dismissal of glossolalic praise in the corporate setting as not edifying for those who do not understand (1 Cor 14:17) must be seen as a part of his attempt to correct the misunderstanding and abuses present at Corinth (cf. 14:23-25). These directives, then, although they are often taken as normative guidelines for "church order" in contemporary worship settings, in reality represent extreme measures designed by Paul to combat a very specific, blatant, and egregious abuse. If at Corinth speaking in tongues had not posed the very real danger of eclipsing intelligible proclamation and instruction, and if at Corinth glossolalia had not been falsely exalted as a sign of "maturity" and "power," it is highly unlikely that Paul would have taken the strongly negative approach to the congregational use of tongues that he does in 1 Corinthians 14. This conclusion is not only supported by Paul's positive exhortations for believers to sing in the Spirit in Ephesians 5:19 and Colossians 3:16,[40] but by other passages which imply a corporate knowledge of speaking in tongues (Rom 8:26; 1 Thess 5:19; and Jude 20). So, in spite of the polemical

---

40. Paul's language in these verses, "speak to one another" (Eph 5:19) and "teach and admonish one another" (Col 3:16), demands a corporate setting.

context in 1 Corinthians 12–14, elsewhere Paul does encourage a public expression of the gift that includes concert singing in tongues and times of corporate, glossolalic prayer. It is imperative, however, that the gift of tongues be exercised in humility and with love. This is "the most excellent way" (1 Cor 12:31).

Chapter 4

SIGNS AND WONDERS
Celebrating God's Kingdom

PENTECOSTALS THE WORLD OVER celebrate the present-ness of the kingdom of God. God's awesome presence in our midst, his gracious willingness to bestow spiritual gifts, his desire to heal, liberate, and transform lives—all of these themes, so central to Pentecostal piety, highlight the fact that God's reign is now present. Pentecostals proclaim a God who is near, a God whose power can and should be experienced here and now. This element of Pentecostal praxis has, for the most part, served as a much-needed corrective to traditional church life, which has far too often lost sight of the manifest presence of God. In a deeply moving essay, Ulrich Luz acknowledges this fact when he declares, "Now we worry about the fact that living religion has to a large extent emigrated from the mainstream churches and flourishes elsewhere . . . in living communities of neocharismatic groups, in colourful open-air meetings, and so on . . . the future belongs to religion and not to the traditional Christian churches."[1]

As traditional churches in the West have increasingly lost touch with the supernatural elements of the Christian faith, Pentecostals have reveled in their worship of an immanent God, a God who speaks to us, a God who is truly with us. Although many in an increasingly secular West struggle to understand this kind of faith, Pentecostal churches around the world are growing with such rapidity that some historians suggest the Azusa Street Revival (1906–9) should be identified as the "Fourth Great Awakening."[2]

---

1. Luz, "Paul as Mystic," 131.
2. See Synan, *Eyewitness Remembers*, 157.

This judgment is not without reason. "More than a million Pentecostal congregations were brought into being around the world as a result of this historic revival."[3] Like it or not, the Pentecostal movement is shaping the contours of Christian faith and praxis throughout the world.

In the following chapter I would like to examine a text that speaks of this present-ness of the kingdom of God that Pentecostals celebrate. However, the force of this text is often blunted by what I believe to be a mistranslation of Luke's language. The text in question, Luke 17:20–21, reads:

> Once, having been asked by the Pharisees when the kingdom of God would come, Jesus replied, "The kingdom of God does not come with your careful observation, nor will people say, 'Here it is,' or 'There it is,' because the kingdom of God is within you."

The key words that I wish to consider are found in verse 21, "the kingdom of God is within you [ἡ βασιλεία τοῦ θεοῦ ἐντὸς ὑμῶν ἐστιν]." In particular, I shall question the way in which the NIV translates ἐντὸς ὑμῶν with the phrase "within you."[4] This translation is found in various other English translations, including the KJV, the TEV, and the translations of J. B. Phillips and William Barclay.[5] The translators of the *Chinese Union Version* also follow this approach and thus render ἐντὸς ὑμῶν with the phrase, *zai nimen xin li*, which also means "within you" or "in your hearts."

This translation suggests that, according to Jesus, the kingdom of God is something that is not visible, something that is purely internal or spiritual. The kingdom of God, according to this reading, "works in men's hearts."[6] But is this quiet, invisible, ethereal, and unobtrusive kingdom really the kingdom that Jesus proclaimed and inaugurated? Are Pentecostals wrong to highlight the powerful presence of God now at work in our midst through "signs and wonders," healings, exorcisms, prophecy, and other visible manifestations? Or perhaps, at the very least, Pentecostals should look elsewhere for support for their exuberant practices.

---

3. Synan, *Eyewitness Remembers*, 157.

4. This is the translation of the NIV 1996 edition. The alternate reading, "among you," is listed in a note. In the NIV 2011 edition, the translation is changed to "in your midst," with the alternate reading, "within you," listed in a note.

5. See *The New Testament in Modern English*, translated by J. B. Phillips (New York: The Macmillan Co., 1958). Phillips' translation reads: "for the kingdom of God is inside you" (p. 163). Note also Barclay, *Luke*, 219: "the kingdom of God is within you."

6. Barclay, *Luke*, 220.

However, before we rush too quickly to this conclusion, we need to acknowledge that this reading of Luke 17:21 has not gone unchallenged. Numerous other English translations follow a different line of interpretation. They translate ἐντὸς ὑμῶν with the words, "among you."⁷ This translation represents a significant shift in meaning from that of the NIV and *The Chinese Union Version* and, as we shall argue, for contextual reasons it is to be preferred.

We shall begin our study by examining the larger context of Luke–Acts, and then focus on the immediate context of Luke 17:21. We shall also note the significant implications for our understanding of and expectation for "signs and wonders" that flow from our analysis of this text.

THE LARGER CONTEXT: THE KINGDOM OF GOD IN LUKE–ACTS

Continuity in Luke–Acts

It has been increasingly recognized that in the New Testament the kingdom of God is understood to be both a present and a future reality.⁸ George Ladd correctly notes that the most distinctive aspect of Jesus' preaching recorded in the synoptic Gospels "was its present in-breaking in history in his own person and mission."⁹ This is undoubtedly the case in Luke's Gospel. The kingdom is both a present realm of redemptive blessing (Luke 4:21; 10:18; 11:20; 16:16; 22:29) and a future eschatological reality (Luke 13:28–29; 19:11).¹⁰

In Luke's Gospel the terms most commonly used to describe this realm of redemptive blessing are "salvation" (σωτήριον, σωτηρία, σώζω) and

---

7. See for example the *New Revised Standard Version*, the *Revised English Bible*, the *New American Bible*, and the *New Jerusalem Bible*. So also Eugene Peterson, in *The Message*, whose translation reads, "God's kingdom is already among you."

8. See the works by Kummel, *Promise and Fulfillment*; Cullmann, *Christ and Time*; Ridderbos, *Coming of the Kingdom*; Schnackenburg, *God's Rule and Kingdom*; Ladd, *Theology of the New Testament* and *Presence of the Future*.

9. Ladd, *Theology of the New Testament*, 70.

10. I agree with Ladd when he declares, "God's rule" is "the best point of departure for understanding" the kingdom of God in the Gospels (Ladd, *Theology of the New Testament*, 60–61; see also Ladd, "Kingdom of God—Reign or Realm?," 230–38). However, "God's rule" implies a realm or sphere of existence where his authority is exercised and recognized. Thus, Jesus speaks of "entering into" the kingdom of God (Luke 16:16; 18:24; cf. Acts 14:22) and in terms that suggest the kingdom is a realm (Luke 7:28; 13:28).

"forgiveness" (ἄφεσις).¹¹ That Jesus is the source of this salvation is clear from the very outset of the Gospel (Luke 1:69, 71, 77; 2:30). Entrance into this realm of redemptive blessing is contingent on a response of "faith" (πίστις) to Jesus and his message. This is clear from the way Luke connects the verb "to save" (σώζω) with "faith" (πίστις), indicating that salvation is contingent on a response of faith (Luke 7:50; 8:12, 50; 17:19; 18:42). That this redemption is experienced, at least in part, in the present is evident by Luke's use of σώζω in the perfect tense (Luke 7:50; 17:18; 18:42). Although salvation has a future referent, it is experienced in the present.

Acts shows direct continuity with these characteristics of the kingdom of God emphasized in Luke's Gospel. It is true that in Acts kingdom terminology is increasingly replaced by other ways of expressing the salvation provided by Jesus. But this is the result of the realization that Jesus is the exalted Lord, not an abandonment of the kingdom as a present or future realm of blessing.¹² Certainly in Acts preaching the kingdom of God means to preach the gospel, the redemptive intervention of God in history in Jesus (Acts 8:12; 28:31). That the kingdom, as a realm of redemptive blessing, has a present dimension is indicated by the present experience of "salvation" and "forgiveness" for those who believe (Acts 2:47; 4:12; 11:14; 15:11; 16:31). In Acts, as in Luke's Gospel, "salvation" (σωτήριον, σωτηρία, σώζω) and "forgiveness" (ἄφεσις) are terms frequently used to describe redemptive blessings.¹³ These terms are again associated with faith (πίστις).¹⁴

Thus, throughout Luke's two-volume work, the kingdom, as a realm of redemptive blessing, can be experienced in the present through faith in the proclamation of Jesus. Certainly a significant difference between Luke's Gospel and Acts is that in the former Jesus proclaims the message, whereas in the later the disciples proclaim a message concerning Jesus. Yet this difference should not be overemphasized. In Acts, the mission that Jesus inaugurated and carried out in the power of the Spirit, is still the mission of Jesus (Acts 16:7), but it is now carried out by the church in the power

---

11. σωτήριον: Luke 2:30; 3:6; σωτηρία: Luke 1:69, 71, 77; 19:9; σώζω: Luke 6:9; 7:50; 8:12, 36, 48; 9:24; 13:23; 17:19; 18:26; 19:10; ἄφεσις: Luke 1:77; 3:3; 4:18; 24:47.

12. Contra Kummel and Merk who maintain that the kingdom is not present during the church period (Kummel, *Promise and Fulfillment*; Merk, "Das Reich Gottes in den lukanischen Schriften," 272–91).

13. σωτήριον: Acts 28:28; σωτηρία: Acts 4:12; 7:25; 13:26, 47; 16:17; 27:34; σώζω: Acts 2:21, 40, 47; 4:9, 12; 11:14; 14:9; 15:1, 11; 16:30–31; 27:20, 31; ἄφεσις: Acts 2:38; 5:31; 10:43; 13:38; 26:18.

14. Acts 10:43; 13:38–9; 14:9; 16:30–31; 26:18.

of the Spirit. The preaching in Acts is still the preaching of the kingdom of the God (Acts 8:12; 14:22; 19:8; 20:25; 28:23, 31).[15] In both Luke and Acts entrance into the realm of God's redemptive blessings is contingent on a response of faith to Jesus. In the Gospel of Luke Jesus is present, calling for a response of faith. In Acts Jesus is still present, in the work of the Spirit through the disciples, calling for a similar response.

In terms of the believers' experience of the kingdom, there is no difference between Luke and Acts. In both Luke's Gospel and the book of Acts entrance into this realm of God's rule constitutes salvation and is contingent on a response of faith to the proclamation of Jesus.

The Kingdom of God and the Content of Salvation

In Acts, as in the synoptic Gospels, the term, "the kingdom of God" (ἡ βασιλεία τοῦ θεοῦ), can refer to a future eschatological realm of divine blessing (e.g., Acts 14:22). For Luke, this future realm is closely linked with the future resurrection (Luke 14:14; 20:35). In Acts 4:2 Luke writes that the apostles "were teaching the people and proclaiming in Jesus the resurrection of the dead (ἐν τῷ Ἰησοῦ τὴν ἀνάστασιν τὴν ἐκ νεκρῶν)." The force of the dative case ("in Jesus") is uncertain. It is possible to interpret ἐν τῷ Ἰησοῦ ("in Jesus") as a dative of reference, indicating that the content of the apostles' preaching included the resurrection of Jesus. The resurrection of Jesus was central to the preaching of the early church (Acts 2:32; 4:9, 33; 26:23). However, it is also possible to interpret this phrase as an instrumental dative, with the apostles speaking of a future resurrection through faith in Jesus. This is most probable since the future hope of the early church clearly included the resurrection of the dead (Luke 14:14, 20:35; Acts 24:15, 21). Luke 20:35 specifically connects the resurrection of the dead with the age to come. Acts 26:23 also indicates that the resurrection of Jesus is only the beginning, one that anticipates the resurrection of his followers as well. In light of these considerations it is evident that participation in the future resurrection of the righteous comprised part of the content of salvation, part of the future realm of divine blessings.

Although the actual resurrection of the body is a future event for Luke, entrance into the realm of divine blessing associated with this resurrection

---

15. Youngmo Cho correctly notes that "for Luke, to be a witness of Jesus means to bear witness to the kingdom of God" (Cho, *Spirit and Kingdom in the Writings of Luke and Paul*, 184).

takes place in the present. This is vividly demonstrated by Luke's use of σώζω ("to save") in the perfect and present tenses throughout Luke–Acts. In Luke 7:50 Jesus declares to the sinful woman, "Your faith has saved (σέσωκέν) you." The perfect tense indicates that the woman experienced salvation at that point in time, although there were dimensions of her salvation that would be realized in the future. In Acts 2:47 Luke describes the growth of the early church in Jerusalem, "The Lord added to their number daily those being saved [τοὺς σῳζομένους]." The present tense of σώζω again indicates a present reception of salvation. For Luke, the present experience of salvation is preparatory for the future resurrection and the life of the age to come.

This is demonstrated further in the ethical content associated with entrance into the kingdom of God. Concern for the poor and the helpless will be rewarded at the resurrection of the righteous (Luke 14:14). To be worthy of the kingdom involves making a radical, uncompromising decision to follow Jesus (Luke 9:57–62; 14:26–35). In Acts, although the ethical implications of life in the kingdom are not a high priority, they are not altogether absent. In Acts 26:18 Luke records Paul's own account of his commissioning. He was commanded to go to the Gentiles "so that they might receive forgiveness of sins (ἄφεσιν ἁμαρτιῶν) and a place among those who are sanctified by faith in me." Here, sanctification (i.e., the act of being set apart) is paralleled with forgiveness of sins and attributed to faith. Preparation for life in the age to come involves ethical transformation.

The present experience of salvation involves more than simply preparation for the future resurrection and life in the age to come. Through faith one actually enters into the realm of God's rule and blessings. For Luke, a result of faith in the message of Jesus is restored fellowship with God. Fellowship with God is an eschatological blessing associated with the future kingdom (Luke 13:29; 14:16–24); yet, it is also a present experience for the disciples of Jesus (Luke 22:27–30). The restoration of fellowship with God is the result of the divine ἄφεσις, a present experience (Luke 7:48; Acts 10:43). In Acts 5:31 Luke records the testimony of Peter and the apostles concerning Jesus, "God exalted him to his right hand as Prince [ἀρχηγὸν] and Savior [σωτῆρα] that he might give repentance and forgiveness of sins [ἄφεσιν ἁμαρτιῶν] to Israel." The thought is this: Jesus is now in a position of authority, reigning at the right hand of God as Lord and Savior. By virtue of this authority Jesus is able to forgive sins. The preaching of the early church centered on the resurrection and exaltation of Jesus because this was so vitally linked to Jesus' present lordship and position of authority

(Acts 2:33). This is why entrance into the future kingdom is contingent on a response of faith, for faith in the proclamation of Jesus involves the recognition of his present lordship by virtue of his resurrection and exaltation.

The Kingdom of God and Visible Signs

The salvation that is associated with the proclamation of the kingdom of God in Luke–Acts involves more than restored fellowship with God and ethical transformation. It is holistic in nature and impacts every aspect of our lives, both as individuals and as members of new "kingdom" communities. Pedrito U. Maynard-Reid correctly notes, "Luke shows that salvation is not limited to the personal, internal, spiritual realm . . . . Healing, deliverance, and dramatic social change accompany" the proclamation of the kingdom throughout Luke–Acts.[16]

This was certainly the case in the ministry of Jesus. Jesus' healings and exorcisms, as well as transformed relationships, serve as dramatic evidence of God's decisive intervention and authority (e.g., Luke 7:21–23; 19:7–9). They are signs that in Jesus God's rule is now being exercised. This is nowhere more clearly stated than in Luke 11:20, where Jesus declares, "But if I drive out demons by the finger of God, then the kingdom of God has come to you."

It is important to note that Luke sees these visible and physical aspects of salvation also at work in the ministry of Jesus' disciples. First the Twelve and then the Seventy are commissioned to "heal the sick" and proclaim that "the kingdom of God is near" (Luke 9:1–2; 10:9). This later commissioning of the Seventy echoes Moses' wish that "all the Lord's people were prophets" (Num 11:29) and thus points forward to Pentecost, when this wish begins to be fulfilled. It would appear that Luke sees the command to "heal the sick" and "proclaim the kingdom of God" as relevant for his church as well as the apostles.

This conclusion is confirmed by the contours of Luke's narrative in Acts. In order to assess the role of healing and visible signs in the narrative of Acts, we must begin with Peter's quotation of Joel's prophecy. Peter, quoting Joel 2:30–31, declares: "I will show wonders in the heaven above, and signs on the earth below, blood and fire and billows of smoke. The sun will be turned to darkness and the moon to blood before the coming of the great and glorious day of the Lord" (Acts 2:19–20). Joel's text only

---

16. Maynard-Reid, *Complete Evangelism: The Luke-Acts Model*, 106.

refers to "wonders in the heavens and on the earth" (Joel 2:30). Yet Luke's skillful editorial work enables him to produce the collocation of "signs and wonders" found in Acts 2:19. With the simple addition of a few words, Luke transforms Joel's text so that it reads: "I will show wonders in the heaven *above*, and *signs* on the earth *below*" (Acts 2:19, added words in italics).

The significance of this editorial work becomes apparent when we read the verses that immediately follow the Joel quotation. Peter declares, "Jesus . . . was a man accredited by God to you by miracles, wonders and signs" (Acts 2:22). The significance of Luke's editorial work is magnified further when we remember that Luke also associates "signs and wonders" with the ministry of the early church. In fact, nine of the sixteen occurrences of the collocation of "signs and wonders" (σημεῖα καὶ τέρατα) in the New Testament appear in the book of Acts.[17] Early in the narrative of Acts, the disciples ask the Lord to stretch out his "hand to heal and perform miraculous signs and wonders" through the name of Jesus (Acts 4:31). This prayer is answered in dramatic fashion. A few verses later we read that, "the apostles performed many miraculous signs and wonders among the people" (Acts 5:12). Similarly, Luke describes how Stephen, one outside the apostolic circle, "did great wonders and miraculous signs among the people" (Acts 6:8). The Lord also enables Paul and Barnabas "to do miraculous signs and wonders" (Acts 14:3; cf. 15:12).

All of this demonstrates that by skillfully reshaping Joel's prophecy, Luke links the miracles of Jesus and those of the early church together with the cosmic signs listed by Joel (Acts 2:19–20). Each of these miraculous events are "signs and wonders" that mark these "last days," that decisive period when God's rule begins to be realized on the earth. Luke, then, is not only conscious of the significant role that miracles played in the ministry of Jesus, he also anticipates that these "signs and wonders" will continue to characterize the ministry of Jesus' followers, including those in his day.[18] According to Luke, healing and other visible manifestations of God's authority represent an integral and ongoing aspect of the ministry of Jesus and his disciples. They are signs that the kingdom of God is invading this present age.

In short, Luke declares that the kingdom of God is inextricably linked to Jesus, who is Lord and Savior. The kingdom of God is none other than

---

17. Acts 2:19, 22, 43; 4:30; 5:12; 6:8; 7:36; 14:3; 15:12.

18. For a fuller discussion of "signs and wonders," see Menzies and Menzies, *Spirit and Power*, 145–58, and Menzies, *Pentecost*, 103–12.

that realm of redemptive blessing where God's rule is exercised and acknowledged. As such, it represents salvation in all of its various aspects. This salvation has a future dimension, but it also can be experienced, in part, in the present through faith in the proclamation of Jesus. Jesus' proclamation of the kingdom included dramatic and visible signs of divine authority, such as healings, exorcisms, and radically altered relationships. Jesus commissioned his disciples to follow his example by healing the sick and proclaiming the kingdom of God as well. Jesus promised his disciples power to accomplish this task. The book of Acts narrates the fulfillment of this promise. Luke envisions that as his church proclaims the good news of the kingdom, which now centers on the death and resurrection of Jesus, visible manifestations of divine authority and liberation will also mark their ministry.

This brief survey of the kingdom concept in Luke–Acts raises significant questions concerning the attempt to translate ἐντὸς ὑμῶν with the phrase "within you." As we have noted, Luke nowhere describes the kingdom of God as something that is simply internal and spiritual. Quite the contrary, the kingdom of God is manifest in dramatic acts of healing and deliverance. It results in a radical reorienting of one's life that has visible and tangible results. Far from being an invisible and inner spiritual impulse, the kingdom of God is pictured as that realm where God's authority is exercised and acknowledged. I. Howard Marshall states the problem succinctly, "Jesus speaks of men entering the kingdom, not of the kingdom entering men."[19]

The evidence from the broader context of Luke–Acts (and, indeed, the entire synoptic tradition) suggests that the translation, "within you," should be discarded. A better option is easily found. With a plural noun, as is the case in Luke 17:21, ἐντός can mean "among" or "in the midst of."[20] Thus, the phrase in question would read, "the kingdom of God is among you" or "the kingdom of God is in your midst" (Luke 17:21).[21] This reading fits nicely into the teaching of Jesus as recorded in Luke–Acts. It is entirely compatible with Jesus' presentation of the kingdom of God as a realm in which God's rule is exercised, often in dramatic and visible fashion. As we have already noted above, a number of translations follow this line of interpretation.

19. Marshall, *Luke*, 655.

20. See Marshall, *Luke*, 655 and the studies cited there.

21. In Chinese, *zhong jian*. This reading is presented as a secondary option in the margin of the *Chinese Union Version*.

However, the question must be asked, does this reading do justice to the immediate context of this saying in Luke's Gospel? To this question we now turn.

THE IMMEDIATE CONTEXT: THE SAYING IN LUKE'S NARRATIVE

In Luke 17:20-21 the Pharisees initiate the conversation by raising a question: when will the kingdom of God come? Jesus responds, "The kingdom of God does not come with your careful observation, nor will people say, 'Here it is,' or 'There it is,' because the kingdom of God is among you."[22] How are we to understand Jesus' response? At first glance it appears that Jesus is now denying what elsewhere is specifically affirmed in Luke–Acts: that the miracles of Jesus and the early church are signs of the presence of God's reign (Luke 7:21-23; 11:20; Acts 2:19-22; cf. 2:43). However, in view of this larger context, we should probably understand Jesus' response in light of the prevailing messianic expectations current within Judaism. As Darrell Bock notes, although Judaism did not have a monolithic picture of the Messiah's coming, "in most conceptions it was a powerful and glorious arrival . . . the arrival of Messiah would be clear and obvious to all."[23] By way of example, Bock cites Psalms of Solomon 17-18, where a powerful Messiah "rules in Israel and rescues it from the nations."[24] Clearly Jesus did not fulfill these expectations of a powerful, nationalistic leader who would bring political liberation to Israel. The recognition that Jesus does not fit conventional expectations is very likely reflected in Luke 7:23, where Jesus responds to John the Baptist's question, "Are you the one who was to come?" After speaking of the blind receiving their sight, the lame walking, and lepers being healed, Jesus declares, "Blessed is the man who does not fall away on account of me" (Luke 7:23). There were indeed dramatic signs, but not the signs that many were seeking.

In Luke 17:20-21 Jesus does not deny that visible signs accompany the coming of the kingdom; rather, he declares to the Pharisees that they are looking for the wrong signs. With his response, Jesus issues a warning: your attempts to calculate the correct time of the kingdom's arrival have

---

22. I have altered the NIV (1996) by inserting "among you" in the place of "within you."

23. Bock, *Luke 9.51—24.53*, 286.

24. Bock, *Luke 9.51—24.53*, 286.

failed, for the kingdom has already arrived—it is already in your midst and its source is standing before you—and yet you have failed to recognize it. Certainly here Jesus places the accent on the present-ness of the kingdom of God. The kingdom has already arrived in his person and thus it is now present in their midst.

This focus on the present-ness of the kingdom raises another crucial question: How then do we reconcile this saying with the future-oriented announcement that follows in Luke 17:22–37? Surely the reference to the "days of the Son of Man" (Luke 17:23) refers to the consummation of the kingdom and the end of this present age.[25] It would appear that Luke here has placed the twin emphases in Jesus' teaching on the kingdom of God, its surprising presence and its future fulfillment, in juxtaposition. Earle Ellis suggests that this alternating present/future perspective on the kingdom is characteristic of Luke and found repeatedly in his Gospel.[26] In Luke's record of John the Baptist's prophecy the promise of a Messiah who will baptize in the Holy Spirit finds a present fulfillment (Luke 3:16), while the promise of fiery judgment refers to a still future event (Luke 3:17). Jesus' warning of future rejection for those who are ashamed of him (Luke 9:26) is followed by the promise that those standing before him will "see the kingdom of God" (Luke 9:27). Luke's version of the Lord's Prayer begins with the petition, "your kingdom come" (Luke 11:2), which is followed by the request for daily bread (Luke 11:3; cf. 11:13, 20). In Luke 12:37–46 references to future judgment are followed by sayings about immediate judgment. Finally, in Luke 16:16 a saying concerning the present proclamation of the kingdom is followed by a parable that speaks of future rewards and punishment (Luke 16:19–31).

All of this indicates that we should not find it strange that Luke highlights the present-ness of the kingdom of God in a saying of Jesus that immediately precedes a prophetic oracle concerning the future coming of the Son of Man. This tension is common to Luke and appears to reflect his concern to provide an accurate and balanced perspective on Jesus' teaching concerning the coming of the kingdom of God. It is possible that Luke in this way seeks to encourage his readers, some of whom may have been discouraged by persecution. Luke reminds them that "God's way of working in the world requires suffering from God's servants" and that those

---

25. Contra Wright, *Surprised by Hope*, 125–27.
26. Ellis, *Luke*, 210.

"hopes which ignore this necessity are premature."[27] An emphasis on the powerful presence of the kingdom of God coupled with a sober assessment of the challenges that will necessarily precede the consummation of God's redemptive plan would serve to encourage those in Luke's missionary communities as they seek to bear witness to Jesus in the face of opposition.

It is by now apparent that the translation "among you" does justice to the immediate context of the saying as well as to the larger context of Luke–Acts. It also accords well with what we know about the actual historical setting of Jesus' ministry. This cannot be said for the alternative translation, "within you."

IMPLICATIONS FOR THE CONTEMPORARY CHURCH

A careful reading of Luke–Acts reveals that the kingdom of God is the dynamic realm of God's redemptive blessing where his rule is exercised and acknowledged. Jesus, as Lord and Savior, is the agent who brings the kingdom of God. Luke, in concert with the other synoptic Gospels, declares that when people respond in faith to the preaching of Jesus or that of his disciples, they enter into the kingdom of God and experience the salvation associated with it. This salvation includes forgiveness, fellowship with God and his people, liberation from the bondage of sin (moral transformation), and the promise of resurrection life. This salvation, however, involves even more. It is holistic in nature and impacts every aspect of our lives, both as individuals and as members of new "kingdom" communities. Thus, life in the kingdom is also marked by dramatic acts of physical healing, powerful displays of victory over demonic power, including exorcisms, and instances of miraculous, divine guidance. Luke tells us that the early church described these dramatic displays of God's in-breaking power as "signs and wonders." Furthermore, he tells us that these "signs and wonders" marked the ministry of Jesus (Acts 2:22) and that they will continue to mark the ministry of Jesus' disciples in these "last days" (Acts 2:19). So, as we read Luke's narrative, we are encouraged to pray, along with the early church, "Lord, . . . enable your servants to speak your word with great boldness . . . Stretch out your hand to heal and perform miraculous signs and wonders through the name of your holy servant Jesus" (Acts 4:29–30).

Pentecostals, then, are right to encourage the "saints" to celebrate the present-ness of the kingdom of God. With good reason we proclaim a God

---

27. Tannehill, *Narrative Unity*, 257.

who is near, a God whose power can and should be experienced here and now. We should expect to experience God's awesome presence in our midst and affirm his desire to heal, liberate, bestow gifts, and transform lives. A deep sense of anticipation should mark our prayer, "your kingdom come" (Luke 11:2). This is all in accordance with Scripture. It is the apostolic way.

Yet, in the midst of this exuberant celebration, Pentecostals face a very present danger. This emphasis on the present-ness of the kingdom and "signs and wonders" that has enabled Pentecostals to make a unique contribution, also renders us susceptible to an unbalanced triumphalism. Our vision can (and at times has) become so fixated on God's power and triumph that we lose the ability to see his hand in the midst of suffering, rejection, and opposition. Our emphasis on the present-ness of the kingdom is easily twisted into an arrogant and unbiblical over-realized eschatology, where there is little room for weakness and where unbiblical displays of power reign supreme. Luther named it well: a "theology of glory" that has little room for a "theology of the cross."[28]

I believe our response to this danger, the corrective that will keep us from lapsing into an arrogant triumphalism, is the Evangelical antidote: an emphasis on the authority of the word of God. If we are careful to judge our message and mission in the light of Scripture, if we seek to evaluate our experiences by the apostolic model, we will not lose our way.

Church history is instructive and calls us to consider our steps with care. As I noted earlier, many charismatic movements have risen, only to succumb to the extremes of fanaticism and heresy. But as Paul reminds us, there is a more excellent way. This is not the cessationist path of denial and rationalistic reductionism. It is the determined yet joyful quest for life in the Spirit directed and guided by the word of God. It is the life modeled by Jesus and the apostolic church. If we are attentive, we will not be distracted by unusual human responses to the working of the Holy Spirit—weeping, shouting, and shaking (although these often require wise pastoral leadership)—nor will we prioritize or seek after novel claims of "glory manifestations" (gold dust, angel feathers, etc.); rather, we will highlight and affirm those attitudes and experiences that are modeled by the early church in the book of Acts. Herein lies the antidote to unbridled triumphalism.[29]

---

28. See Kärkkäinen, "Theology of the Cross: A Stumbling Block to Pentecostal /Charismatic Spirituality?," 150–63. Martin Mittelstadt offers an antidote for this danger in his fine study, *Spirit and Suffering*.

29. Lora Timenia provides the Pentecostal movement with critically-needed tools and wise counsel for evaluating unusual spiritual experiences and phenomena, including

The British Pentecostal statesman Donald Gee was known for his balance, wisdom, and candor. His wise counsel to a young and at times immature Pentecostal church is worth repeating. He noted that the more unusual or bizarre forms of behavior that often accompany the coming of the Spirit (shouting, barking, laughing, shaking, etc.) are not in and of themselves "manifestations" of the Spirit. Rather, he noted, these are human responses to the work of the Holy Spirit. The manifestations of the Spirit are, in Gee's view, outlined by Paul in 1 Corinthians 12–14. So, Gee exhorted, we should acknowledge these human reactions to the work of the Spirit for what they are: human responses to God's presence. We need not be overly concerned about them, but we certainly should not lift them up as models for all to follow. The experiences of the apostolic church should serve as our guide. Gee observed that pastoral leadership in these matters is essential; for, while these human responses are relatively common and not intrinsically wrong, they can at times get in the way of what God desires to accomplish. When that happens, wise leadership will offer the guidance that is needed to maintain order.[30]

A Pentecostal approach to "signs and wonders" will seek to follow after the New Testament model.[31] It affirms the present-ness of the kingdom of God and God's desire to pour out his Spirit upon us. Our posture is one of openness and expectation, for the calling and power of the apostolic church are ours as well. Their experience is our inheritance. At the same time, Pentecostals, following in the footsteps of William Seymour, Donald Gee, and others, will allow the biblical record to guide and direct our experience. This is the standard by which we evaluate every doctrine, practice, and experience. If we deviate from this path, we will lose our way.

---

contemporary "glory manifestations." Her sympathetic yet critical analysis of four influential proponents of 'Toronto Blessing' revivalism in the Philippines is marked by careful research, informed analysis, and a pastoral heart (Timenia, "Toronto Blessing," 88–157).

30. See Gee, *All with One Accord*, 24–28, 56–59; Gee, *Is It God?*, 3–7; Gee, *Concerning Spiritual Gifts*, 86–101; Gee, *Why Pentecost?*, 37–40.

31. So, I would maintain, churches that are unwilling to evaluate their doctrine, practice, or experience according to the New Testament standard do not stand in the Pentecostal tradition. Although we might not all agree on every point of interpretation, we can and must agree that the standard is the New Testament and strive to follow the models presented there.

CONCLUSION

Although the NIV translates ἐντὸς ὑμῶν in Luke 17:21 with the phrase "within you" and the *Chinese Union Version* follows a similar approach, I have argued that this translation misses the mark. In Luke–Acts and the entire synoptic tradition Jesus never refers to the kingdom of God as an inner, invisible, and purely spiritual impulse. The notion that the kingdom of God is "within you" runs counter to the way that the kingdom of God is presented throughout Luke's two-volume work. In Luke–Acts the kingdom of God is the dynamic realm of God's redemptive blessing where his rule is exercised and acknowledged. As such, the kingdom is manifest in dramatic acts of healing and deliverance; and it results in a radical reorienting of one's life that has visible and tangible results. Jesus, as Lord and Savior, is the agent who brings the kingdom of God. Thus, the kingdom, as a realm of redemptive blessing, can be experienced in the present through faith in the proclamation of Jesus. "Salvation" and "forgiveness" are terms frequently used to describe these redemptive blessings. These blessings include restored fellowship with God and ethical transformation. However, the salvation that is associated with the proclamation of the kingdom of God in Luke–Acts involves more than this. It is holistic in nature and impacts every aspect of the disciple's life, both as an individual and as a member of a kingdom community. No wonder, then, that, "Jesus speaks of men entering the kingdom, not of the kingdom entering men."[32]

In the light of these considerations, I have suggested that we translate ἐντὸς ὑμῶν in Luke 17:21 with the phrase, "among you" or "in your midst." If we employ this translation, the text in question would read, "the kingdom of God is among you" or "the kingdom of God is in your midst" (Luke 17:21).[33] This reading resonates nicely with the teaching of Jesus as recorded in Luke–Acts. It is entirely compatible with Jesus' presentation of the kingdom of God as a realm in which God's rule is exercised, often in dramatic and visible ways. Additionally, this reading fits well into the immediate context of Luke 17:20–21. It serves to challenge the Pharisees' nationalistic and political understanding of the kingdom of God and it highlights the present-ness of the kingdom in a manner consistent with Luke's usage elsewhere.

---

32. Marshall, *Luke*, 655.
33. In Chinese, *zhong jian*.

It would appear that Pentecostals have read Luke 17:20–21 rather well. I would encourage every Christian to follow their lead and joyfully celebrate God's awesome presence in our midst, his desire to heal, deliver, and transform lives. Luke declares that "signs and wonders" marked the ministry of Jesus (Acts 2:22) and that they will continue to mark the ministry of Jesus' disciples in these "last days" (Acts 2:19). Let us allow the biblical record to guide and direct our doctrine, practice, and experience. And let us not forget, the kingdom of God is in our midst.

Part III

PENTECOSTAL THEOLOGY
Its Evangelical Trajectory

Evangelicals affirm that faith in Christ involves a personal relationship with the resurrected Lord, Jesus Christ. They proclaim that through repentance and faith in Christ we are enabled to enter into intimate, filial relationship with God. Paul declares that in Christ we become a "new creation" (2 Cor 5:17) and members of God's family (Eph 2:18; Rom 8:15–16). Pentecostals also stand squarely on these foundational truths. Yet they uniquely highlight a significant result of this new filial relationship with God in Christ. Out of this intimate understanding of our relationship with the Father, Pentecostals affirm, a new language of prayer and worship flows—language and worship which express our sense of "sonship" with God. Jesus modeled this kind of prayer and worship (Luke 11:1–13; cf. 10:21). And he calls and enables his disciples to follow him and participate in this amazing, intimate relationship with the triune God.

This new language of prayer and worship also calls the church to expand its understanding of God's great mission and to engage in the global quest to give every person on this planet the opportunity to hear the gospel and worship Jesus in their own mother tongue. Luther's translation of the Bible into German and his revolutionary use of German, the language of the people rather than a special "religious" language, in hymns and worship represent important initial steps in this regard. Pentecostals take this emphasis on personal relationship with God in Christ one step further. They affirm that, as a result of our relationship with Christ, believers may also experience Spirit-inspired prayer and worship that is uttered in the languages of heaven (1 Cor 13:1). This experience too, as we shall see, has significant missiological implications.

Chapter 5, "Jesus, Intimacy, and Language," develops these themes and places Pentecostals in a trajectory of prayer, worship, and mission that is initiated by Jesus, recaptured by Luther, and which finds its ultimate fulfillment in the intimacy of Spirit-inspired prayer—prayer modeled by Jesus (Luke 10:21–22), encouraged by Paul (Romans 8:15–17, 26–27), and affirmed by modern Pentecostals.

This trajectory of Spirit-inspired prayer and worship culminates in a practice dear to the heart of all Evangelicals, evangelism. Since Evangelicals believe that the gospel centers on a call to enter into a personal relationship with Jesus Christ, they highlight the importance of evangelism. Active participation in God's great mission is not optional for Evangelicals. It is central to the Christian life, which is fundamentally a life of obedient service for Christ. Pentecostals also stress the inextricable link between discipleship and missions. In fact, we shall argue in chapter 6, "Missional Spirituality," that Pentecostals, with their fresh reading of Luke–Acts, offer important, new theological insight into this missiological understanding of discipleship.

Chapter 5

JESUS, INTIMACY, AND LANGUAGE

My favorite noodle shop is housed in a small space below a tall building of apartments. The Muslim family that runs the shop hail from the city of Lanzhou and thus their shop is called, *Lanzhou La Mian* (or "Lanzhou 'pulled' noodles"). Not long ago I found myself alone in the shop with the patriarch of the family, Mr. Ma. So, I took this opportunity to speak to him about his relationship with God. I asked, "You believe in God, don't you?" After his affirmative response, I replied, "I too believe in God." Then I asked, "You often pray, don't you?" Again, when he replied "yes," I noted that I too often pray. Then I asked him, "What language do you use when you pray?" He answered, "Arabic." I then asked, "What language do you speak at home with your family?" "Mandarin [Chinese]," he replied. "Do you ever pray in Mandarin?," I asked. "Arabic," was his only response. It was evident that for Mr. Ma and I suspect most, if not all, of the Muslims around the world, Arabic is the language of prayer, the language of heaven.

A few weeks later I found myself in one of Bangkok's major airports. As I waited for my bag to emerge on the conveyor belt, I noticed two orthodox Jews. These two young men, roughly forty years of age, were standing nearby, also waiting for their bags. They were both dressed alike, in the traditional and distinctive black suit and white shirt of the orthodox Jews, complete with a hat partially covering a small box containing Hebrew Scriptures. Scriptures printed on leather strips were also wrapped around their arms. A prayer shawl with tassels hung low beneath their dark suitcoats.[1]

---

1. The small, black leather boxes that contain texts from the Torah are worn on the head and thus called head *tefillin* (also known as phylacteries). The leather strips wrapped around the arms and hands are called hand *tefillin*. This form of clothing is based on a

There was no mistaking who these men were and what they believed. I decided to seize this opportunity, so I walked over and began a conversation with the Jewish man nearest to me.

I began by asking the man, "Where are you from?" He looked at me and shrugged, as if to say "isn't it obvious?," and then replied: "We are from Israel." I continued, "But where did your family live before moving to Israel?" He nodded and stated, with a look of understanding, "Russia."

I then asked my newfound friend, "What language do you use when you pray?" His facial expressions again revealed his surprise. The answer to this question was even more obvious than the first. "Hebrew," he declared. Clearly, this orthodox Jew felt that there was really only one language for prayer. His response reminded me of the intertestamental Jewish discussions concerning prayer and the language of heaven. There were essentially two perspectives. One group maintained that the language of heaven was an esoteric language, not known on earth. It was a special language, the language of God and his angels. Yet a second group insisted that God spoke Hebrew. This was the language of heaven and if one wanted his or her prayers to be heard, he or she must pray in Hebrew. This was the only language that God heard and understood.[2]

These two experiences reminded me of an important fact. Many people around the world believe that there is a special religious language, a special language for prayer. For Muslims, that language is Arabic. It is the language of their Scriptures and the language of prayer. For Jews, that special spiritual language is Hebrew. They both affirm that, if you want to pray to God and be heard, you must use this special language.

I am tremendously thankful that Jesus' teaching on prayer is different. *Jesus teaches his disciples to pray in their mother tongue*, not in the special religious language of his Jewish contemporaries. This wonderful fact is filled with significance for us. It means that "in Christ" we can use our heart-language to speak with God and address him as "Father." To this important topic we now turn.

---

literal reading of Exod 13:9–10, 16; and Deut 6:8; 11:18. The prayer shawls with tassels, also known as *tallit*, are based on Num 15:38–40.

2. Poirier, *Tongues of Angels*, see chapters 2 and 3 for texts supporting the Hebrew view and chapters 4 and 5 for texts voicing the esoteric view.

JESUS, INTIMACY, AND LANGUAGE

JESUS' ABBA PRAYER

The disciples asked Jesus to teach them to pray (Luke 11:1). Jesus responds with the Lord's prayer (Luke 11:2-4). Note how this amazing prayer begins with one, wonderful word, "Father." The word, "Father," is the English translation of the Greek, Πάτερ, found in Luke's text. Yet in view of several key passages found elsewhere in the New Testament, it is almost certain that the original instruction on prayer that Jesus offered his disciples was uttered in Aramaic.

The first text that supports this judgment is found in Mark 14:35-36. Here, we find Jesus, on the night before his crucifixion, praying in Gethsemane. It is one of the most stressful, emotional moments in Jesus' life. The text reads:

> Going a little farther, he fell to the ground and prayed that if possible the hour might pass from him. "*Abba*, Father," (Αββα ὁ πατήρ) he said, "everything is possible for you. Take this cup from me. Yet not what I will, but what you will." (Mark 14:35-36)

This passage from Mark's Gospel reveals that Jesus' prayers were typically uttered in Aramaic and that he routinely used the term, *Abba*, to address God the Father. This assessment is confirmed by two passages, close parallels, in the Pauline epistles (Rom 8:15-16 and Gal 4:6-7). Romans 8:15-16 reads:

> The Spirit you received does not make you slaves, so that you live in fear again; rather, the Spirit you received brought about your adoption to sonship. And by him we cry, "*Abba*, Father" (Αββα ὁ πατήρ). The Spirit himself testifies with our spirit that we are God's children.

This same phrase, Αββα ὁ πατήρ, is echoed in Galatians 4:6. These two Pauline texts both highlight a beautiful truth: the Holy Spirit reveals to us that in Christ we have been "adopted" into God's family. Thus, Paul declares, the Spirit enables us to cry out "*Abba*, Father" (Rom 8:15; Gal 4:6). This declaration raises an important question: What inspired Paul to describe our sense of "adoption," our experience of "sonship," in this way? What motivated Paul to speak of the Spirit moving us to cry, "*Abba*, Father?" In light of Mark 14:36 there can only be one answer: Jesus. It was Jesus' prayers and his teaching on prayer (11:1-4; cf. Matt 6:9-13) that inspired Paul's choice of words at this point.

All of these texts—the three occurrences of *Abba* in the New Testament—demonstrate two surprising and vitally important facts about Jesus' prayer life and his instruction to his disciples regarding prayer. Both of these facts must have shocked and scandalized many of Jesus' Jewish contemporaries. Yet, I would add, to us they come as an incredible gift.

First, following his own, personal practice (Mark 14:36), Jesus taught his disciples to pray in their mother tongue, Aramaic.[3] He did not follow Jewish custom and teach them to pray in the "religious" language of the Jewish people (Hebrew), the language of their Scriptures and their communal prayers.[4] Jesus broke from these conventions and encouraged his disciples to pray in their heart-language. In view of the fact that many rabbis considered Hebrew to be the language of heaven—and thus, by extension, the only language that God heard—this is, indeed, a striking turn of events.[5] It is a fact that, we shall argue, has dramatic ramifications for the Christian life.

Secondly, again, following his personal practice, Jesus taught his disciples to address God as "Father" (*Abba*) when they prayed. The significance of the term, *Abba*, has been hotly debated by scholars and theologians. However, this much appears to be clear. *Abba* was clearly a term of respect and could be used by a student addressing his teacher. Yet more commonly it was also used by a small child when calling out to his or her father. Kenneth Bailey, who served as a missionary in the Middle East for over forty years, describes discussing this term, *Abba*, with a group of Palestinian women. One exclaimed, "*Abba* is the first word we teach our children."[6]

It must have shocked many of Jesus' contemporaries when they heard him or his disciples address God as *Abba*. Although God is often described as being like a father in the Old Testament, nowhere is he there addressed directly as "Father." If we expand our survey of the relevant Jewish literature beyond the Jewish Scriptures, we find that direct address in prayer as

---

3. Bailey, *Jesus Through Middle Eastern Eyes*, 95.

4. As Bailey notes, "The Aramaic-speaking Jew in the first-century was accustomed to recite his prayers in Hebrew, not Aramaic" (*Jesus Through Middle Eastern Eyes*, 95).

5. Poirier, *Tongues of Angels*, 16: "b. Sabb. 12b:. . .and [did not] R. Yochanan say, 'Everyone who petitions for his needs in Aramaic, the ministering angels will not attend to him, because the ministering angels do not understand Aramaic!'" I want to thank Russell Spittler for pointing me to this reference. See Spittler, "Review of John C. Poirier's *The Tongues of Angels*," 146–52.

6. Bailey, *Jesus Through Middle Eastern Eyes*, 97.

"Father" is exceedingly rare.[7] So, when Jesus taught his disciples to pray in Aramaic and to begin their prayers by addressing God as "*Abba*, Father," he was defying tradition. Jesus rejected the widely-held belief that we must use a special "religious" language when communicating with or about God. Additionally, he called and enabled his disciples to enter into a filial relationship with God characterized by deep intimacy. This intimate, filial relationship, so beautifully illustrated in the parable of the Gracious Father (Luke 15:11–32), is powerfully expressed with one word: *Abba*.

This countercultural practice of Jesus, calling his disciples to pray in their mother tongue and with the deeply intimate term, *Abba*, has significant implications for how we understand our own relationship with God, our relationship with other Christians, and our relationship with non-Christians. It calls us, first, to recognize God's deep desire to enter into intimate relationship with us. This amazing relationship, as we have noted, is pictured throughout the New Testament, but perhaps nowhere more beautifully than in Jesus' parable of the Gracious Father and Paul's declaration in Romans 8:15–17.

The second implication flows naturally from the first. If, for those in Christ, God is our Father (Matt 6:9), then this means that we in the body of Christ are all brothers and sisters. We are family. This fact calls us to exercise patience and grace in our relationships with fellow believers in the church. As a friend from Yugoslavia of the former Soviet Union prior to its collapse wryly commented, "The Russians, they are our brothers. Do you know the difference between friends and brothers? You can choose your friends." In the church, we are not allowed to pick and choose those with whom we will fellowship. No, this is God's doing. He has brought us together and, although formerly we were "foreigners and aliens," he has enabled us to become members of his household (Eph 2:19). So, we are called to treat one another as family, accepting, helping, and encouraging one another to grow and mature in Christ (Eph 4:11–16).

The third implication of Jesus' unique perspective on prayer impacts our relationships with non-Christians. Jesus' call for his disciples to pray in their mother tongue clarifies our task. It defines our mission. It calls us to recognize that everyone should have the opportunity to communicate with God in their own mother tongue. The intimacy of the *Abba* prayer, which is heightened and expressed through the use of the vernacular, the language of the heart, provides strong, experiential motivation, then, for

---

7. Bailey, *Jesus Through Middle Eastern Eyes*, 97.

PART III: PENTECOSTAL THEOLOGY

Christians to engage in cross-cultural, incarnational mission. It compels us to take risks, to suffer hardship if necessary, and above all to bridge every cultural and linguistic barrier so that all might hear the gospel, come to know Christ, and thereby relate to God as "Father."

LUTHER'S INSIGHT

Not long ago, October 31, 2017, we celebrated the five-hundred-year anniversary of the Protestant Reformation. On this day in 1517 Martin Luther tacked his ninety-five theses to the door of the Wittenberg Church and unwittingly launched a series of events that would dramatically change the world. The Reformation had begun.

All Evangelicals, including Pentecostals, are the offspring of Luther and the Reformation. Four main church groups emerged from the Reformation—Lutherans, Presbyterians, Anglicans, and the Free Churches (Anabaptists, Mennonites, Brethren, among others)—and the Evangelical movement emerged from these groups. As we have seen, the Pentecostal movement sprung from these roots as well, nurtured largely by American revivalism and the Holiness movement.[8]

The Reformation was marked by four foundational truths:

- The Bible alone (not human or church traditions) is authoritative
- Faith alone (not good works) leads to salvation
- Christ alone (not other mediators, such as priests) provides our salvation
- Two sacraments or ordinances: water baptism and the Lord's Supper

The Reformation was launched by Luther's bold reaffirmation of the gospel. As a young monk dedicated to serving God, Luther went through a period of intense personal struggle with his own feelings of sinfulness and unworthiness. Luther knew that he did not meet God's standard of righteousness. As a result, he was deeply frustrated and filled with anger towards God. He descended into despair. Then, as a result of his study of the New Testament, and particularly Romans 1:16–17, Luther came to the realization that "the righteousness of God" comes from Christ, not our good works. He came to understand the gospel—that when we repent and

---

8. My summary of the Reformation's central doctrines and impact draws upon a series of emails that I received (August 18 through October 30, 2017) from the late, Dr. Calvin Holsinger.

place our faith in Christ, we are justified and become children of God—at a time when the church had lost sight of this foundational truth. Luther grasped and experienced the liberating truth that in Christ, when God looks at us, he sees Christ's righteousness rather than our sin. Luther's life was thus transformed.[9]

It should be noted that Luther's insights flowed from his study of the Bible, especially the New Testament. In Luther's day, the curriculum for young men entering the priesthood and monastic life did not feature extensive study of the Bible. In their first year, the young students were given a Latin Bible. However, this was normally taken away after the novice became a monk and the advanced curriculum focused on other matters, including Greek philosophy (especially the writings of Aristotle, which Luther came to loathe) and the traditions of the church.[10] Nevertheless, Luther was determined to study the Bible and in its original languages. Erasmus' Greek New Testament had just been published (1516) and the Renaissance emphasis on going "back to the sources" encouraged Luther in this regard. So, motivated by his own personal questions, Luther poured over the Scriptures and reappropriated the apostolic message.

Luther's reaffirmation of the gospel had a profound impact on his life. He went from "hating God" to "loving him." He went from a man filled with anger and despair, to a man filled with purpose and hope.[11] This newfound, intimate relationship with God rooted in the gospel not only transformed Luther's personal life, it also propelled Luther into a leadership role in the church. Although Luther was an unlikely prophet or revolutionary leader, in the providence of God he was thrust onto the world scene through a series of events that he could never have imagined on that fateful day, October 31, 1517.

What is particularly remarkable about Luther's Reformation for our purposes is the impact that Luther and the Reformation had upon corporate worship. Prior to Luther, the medieval church had functioned with a single, "religious language." Worship was conducted entirely in Latin. Sermons were uttered in Latin. The Scriptures were written and read out loud in Latin. The choirs, comprised of priests and monks, sang in Latin. The church members, most of whom did not understand Latin,

---

9. My brief summary of Luther's life and ministry draws upon many sources, but I am particularly indebted to Eric Metaxas' wonderful book, *Luther*.

10. Metaxas, *Luther*, 53, and for his loathing of Aristotle, 69.

11. Metaxas, *Luther*, 93–99.

were encouraged to dutifully participate and go through the motions. The priests, who spoke Latin and thus wielded unquestioned authority in religious matters, served as the guides of the people, their mediators with God. God, after all, spoke Latin.

When Luther grasped the gospel and encountered Christ as his Savior, he determined to change this sad state of affairs. He translated the Bible into German, the language of the people. In fact, Luther's German Bible is famous for unifying the German language and in this way establishing the foundation for modern German. Luther's motivation for translating the Bible into German was clear: he wanted all people, not just the scholars and priests, to have access to the word of God. He desired to make the Bible available in the vernacular, the language spoken by ordinary people. Luther was not the first person to have this dream. Jan Hus held similar views almost one hundred years prior and, as a result, was burned at the stake in 1415. Hus was greatly influenced by John Wycliffe, an English Roman Catholic priest who in the fourteenth century AD sought to make the Bible available in the vernacular. Wycliffe's views, however, were later deemed heretical at the Council of Constance (1415 AD). So, while Luther stood on the shoulders of Wycliffe and Hus, he was perhaps the first Christian of the medieval era who was able to see his dream of vernacular worship become a reality on a significant scale.

Luther not only translated the Bible into German, the mother tongue of the masses, he also introduced vernacular language sermons and congregational singing to Christian worship services.[12] Latin sermons gave way to preaching in German and Lutheran churches were filled with the sound of German hymns, many penned by Luther himself, sung by the people. It is significant that Luther's emphasis on praying, preaching, singing, and reading God's word in one's mother tongue flowed from his reaffirmation of the gospel and his newfound, intimate relationship with God in Christ. The trajectory of the gospel leading to intimate relationship with God, which in turn produces vernacular language prayer and culminates in a passion for Christ to be proclaimed in every language among all peoples, begins with Jesus and is given unique impetus with his *Abba* prayer. This trajectory can then be traced in Luther's experience and ministry. It finds striking fulfillment in Pentecostal experience, worship, and missions. To this Pentecostal fulfillment we now turn.

---

12. Metaxas, *Luther*, 287, 374–77.

JESUS, INTIMACY, AND LANGUAGE

THE PENTECOSTAL CONTRIBUTION

Like Luther in his day, Pentecostals in the modern era have highlighted how our intimate relationship with God, experienced through faith in Christ, impacts the language of prayer and worship. Pentecostals, like Jesus and Luther, stress the use of the vernacular in worship. However, following Jesus and Paul, Pentecostals challenge the limitations of a "religious language" in an additional way. Pentecostals not only emphasize the use of our human mother tongues in prayer and worship, they also encourage the use of the divine mother tongue, the language of the Spirit, in prayer and worship. The Apostle Paul was very familiar with this divine mother tongue, this heavenly language. In chapter 3 above we examined the many references in the Pauline epistles to glossolalia as a form of Spirit-inspired, doxological prayer.[13] These texts, which describe the Spirit praying through the believer, link speaking in tongues with a strong sense of communion with Christ. This is perhaps most beautifully expressed in the *Abba* prayer of Romans 8:15–16 and Galatians 4:6. Paul declares that, "the Spirit himself testifies with our spirit that we are God's children" (Rom 8:16). While the *Abba* prayer references charismatic prayer more broadly, it clearly includes glossolalic prayer. Furthermore, Paul's words here paint a powerful picture of what happens as the Spirit prays through us. We are caught up in the love of Christ and filled with joy as we begin to glimpse the significance of our divine adoption. Is it any wonder that human words fail to adequately express what we feel?

Many Christians, especially those educated in the West, struggle with the notion that unintelligible speech can be edifying and convey intimacy.[14] Yet there are many examples of that which transcends rational description or understanding serving as a powerful vehicle for expressing deep emotions. Poetry and music are great examples. There is, however, perhaps an even closer and better analogy for tongues. The term "idiolect" is used to describe an intimate language that is only understood and shared by a select few. Twins in infancy, for example, often use a language all their own. Only they can communicate by means of this idiolect. The use of an idiolect implies familiarity, trust, and intimacy. The Pauline passages noted above support this description of glossolalia as a kind of idiolect. Glossolalia, like

---

13. 1 Cor 12:2–3; 14:14–17; Rom 8:15–16; Gal 4:6; Eph 5:18; 6:18; Col 3:16; 1 Thess 5:19; note also Jude 20.

14. See, for example, MacArthur, *Strange Fire*, 75.

an idiolect shared by twins, is an ongoing reminder of our close, filial relationship to God in Christ. It is a reminder that is unique to each individual, made possible by the inspiration of the Holy Spirit, and expressed in a form of intimate language.

The trajectory we have mapped out above moves from reception of the gospel to intimate relationship with God, which in turn produces vernacular language prayer and culminates in a desire to take the gospel to the ends of the earth. It therefore not only stresses the importance of entering into intimate relationship with God in Christ, but it also highlights the priority of cross-cultural missions. Here again I would argue that Pentecostals have taken the missions mandate a step beyond anything Luther could envision or contemplate. In view of the fact that the Pentecostal movement, with its explosive growth, has produced "one of the most dramatic shifts in Christianity since the Reformation,"[15] this is a judgment that would be hard to challenge. The missiological power of the modern Pentecostal movement should come as no surprise to students of the Bible, for the themes of the Spirit's power, bold cross-cultural witness, and glossolalic prayer are inextricably linked in Luke's account of the Pentecostal outpouring of the Spirit (Acts 2).

In Acts 2:4 we read that those present were all filled with the Holy Spirit and began to "speak in other tongues [λαλεῖν ἑτέραις γλώσσαις] as the Spirit enabled them." This phenomenon creates confusion among the Jews of the crowd who, we are told, represent "every nation under heaven" (Acts 2:5). The crowd gathered in astonishment because "each one heard them speaking in his own language" (διαλέκτῳ; Acts 2:6). These details are repeated as Luke narrates the response of the astonished group: "Are not all these men who are speaking Galileans? Then how is it that each of us hears them in his own native language" (διαλέκτῳ; Acts 2:7–8)? After the crowd lists in amazement the various nations represented by those present, they declare, "we hear them declaring the wonders of God in our own tongues" (γλώσσαις; Acts 2:11)! Since Acts 2:11 clearly relates γλώσσαις to the various human languages of those present in the crowd, most scholars understand the "tongues" (γλώσσαις) of Acts 2:4 and 2:11 as referring to intelligible speech. The disciples are enabled by the Spirit to declare "the wonders of God" in human languages that they had not previously learned.

It is important to note that this language miracle at Pentecost is not a literal reversal of Babel. The disciples of Jesus who were "filled with the

---

15. Tennent, *Theology in the Context of World Christianity*, 2.

Holy Spirit and began to speak in other tongues" (Acts 2:4) did not speak a single tongue that all understood. Rather, they spoke in *the multiple mother tongues* of each individual present. The cultural distinctives were not obliterated. On the contrary, the Holy Spirit enabled his disciples to embrace them and to minister through them. There were many languages, but only one message. And the message was simply this: Jesus is the resurrected and exalted Lord and only Jesus is worthy of our praise and worship (Acts 2:33).

Luke's account of Pentecost, then, highlights the significance of Jesus' *Abba* prayer for Christians today.[16] It calls us to see that we too have a clear mandate to take the gospel of Jesus Christ to the ends of the earth. The fact that the Spirit inspires the disciples at Pentecost to speak in multiple and diverse tongues—indeed tongues unknown to them—this fact should encourage us to recognize that we too are called to identify with and embed ourselves within the cultures of the diverse people groups that populate this planet. In short, like Jesus, we too must become incarnate. This is the nature of our mission and Jesus' *Abba* prayer, understood in the light of Pentecost, clarifies and reinforces this fact.

Our destiny as Christians, described in the book of Revelation, confirms this judgment. This eschatological vision helps us grasp the missiological significance of Jesus' *Abba* prayer. We have already noted how Paul describes the Spirit-inspired *Abba* cry—a cry that issues from our intimate encounter with God in Christ—with the verb κράζω (Rom 8:15, Gal 4:6). This verb is also echoed in the cry that is recorded in Revelation 7:9–10:

> After this I looked, and behold, a great multitude that no one could number, from every nation, from all tribes and peoples and languages, standing before the throne and before the Lamb, clothed in white robes, with palm branches in their hands, and crying out [κράζουσιν] with a loud voice, "Salvation belongs to our God who sits on the throne, and to the Lamb!"

Once again we see an emphasis on unity within cultural diversity. The "great multitude" come from every nation, tribe, and language, and yet they all voice the same cry, "Salvation belongs to our God . . . and to the Lamb!" The fact that Jesus calls and enables us to enter into intimate, filial relationship with God is beautifully expressed in the freedom we find in communicating with God *in our diverse mother tongues*. Indeed, Jesus,

---

16. It is significant that in the context of Jesus' teaching concerning the Lord's prayer (Luke 11:1–4), Luke also relates Jesus' call for his disciples to pray for the Holy Spirit (Luke 11:13).

Luke, Paul, and John, in various ways, all encourage us to express our filial relationship with God, which is rooted in the atoning death of our Savior, Jesus, the Lamb of God, through Spirit-inspired prayers formed in the languages of our hearts. There is no need for pretense. There is no special religious language that we must use. We do not need to adopt an alien culture or manner of speech. We are free to express our joy and love in the intimate language of our deepest self. Sometimes this joyful communion takes the form of prayer in a heavenly language, an idiolect of the Spirit. This deep communion with God is the very purpose for which we were created and an experience that, Jesus tells us, no one should miss (John 3:16).

All of this suggests that Pentecostals, by appropriating the rich insights into the work of the Spirit found in the New Testament, are following in the footsteps of Jesus and Luther. They too challenge the use of "religious language" by encouraging the use of the vernacular in worship. Yet Pentecostals go further than Luther in that they also encourage the use of the divine mother tongue, the language of the Spirit, in prayer. This Pentecostal practice finds biblical support in Paul's descriptions of glossolalia as Spirit-inspired doxological prayer. For the Pentecostal, prayer in tongues is an ongoing reminder of our close, filial relationship to God in Christ. This intimate relationship with Christ also serves as a powerful motivation for involvement in missions. By interpreting Luke's account of Pentecost against the backdrop of Jesus' *Abba* prayer, Pentecostals are able to highlight in a unique way the missiological significance of this prayer for Christians today. The results can be seen all around the globe.

CONCLUSION

Evangelicals the world over are known for their emphasis on the gospel, personal relationship with God in Christ, and involvement in missions. Jesus' *Abba* prayer (Luke 11:1–4), I have argued, encapsulates each of these important distinctives. This beautiful prayer is a summary of Jesus' "good news" and, by defying traditional Jewish conventions regarding the language and form of prayer, it calls us to enter into the deep communion with God that only Jesus makes possible. Furthermore, by challenging the notion of a special "religious language," the *Abba* prayer provides a clear rationale and powerful motivation for engagement in cross-cultural missions. In short, Jesus' *Abba* prayer in a concise and compelling way ties together the great themes of the Evangelical movement.

JESUS, INTIMACY, AND LANGUAGE

This fact is beautifully illustrated in the life and ministry of the great reformer, Martin Luther. Luther's grasp of the gospel—at a time when the church had sadly lost sight of its message and power—transformed his relationship with God. His new, intimate relationship with God, now understood to be accessible through faith in Christ, moved him to change the traditional patterns of prayer and worship in his day. Luther translated the Bible into German, the language of the people, and encouraged vernacular prayer and worship so that all people might have access to the gospel and, through it, relationship with God.

I have argued that this trajectory—which moves from reception of the gospel to intimate relationship with God, which in turn produces vernacular language prayer and culminates in a desire to take the gospel to the ends of the earth—is also found in the modern Pentecostal movement, yet in a fresh way. Like Luther and following Jesus, Pentecostals also challenge the limitations of "religious language." Yet Pentecostals not only emphasize the use of our human mother tongues in prayer and worship, they also encourage the use of the divine mother tongue, an idiolect shared with the Spirit, in prayer and worship. Glossolalic prayer for Pentecostals serves as an ongoing reminder of their close, filial relationship to God in Christ. This intimate relationship with Christ also provides powerful motivation for bold, cross-cultural witness. Indeed, by interpreting Luke's Pentecost narrative against the backdrop of Jesus' *Abba* prayer, Pentecostals uniquely highlight the missiological significance of this prayer for Christians today.

Chapter 6

MISSIONAL SPIRITUALITY

A Pentecostal Contribution to Spiritual Formation

THE PENTECOSTAL MOVEMENT HAS attracted millions of people around the world, producing "one of the great religious migrations of modern times."[1] All knowledgeable observers agree that this amazing movement is changing the face of the Christian church. Additionally, in many countries, such as in Brazil and Korea, it is hard to overestimate its impact on the larger society. So, it should come as no surprise when Allan Anderson describes the modern Pentecostal movement, broadly conceived, as "the fastest growing group of churches within Christianity today."[2]

Yet, as we have noted, in spite of its amazing growth and impact, many Christians still do not see the Pentecostal movement as having much to offer theologically. Conventional wisdom suggests that the Pentecostal movement is a movement of action rather than reflection, experience rather than doctrine. Our cultured friends, who prefer to worship in a more serene and cognitive manner, speak of Pentecostal exuberance in polite but condescending tones. Their negative responses often betray their own, unexamined assumptions, primary of which is this: the "enthusiasm" of the early church was unique to the apostolic era and is no longer appropriate for Christians today. "Visions and dreams, prophecy and tongues, loud and joyful praise, are all anachronisms," they maintain, "and should not be viewed as contemporary models." Implicit in this critique is the assumption

---

1. Wacker, *Heaven Below*, 1.

2. Anderson, *Introduction to Pentecostalism*, 1. Anderson's statement refers to the "Pentecostal and Charismatic movements in all their multifaceted variety" (p. 1).

that Pentecostals are driven by emotion and need to spend more time studying the word.

This judgment, I would suggest, misses something important. As we have noted, Pentecostals have always been "people of the book" and committed to the Bible. In fact, the origins of the Pentecostal movement may be traced to a Bible college and serious study of the Scriptures. Pentecostal experience flows from a desire to embrace the biblical record and encounter God in Christ through the Holy Spirit like the apostolic church did.[3] Indeed, a Pentecostal approach to the Bible may be summed up with the simple phrase: "their stories are our stories."[4] This approach has enabled the Pentecostal movement, at least in modern times, to bring together an emphasis on experience with a commitment to the authority of the Bible. Rather than competing with one another, most Pentecostals see these twin themes as complementary.

This blending of a desire for authentic, apostolic experience with a commitment to the Bible has uniquely marked the Pentecostal movement. It has encouraged Pentecostals to reexamine the New Testament, and particularly the book of Acts, in an attempt to recover the calling and experience of the apostolic church. This approach, I would suggest, has led to fresh and important insights into Luke's theological perspective and his missiological purpose. I believe these insights have profound implications for the life of the church.

In this chapter, then, I will argue that Pentecostals have an important theological contribution to make to the larger church world and that this contribution directly impacts a theme of great importance for all Christians: the Holy Spirit's contribution to spiritual formation. I hope to accomplish this task by first outlining what I would describe as a uniquely Pentecostal contribution to spiritual formation. Then, I will argue that this contribution is rooted in a reading of Luke–Acts that captures well Luke's intent.

MISSIONAL SPIRITUALITY

Pentecostal experience and praxis are shaped, in large measure, by the stories contained in the book of Acts. The central texts that Pentecostals around the world memorize and feature are Acts 1:8, "But you will receive

---

3. As Keith Warrington notes, Pentecostal theology is, at its heart, a theology of encounter. See Warrington, *Pentecostal Theology: A Theology of Encounter*, 21.

4. See Menzies, *Pentecost*, especially chapter 1.

power when the Holy Spirit comes on you; and you will be my witnesses in Jerusalem, and in all Judea and Samaria, and to the ends of the earth," and Acts 2:4, "All of them were filled with the Holy Spirit and began to speak in other tongues as the Spirit enabled them." These texts and the related stories of bold missionary endeavor that follow in the book of Acts provide the templates for our understanding of baptism in the Spirit. They shape Pentecostal experience and give direction to our mission. Within the larger Christian family this emphasis is unique and it gives the Pentecostal movement a profoundly missional ethos. This is, in my opinion, one of the key reasons why Pentecostal churches around the world have grown at such an amazing rate. It is certainly a central reason why scores of missionaries, most with meager financial backing, left the Azusa Street Revival and traveled to diverse points of the globe to proclaim the "apostolic" faith. I would suggest it is also why Pentecostals today constantly share their faith with others. Bold witness for Jesus is recognized as our primary calling and the central purpose of our experience of the Spirit's power. Missions is woven into the fabric of our DNA.

This perspective, this missiological emphasis gleaned from Luke–Acts, is unique to Pentecostals. While Pentecostals have featured Luke's writings and the book of Acts, other Protestant churches have highlighted the Pauline epistles. The great truths of the Reformation were largely gleaned from Romans and Galatians and the writings of Paul. The cry, "justification by faith," mimics Paul. So, following in the footsteps of Luther and Calvin, the Protestant churches have featured the Pauline epistles.

This Pauline emphasis has, to a large extent, shaped the Evangelical movement. We have already noted how Evangelicals of the past century overreacted to liberal scholarship that challenged the historical reliability of Luke's writings.[5] They maintained that Luke and the other Gospel writers were historians, *not* theologians. Even today Evangelicals are reluctant to speak of the theological purpose of Luke and his narrative.[6] Of course this approach establishes a canon within the canon by elevating Paul's epistles to a place of primacy.

---

5. See Menzies and Menzies, *Spirit and Power*, 37–45.

6. For example, Anthony Thiselton repeatedly questions the wisdom of those who "wish to drive a wedge between Luke and Paul" and flatly states, "Luke and Paul do not stand on equal footing." Thiselton justifies this latter statement by insisting that it remains uncertain whether Luke intended to offer instruction for the church, a blueprint for later Christians, with his writings. See Thiselton, *Holy Spirit*, 490 and 496 for the quotes cited above.

Evangelicals have, in their own way, highlighted the missionary call. Normally this has come by way of the Great Commission in Matthew 28:18–20. This text has perhaps been more acceptable to Evangelicals than the commissioning material in Acts, since here Jesus is the one who has "all authority" and there is no overt commission for his disciples to work "signs and wonders." Yet, even here, tensions persist. Is this commission valid for everyone in the church? And how does Jesus' authority relate to the disciples whom he sends out? Here the Pentecostal reading of Acts provides clear and ready answers. On the basis of their reading of Acts, Pentecostals affirm that every disciple is called and empowered; and every disciple is encouraged to expect that "signs and wonders" will accompany their witness. Evangelicals tend to be, at best, less clear on these matters.

More recently, third wave Evangelicals have highlighted the role of spiritual gifts in evangelism.[7] But, as I have pointed out elsewhere, this perspective, rooted as it is in Paul's gift language, fails to offer a solid rationale for a high sense of expectancy with respect to divine enabling.[8] When it comes to spiritual gifts, the attitude of many is quite passive: "Perhaps verbal witness is not our gift." What is lacking here is a clear promise of empowering that extends to every believer. Pentecostals find this in the narrative of Acts (Acts 1:8; 2:19). Furthermore, Luke highlights more than simply "signs and wonders." His narrative is also filled with examples of bold, Spirit-inspired witness in the face of opposition and persecution (e.g., Luke 12:11–12; Acts 4:31). This staying power is an undisputable focus in Luke's narrative and it has been central to Pentecostal missions as well. Here again we need to hear Luke's unique contribution.

I do not wish to minimize in any way the significance of the great doctrinal truths of Paul's writings. I merely point out that since Paul was, for the most part, addressing specific needs in various churches, his writings tend to feature the inner life of the Christian community. His writings, with some significant exceptions, do not focus on the mission of the church to the world. So, for example, Paul has much to say about spiritual gifts and how they should be exercised in corporate worship (1 Cor 12–14); however, he is relatively silent when it comes to the Pentecostal outpouring of the Spirit. It is probably fair to say that while Paul features the "interior" work of the Spirit (e.g., the fruit of the Spirit, Gal 5:22–23); Luke features

---

7. See, for example, Wimber and Springer, *Power Evangelism*.
8. Menzies and Menzies, *Spirit and Power*, 145–58.

his "expressive" work (Acts 1:8).⁹ Thus, by appropriating in a unique way the significant contributions of Luke–Acts, Pentecostals have developed a piety with a uniquely outward or missiological thrust. Pentecostal spirituality is missional spirituality.

This Lukan and missiological emphasis, transmitted largely through the stories in the book of Acts, also points to a significant difference that distinguishes the Pentecostal movement from the charismatic movement. Whereas the Pentecostal movement from the very beginning has been a missionary movement, the charismatic movement has largely been a movement of spiritual renewal within existing, mainline churches. Here, the names are instructive. The term "Pentecostal" points us to Pentecost and the missionary call and power that is given to the church (Acts 1–2). The term "charismatic," by way of contrast, points to the spiritual gifts that serve to edify the church, particularly as it gathers together for corporate worship (1 Cor 12–14). Both movements have blessed the wider church and brought fresh insights and much-needed spiritual energy. However, the missiological legacy of the Pentecostal movement is conspicuous. The same cannot be said for the charismatic movement.

Our unique appropriation of Luke–Acts not only distinguishes Pentecostals from our Evangelical and charismatic brothers and sisters, it also highlights a significant difference that separates us from the liberal wing of the Protestant church. It should be noted that many liberals, unlike their Evangelical counterparts, have given more attention to the Gospels, and particularly Jesus, than to Paul. In fact, some liberals go so far as to claim that Paul distorted or obscured the "pure" teachings of Jesus. It would appear, at least with this emphasis on the Gospel narratives, that liberals and Pentecostals might find some common ground. But, here again, we encounter a major difference. Whereas liberals seek to understand Jesus in the light of a critical scholarship that discounts the possibility of the miraculous; Pentecostals, without hesitation, embrace the miracle-working Jesus of the New Testament who is both fully human and fully divine. The difference is profound. One has an apostolic faith to proclaim. The other is left with little but pious platitudes. Again, it is not difficult to see why one is a missionary movement and the other is not.

All of this suggests that Pentecostals, with their simple approach to the book of Acts ("their stories are our stories"), have uniquely highlighted

---

9. For more on the relationship between Luke's perspective on the work of the Spirit and that of Paul, see Menzies, "Subsequence," 342–63.

an important aspect of the work of the Holy Spirit and Christian discipleship. Pentecostals assert that every Christian is called and empowered (at least potentially) to be bold, Spirit-inspired witnesses for Jesus. As Peter declared in his Pentecost sermon, the church is nothing less than a community of end-time prophets. Thus, from a Pentecostal perspective, one cannot separate missions from discipleship or bold witness from Christian character. The call comes to every believer and the enabling of the Spirit is promised to all.

MISSIONAL SPIRITUALITY AND LUKE'S PURPOSE

This all sounds very inspiring, but the question must be asked: Is this really the message Luke intended to communicate? How did Luke expect his story to be read? As we have noted, many Christians have not read Luke–Acts in this way. Non-Pentecostal Evangelicals generally maintain that Luke wrote to provide an historical account of the beginnings of the church so that subsequent readers might have an accurate account of the gospel message and be assured of the historical basis upon which it stands. So far, so good; but there is more. These Evangelicals also insist that since Luke's historical narrative treats a unique era in the life of the church, it should be understood that the events he describes are not presented as models for the missionary praxis of subsequent generations of Christians.[10] In short, Evangelicals generally assume that Luke the historian wrote to provide the church with its message, not its methods.

This assumption has produced a chorus of Evangelical scholars who, with one voice, constantly tell us that Pentecost is a unique and unrepeatable event.[11] As a young student, I was puzzled by these statements. In what sense is Pentecost unique? Any event in history cannot be repeated,

---

10. See, for example, Witherington, *Acts*, 132; Bock, *Acts*, 108–39 (cf. Bock, *Luke 9.51—24.53*, 189–90); and Hacking, *Signs and Wonders*, 251–58. Witherington highlights the "unique" nature of Pentecost. Bock also fails to develop the theological implications of Acts 1–2 for the missionary praxis of the contemporary church (see my review of Bock's Acts commentary in *Pneuma* 30 [2008] 349–50). Hacking argues that the miracles of Jesus and the apostles were not intended to serve as models for the post-apostolic church and that the commissioning accounts are relevant only to a select few (see my review of Hacking's book in *EQ* 79 [2007] 261–65).

11. Dunn, *Baptism in the Holy Spirit*, 53: "Pentecost can never be repeated—for the new age is here and cannot be ushered in again." Note also Witherington, *Acts*, 132: "[of Pentecost]. . .in crucial ways it is unique."

but many events in the narrative of Acts are clearly presented as models for Luke's church. They are recorded by Luke precisely so that they will be repeated in the lives of his readers. Why do Evangelical scholars insist that Pentecost is unique and unrepeatable? Their response is connected to their view of Luke's purpose.

Although I would acknowledge that Luke does stress the reliability of the apostolic witness and the remarkable nature of the origins of the Christian movement, his purposes go beyond this, beyond simply "confirming the gospel."[12] Luke's narrative is far more than a nostalgic review of how it all began. For Luke, the story does not end with the apostles and their witness. The story continues, as the ending of Acts anticipates, with the readers taking up the mantle of ministry modeled by Jesus and his disciples. Luke narrates the story of Jesus and the early church in order to challenge his church (and every church in "these last days") to take up its prophetic calling by listening to the voice of the Spirit and bearing bold witness for Jesus. Luke's two-volume work is a missionary manifesto. Through it, Luke seeks to remind his Christian readers of their true identity—they are a community of prophets called to be a "light to the nations"—and to encourage them, even as they face opposition and persecution,[13] to listen to the voice of the Spirit and, through his power, to bear witness for Jesus. Of course, Luke accomplishes this by providing various models: above all, Jesus, but also other models such as Peter, Stephen, Philip, and Paul. With great literary skill and artistry, Luke provides his intended readers, the persecuted Christians of his church, with theological and methodological guidance for their mission.[14]

If this summary of Luke's purpose (or, at least one of his central purposes) is correct, then Pentecostals read Luke–Acts well. They read Luke's narrative as Luke had hoped his readers would: as providing models for life and action, models for the mission every believer is called to

12. Maddox, *Purpose of Luke-Acts*. Maddox argues that Luke writes to reassure his largely Gentile church of the reliability of the gospel in spite of Jewish hostility and rejection.

13. Mittelstadt, *Spirit and Suffering*, and Cunningham, *Persecution*, argue convincingly that Luke wrote to a church that was experiencing persecution. See especially Cunningham, *Persecution*, 328–36.

14. I agree with Karris, who posits that Luke wrote shortly after the destruction of Jerusalem and its temple (around 75 AD) and that he wrote to "communities whose missionary work and daily existence are prone to danger and suffering—both from Jew and Gentile, but primarily from the Jewish synagogal authorities" (Karris, "Missionary Communities," 96). For supporting arguments, see also Menzies, "Persecuted Prophets," 52–70.

embrace.[15] In this chapter I would like to focus on one text that I believe offers considerable support for this Pentecostal reading of Luke–Acts. It is a classic text that calls us back to the missional spirituality of the apostolic church: Acts 2:17–21.

PENTECOST AS A PARADIGM (ACTS 2:17–21)

Every New Testament scholar worth his salt will tell you that Luke 4:16–30, Jesus' dramatic sermon at Nazareth, is paradigmatic for Luke's Gospel. All of the major themes that will appear in the Gospel are foreshadowed here: the work of the Spirit; the universality of the gospel; the grace of God; and the rejection of Jesus. And this is the one significant point where the chronology of the Gospel of Luke differs from the Gospel of Mark. Here Luke takes an event from the middle of Jesus' ministry and brings it right up front to inaugurate the ministry of Jesus. Luke does this because he understands that this event, particularly Jesus' recitation of Isaiah 61:1–2 and his declaration that this prophecy is now being fulfilled in his ministry, provides important insights into the nature of Jesus and his mission. This passage, then, provides us with a model for Jesus' subsequent ministry.

It is interesting to note that Luke provides a similar sort of paradigmatic introduction for his second volume, the book of Acts. After the coming of the Spirit at Pentecost, Peter delivers a sermon (Acts 2:14–41) that in many ways parallels that of Jesus in Luke 4. In his sermon, Peter also refers to an Old Testament prophecy concerning the coming of the Spirit, this time Joel 2:28–32, and declares that this prophecy too is now being fulfilled (Acts 2:17–21). The message is clear: Just as Jesus was anointed by the Spirit to fulfill his prophetic vocation, so also Jesus' disciples have been anointed as end-time prophets to proclaim the word of God. The text of Joel 2:28–32 that is cited here, like the paradigmatic passage in Luke 4, also shows signs of careful editing on the part of Luke.

The text of Acts 2:17–21 reads:

> [v. 17] *In the last days, God says,* [Joel: "after these things"]
> I will pour out my Spirit on all people.
> Your sons and daughters will prophesy
> *Your young men will see visions,* [Joel: these lines are inverted]
> *Your old men will dream dreams.*

---

15. Green, "Learning Theological Interpretation from Luke," 66: "Luke's Model Readers will embrace this narrative as their own, and seek to continue it in their lives."

> [v. 18] *Even* on *my* servants, both men and women, [additions to Joel]
> I will pour out my Spirit in those days,
> *And they will prophesy.*
> [v. 19] I will show wonders in the heaven *above*
> And *signs* on the earth *below*,
> Blood and fire and billows of smoke.
> [v. 20] The sun will be turned to darkness and the moon to blood
> Before the coming of the great and glorious day of the Lord.
> [v. 21] And everyone who calls on the name of the Lord will be saved.
> (Acts 2:17–21; modification of Joel 2:28–32 italicized)

Luke carefully shapes this quotation from the LXX in order to highlight important theological themes. Three modifications are particularly striking:

First, in verse 17 Luke alters the order of the two lines that refer to young men having visions and old men dreaming dreams. In Joel, the old men dreaming dreams comes first. But Luke reverses the order: "Your young men will see visions, your old men will dream dreams" (Acts 2:17). Luke rearranges these two lines drawn from Joel so that the reference to "visions" precedes the comment about "dreams." A survey of Acts reveals that this alteration is not simply an insignificant stylistic change. This is not merely a whim or slip of the eye. On the contrary, this subtle shift is intentional. Luke gives the reference to "visions" pride of place in order to emphasize its importance. With this modification of the LXX, Luke highlights a theme that he sees as vitally important and which recurs throughout his narrative.[16]

A survey of the key terms is instructive. First, we find that the terms associated with dreams and dreaming occur only here in the book of Acts. The term translated "shall dream" is a future passive of ἐνυπνιάζω. This verb occurs only here and in Jude 8 in the entire New Testament. The noun, ἐνύπνιον ("dream"), is found nowhere else in Acts or the rest of the New Testament. Clearly, Luke is not big on dreaming.[17]

Luke, however, loves to recount stories that reference guidance through "visions." At first glance this may not appear to be the case. The noun translated "visions" in verse 17, ὅρασις, occurs four times in the New Testament and only here in Acts. The other three occurrences are all found in Revelation. But appearances are often misleading and this is the case

---

16. This insight into Luke's special use of "vision" was inspired by a conversation with Dr. David Yonggi Cho during my visit to Seoul in 2007.

17. Note how Luke describes revelatory experiences at night, which might have taken place during sleep, as "visions" and not "dreams" (e.g., Acts 16:9–10).

here. Luke uses another term, a close cousin to ὅρασις, the neuter noun, ὅραμα, often and at decisive points in his narrative to refer to "visions." The noun ὅραμα occurs twelve times in the New Testament and eleven of these occurrences are found in the book of Acts.[18] Luke is, indeed, fond of visions. Although in Acts 2:17 Luke retains the language of the LXX (ὅρασις), elsewhere in his narrative he employs his preferred, very similar term (ὅραμα), to speak of "visions."

References to visions are not only plentiful in Luke's narrative, they also come at strategic moments.[19] Thus, Luke's alteration at this point appears to be theologically motivated. Of course, visions are not the only way that God guides the church in the book of Acts. Yet Luke's point is hard to miss: By linking the "visions" of Joel's prophecy (Acts 2:17) with the visions of the early church, Luke is in effect saying that in "these last days"—that period inaugurated with Jesus' birth and leading up to the Day of the Lord—the mission of the church must be directed by God, who will lead his end-time prophets in special and personal ways, including visions, angelic visitations, and the prompting of the Spirit, so that we might fulfill our calling to take the gospel to "the ends of the earth." In short, for Luke, the experience of the early church, a church that is supernaturally led by God, serves as a model for his church (and ours).

Second, with the addition of a few words in verse 19, Luke transforms Joel's text to read: "I will show wonders in the heaven *above*, and *signs* on the earth *below*." In this way, Luke consciously links the miracles associated with Jesus (notice the very first verse that follows the quotation from Joel: "Jesus . . . was a man accredited by God to you by miracles, wonders and signs," Acts 2:22) and the early church (e.g., 2:43) together with the cosmic portents listed by Joel (Acts 2:19–20). All are "signs and wonders" that mark the end of the age. For Luke, "these last days"—remember, Luke's church and ours are firmly rooted in this period—represents an epoch marked by "signs and wonders." Luke, then, is not only conscious of the significant role that miracles have played in the growth of the early church, he also anticipates that these "signs and wonders" will continue to characterize the ministry of the church to whom he writes.

---

18. Acts 7:31; 9:10, 12; 10:3, 17, 19; 11:5; 12:9; 16:9–10; 18:9; and then also in Matt 17:9.

19. For the strategic role of visions in the narrative of Acts see: Acts 9:10–12; 10:3, 17, 19; 11:5; 16:9–10; 18:9–10.

Third and most important for our purposes, Luke inserts the phrase, "And they will prophesy," into the quotation in verse 18. This insertion simply emphasizes what is already present in the text of Joel. The previous verse has already reminded us that this end-time outpouring of the Spirit of which Joel prophesies is nothing less than a fulfillment of Moses' wish "that all the Lord's people were prophets" (Num 11:29). Acts 2:17 quotes Joel 2:28 verbatim: "I will pour out my Spirit on all people. Your sons and daughters will prophesy." Now, in verse 18, Luke echoes this refrain. Luke highlights the fact that the Spirit comes as the source of prophetic inspiration because this theme will dominate his narrative. It is a message that Luke does not want his readers to miss. The church in "these last days," Luke declares, is to be a community of prophets—prophets who are called to bring the message of "salvation to the ends of the earth" (Isa 49:6). And now Luke reminds his readers that they also have been promised power to fulfill this calling. The Spirit will come and enable his church—Luke's and ours—to bear bold witness for Jesus in the face of opposition and persecution.

This theme of bold, prophetic witness is anticipated in Luke's Gospel. Jesus is anointed with the Spirit so that he might "preach the good news to the poor," so that he might "proclaim freedom for the prisoners" and "proclaim the year of the Lord's favor" (Luke 4:18–19). The parallels between Jesus' experience at the Jordan and that of the disciples at Pentecost are striking and should not be missed. Both occur at the beginning of the respective missions of Jesus and the early church, both center on the coming of the Spirit, both are described as a prophetic anointing in the context of a sermon that cites Old Testament prophecy. Through his careful shaping of the narrative, Luke presents Jesus, the ultimate prophet, as a model for all of his followers, from Pentecost onward. Luke's church has a mission to carry out, a message to proclaim.

This motif of bold, Spirit-inspired witness is also highlighted in the teaching of Jesus. Luke foreshadows events that will follow in his second volume by relating the important promise of Jesus recorded in Luke 12:11–12: "When you are brought before synagogues, rulers and authorities, do not worry about how you will defend yourselves or what you will say, for the Holy Spirit will teach you at that time what you should say."

Immediately after Pentecost, in the first story Luke recounts, we begin to see how relevant and important this promise of Jesus is for the mission of the church. Luke describes the dramatic story of Peter and John's encounter with a crippled beggar and the beggar's miraculous healing. A large crowd gathers, gaping at this marvelous event. The story builds to a climax as the Jewish leaders arrest Peter and John for preaching about the resurrection of Jesus. "You killed the author of life," Peter declares, "but God raised him from the dead. We are witnesses of this" (Acts 3:15). The Jewish leaders, upset with this turn of events, move in and arrest Peter and John. After spending the night in prison, Peter and John are called before the leaders and questioned. Peter is filled with the Holy Spirit and begins to bear bold witness for Jesus (Acts 4:8). Peter and John's courage is so striking that it leaves the Jewish leaders astonished and amazed. Finally, after deliberations, the leaders command the apostles to stop preaching about Jesus. But Peter and John reply with incredible boldness. They declare, "Judge for yourselves whether it is right in God's sight to obey you rather than God. We cannot help speaking about what we have seen and heard" (Acts 4:19–20).

This is merely the beginning of the persecution the end-time prophets must face. Very soon the apostles are again arrested. The Jewish leaders interrogate the apostles and angrily declare, "We gave you strict orders not to teach in this name [the name of Jesus] ... Yet you have filled Jerusalem with your teaching" (Acts 5:28). Peter and the apostles incur the wrath of their opponents when they declare, "We must obey God rather than men! The God of our fathers raised Jesus from the dead.... We are witnesses of these things, and so is the Holy Spirit" (Acts 5:29–32). The apostles are flogged and warned not to speak about Jesus. But the beatings do not have their desired effect. The apostles rejoice that they have been "counted worthy of suffering" for Jesus and continue to proclaim "the good news that Jesus is the Messiah" (Acts 5:41–42).

The persecution intensifies. What began with warnings in Acts 4 and led to beatings in Acts 5, now extends to Stephen's martyrdom in Acts 7. Just as the apostles were strengthened by the Spirit to bear bold witness for Jesus, so also Stephen's witness unto death is inspired by the Spirit (Acts 6:10). In the midst of his sermon to his persecutors recorded in Acts 7, Stephen declares, "You always resist the Holy Spirit! Was there ever a prophet your fathers did not persecute?" (Acts 7:51–52). The powerful irony should not be missed, for this same crowd moves to kill Stephen, a man "full of the Holy Spirit" (Acts 7:55).[20] The witness of another prophet is rejected.

---

20. Karris notes that in Acts 7:55–56 the promises of Luke 6:22–23 and 12:8 are fulfilled and concludes: "Luke 6:22–23 and 12:8 are meant for the edification of Luke's persecuted and harassed readers" (Karris, "Missionary Communities," 95).

PART III: PENTECOSTAL THEOLOGY

This pattern of bold, Spirit-inspired witness in the face of opposition continues with Paul, the dominant character in the latter portion of Acts. Paul is chosen by the Lord to take the gospel to the Gentiles. We are told that his journey will not be easy. The Lord, speaking to Ananias, declares, "I will show him how much he must suffer for my name" (Acts 9:16). And suffer he does. Yet, in the face of mind-numbing opposition, Paul is guided and strengthened by the Holy Spirit. A trail of churches filled with believers who worship Jesus are left in his wake. The narrative of Acts ends with Paul in prison in Rome, where he "boldly and without hindrance" preached about Jesus (Acts 28:31).

Luke's motive in presenting these models of Spirit-inspired ministry—Peter, John, Stephen, and Paul, to name a few—should not be missed. Luke has more in mind than simply declaring to his church, "This is how it all began!" Certainly Luke highlights the reliability of the apostolic witness to the resurrection of Jesus. And he wants to be sure that we are all clear about their message, which is to be handed on from generation to generation, people group to people group, until it reaches "the ends of the earth." Yet Luke also narrates the ministry of these end-time prophets because he sees them as important models of missionary praxis that his church needs to emulate. These characters in Acts demonstrate what it truly means to be a part of Joel's end-time prophetic band and thus challenge Luke's readers to fulfill their calling to be a light to the nations.[21] As they face opposition by relying on the Holy Spirit, who enables them to bear bold witness for Jesus no matter what the cost, these end-time prophets call Luke's church to courageously follow the path first traveled by our Lord.

CONCLUSION

This analysis of Acts 2:17–21, I would suggest, sheds significant light on Luke's larger purpose. Luke is a missiologist and with his two-volume work he has produced a manifesto for the Christian mission.[22] Through his manifesto, Luke seeks to remind his readers of their true identity—they are a community of prophets called to be a "light to the nations." He also seeks to encourage these Christians, even as they face opposition and persecution, to listen to the voice of the Spirit and, through his power, to bear bold

---

21. This conclusion is supported by Stronstad's insightful study, *Prophethood of All Believers*.

22. Matson, *Household Conversion Narratives in Acts*, 184: "Luke is a missiologist."

witness for Jesus. Luke accomplishes these objectives by providing various models: above all, Jesus, but also other models such as the Twelve, the Seventy, Stephen, Philip, and Paul. With great literary skill, Luke provides his intended readers, the persecuted Christians of his church, with encouragement and guidance for their mission.

This conclusion also indicates that Pentecostals, with their simple, narrative approach to Acts—"their stories are our stories"—actually read Luke–Acts well. They read Luke's narrative as Luke hoped his readers would: as providing models for life and action, models for the mission every believer is called to embrace. This approach has enabled Pentecostals to highlight in a unique way an important aspect of the work of the Holy Spirit and Christian spirituality. The Pentecostal affirms that every Christian has been called and promised the power needed to become bold, Spirit-inspired witnesses for Jesus. The church is nothing less than a community of end-time prophets. By appropriating Luke's dynamic message, Pentecostals have developed a piety with a uniquely outward thrust. This is missional spirituality and it flows from the apostolic church.

Part IV

PENTECOSTAL THEOLOGY
Its Evangelical Future

Chapter 7

THE NATURE OF PENTECOSTAL THEOLOGY
A Response to Kärkkäinen and Yong

My first encounter with the writings of Veli-Matti Kärkkäinen and Amos Yong occurred back in 2003. As a coeditor of the *Festschrift* for Russell Spittler, *The Spirit and Spirituality*, I read their thoughtful and finely written pieces for this volume.[1] At that time I remember being impressed with their intellectual gifts and literary skills. This initial impression was surely on mark. These two scholars have been among the most prolific theologians of the past decade. Just listing their literary production would take up more space than I have planned for this short chapter. In theological circles, Kärkkäinen and Yong have become household names, and this is particularly so for Pentecostals. Both Kärkkäinen and Yong grew up in Pentecostal churches and write from a Pentecostal, or perhaps better (as I shall argue), a pneumatological viewpoint. Currently, they both teach at Fuller Theological Seminary.

This brief chapter is a response to Kärkkäinen's essay, "Pentecostal Pneumatology of Religions: The Contribution of Pentecostalism to Our Understanding of the Work of God's Spirit in the World," which appeared in a multi-author collection of essays entitled, *The Spirit in the World*.[2] I have chosen to respond to this essay because in a short space it touches upon three issues of crucial importance for Pentecostal theology and, indeed, the Pentecostal movement. These issues are: (1) Pentecostal identity; (2) the locus of authority for theological reflection; and (3) a Pentecostal

1. Ma and Menzies, *Spirit and Spirituality*.
2. Kärkkäinen, *Spirit in the World*, 155–80.

approach to other religions. However, in order to place our discussion of these important issues in their proper context, I shall first summarize the salient features of Kärkkäinen's chapter.

SUMMARY

In this essay Kärkkäinen begins by drawing with broad strokes an overview of the current state of pneumatology in contemporary theology. He pays special attention to contributions or characteristics that mark the work of mainline or ecumenical theologians. According to Kärkkäinen, the key point to note is that contemporary reflection seeks to understand the Spirit's role more broadly, not simply as the source of spiritual life, but also as a catalyst for positive developments in politics, society, the environment, and science.[3] Additionally, contemporary theologians seek to relate the work of the Spirit to specific contexts, whether these contexts are understood in terms of economics (the poor and marginalized), gender (women), or culture (e.g., Africa, Asia, Latin American). Finally, Kärkkäinen notes that "contemporary theology includes an enthusiasm over relating the Spirit of God to other religions" and he cites Yong with approval when he says that we "can talk about the 'turn to the Spirit' in the Christian theology of religions."[4]

Kärkkäinen then considers the shape of Pentecostal theology. He begins with the ubiquitous warning that, due to the cultural and theological diversity within the movement, we really need to speak of Pentecostalisms (plural) rather than Pentecostalism, a unified group. Nevertheless, after this word of caution, he proceeds to outline what he feels are the central features of a Pentecostal pneumatology. The most foundational feature of a Pentecostal approach to the work of the Spirit is summed up with the word, empowerment: "Whereas for most other Christians the presence of the Spirit is just that, *presence*, for Pentecostals the presence of the Spirit

---

3. Kärkkäinen's upbeat account might be balanced by Peter Kuzmic's review of Jürgen Moltmann's *The Spirit of Life: A Universal Affirmation* (trans. M. Kohl; London: SCM Press, 1992). Kuzmic writes, "reading Moltmann I had the impression that he wrote a quasi-pneumatological manifesto for an unattainable, humanly created new world order. His implicit optimism in regard to human will and nature ... coupled with many explicit and implicit indications of pantheism, do tend towards a utopianism whose most serious temptation is to ignore the reality of the human condition" (Kuzmic, "Croatian War-Time Reading," 17-24, quote from p. 20).

4. Kärkkäinen, "Pneumatology of Religions," 159 (both quotes).

in their midst implies *empowerment*."[5] Kärkkäinen correctly notes that Pentecostals call the initial experience of empowerment, Spirit baptism. He also acknowledges that "the large majority of Pentecostals" affirm speaking in tongues as the "initial physical evidence" of this experience.[6] This emphasis on the empowering work of the Holy Spirit, drawn as it is from the New Testament and especially the book of Acts, gives the movement a distinctively eschatological and missiological emphasis: "From the beginning, Pentecostals were convinced that the twentieth-century outpouring of the Spirit marked the beginning of the return of Jesus Christ to establish the kingdom. In the meantime, based on biblical promises such as Acts 1:8, Christians were supposed to be empowered by the Spirit to bring the gospel to all nations."[7]

Against this backdrop, Kärkkäinen seeks to compare this classical Pentecostal pneumatology with the more recent emphasis on pneumatology found in the theological reflection within mainline denominations. Although Kärkkäinen sees significant points of convergence—the dynamic, holistic emphases of mainline theologians are somewhat paralleled by the Pentecostal affirmation that the Spirit is active and present, can be experienced, and bestows healing and deliverance—however, there is a significant difference. Pentecostals, unlike their mainline counterparts, are reluctant "to consider the role of the Spirit in relation to science . . . politics, environment, issues of equality, and similar public matters."[8] This reluctance to conceive of the Spirit's work more broadly extends to the question of other religions.

This reluctance of Pentecostals to contemplate the work of the Spirit more broadly serves as an introduction to Kärkkäinen's final section, which is in reality a call for Pentecostals to consider once again the possibility of the Spirit's work in other religions. Kärkkäinen chides Pentecostals for not developing a Spirit-oriented theology of religions and suggests that the problem is our location in the camp of conservative Christianity. He traces Pentecostal responses in various encounters or dialogues with Roman Catholics, the Reformed tradition, and the WCC and notes that in each instance Pentecostals insist that, "there cannot be salvation outside the church." Indeed, "Most Pentecostals limit the saving work of the Spirit to

---

5. Kärkkäinen, "Pneumatology of Religions," 163 (italics his).
6. Kärkkäinen, "Pneumatology of Religions," 164.
7. Kärkkäinen, "Pneumatology of Religions," 165–66.
8. Kärkkäinen, "Pneumatology of Religions," 167.

the church and its proclamation of the gospel, although they acknowledge the work of the Holy Spirit in the world, convincing people of sin."[9] Yet, in spite of the clarity of this Pentecostal response, Kärkkäinen suggests that this response is insufficient. He points with approval to the more open, "inclusivist" perspective of Amos Yong, who writes:

> Religions are neither accidents of history nor encroachments on divine providence but are, in various ways, instruments of the Holy Spirit working out the divine purposes in the world and that the unevangelized, if saved at all, are saved through the work of Christ by the Spirit (even if mediated through the religious beliefs and practices available to them).[10]

Kärkkäinen also appears quite sympathetic to Yong's definition of a Pentecostal theology of religions, "as the effort to understand both the immensely differentiated experiences of faith and the multifaceted phenomena of religious traditions and systems that is informed by experiences of the Spirit in the light of Scripture, and vice versa."[11] Kärkkäinen concludes his discussion at this point with a cryptic and somewhat contradictory statement, "Moreover, this endeavor should be attempted without giving up the priority of evangelism on the one hand or, on the other hand, commitment to the authority of Scripture."[12] Is this really possible? This is a question that we shall return to below.

Kärkkäinen's conclusion is ostensibly a list of potentially fruitful research topics for the future, but in reality it appears to be a rather clear call for Pentecostals to engage and dialogue with mainline theologians as we develop a theology of religions.

As I have noted above, although this article focuses more specifically on a Pentecostal theology of religions, it actually serves to illustrate several issues of importance for Pentecostals as we seek to be faithful and relevant in our understanding and application of the Scriptures.

---

9. Kärkkäinen, "Pneumatology of Religions," 172 (both quotes).

10. Kärkkäinen, "Pneumatology of Religions," 174, citing Yong, *Spirit Poured Out on All Flesh*, 235–36.

11. Kärkkäinen, "Pneumatology of Religions," 174, citing Yong, *Discerning the Spirit(s)*, 24.

12. Kärkkäinen, "Pneumatology of Religions," 174, does not quote Yong verbatim here, but suggests that this conclusion is drawn from Yong, *Discerning the Spirit(s)*, 24–25.

PENTECOSTAL IDENTITY

Let us begin with the matter of Pentecostal identity. Kärkkäinen gives voice to what in academic circles is becoming an uncritically accepted consensus: It is virtually impossible to speak coherently about Pentecostal theology because of its bewildering diversity. Kärkkäinen identifies a number of daunting challenges that make it difficult to speak of a Pentecostal pneumatology, but this matter of diversity is "undoubtedly the most radical one."[13] Kärkkäinen suggests that this diversity has two dimensions: "the cultural and the theological-ecumneical."[14]

I would suggest that this angst over the wide-ranging diversity of the movement misses several important factors. First, while it is true that the Pentecostal movement is "spread across many cultures, linguistic barriers, and social locations,"[15] it is also possible to highlight the central theological themes that animate these Pentecostal churches, irrespective of their cultural location, as Kärkkäinen himself does. Although Kärkkäinen's description is a bit more vague than I would prefer, it should be acknowledged that he is intentionally offering a very brief overview. I have provided a more nuanced description of core Pentecostal beliefs in my book, *Pentecost: This Story is Our Story*. These themes (for Kärkkäinen, an empowering baptism in the Spirit marked by speaking in tongues) are able to unite Pentecostals in Africa, Asia, and Latin America precisely because they are rooted in the Bible, and particularly the book of Acts. Although Pentecostal proclamation and praxis may address felt needs in various regions in a manner that former Christian theologies and movements, often steeped in a modernistic view of the world, did not, this is due to the Pentecostals' unwavering acceptance of the biblical, supernatural worldview rather than a syncretistic reliance on traditional pagan religious practices.[16] Pentecostals around the world accept the biblical "map of the universe" (to use Obu Kalu's language) and this resonates with the heart-felt needs of most people on the planet. Kalu's insightful chapter in this same book, *The Spirit in the World*, makes this point. He notes that there is "a confluence of the spiritual and material worlds, [which deny] the myth of materialism" in both the

---

13. Kärkkäinen, "Pneumatology of Religions," 161.

14. Kärkkäinen, "Pneumatology of Religions," 161.

15. Kärkkäinen, "Pneumatology of Religions," 161.

16. I am not saying that syncretism is not possible; rather, I suggest that when a person or church engages in unbiblical, syncretistic practices, this marks them as being outside the boundaries of what it means to be Pentecostal.

Bible and traditional African religions.[17] Kalu cites with approval the call by Philip Jenkins, which he sees as building on the work of John Mbiti and Kwame Bediako, for scholarship to pay attention "to the centrality and uses of the Bible among Christians in various regions of the world."[18] This fact should not be overlooked: Whereas mainline or ecumenical theologians have labored in Bultmannian fashion to demythologize the biblical message in an attempt to make its message more meaningful to a contemporary audience,[19] Pentecostals have not been distracted by perceived contradictions, outdated worldviews, or cultural distance. We simply accept the stories of the Bible as our stories, models for our lives and ministries. The biblical "map of the universe" becomes our map, and it appears that this is a map that people from every culture on the planet find meaningful and useful. So, in the midst of cultural diversity, the biblical narrative gives cohesion to the Pentecostal message and practice. This important unity that unites people across cultures should not be minimized.

There is another reason that many academics appear blind to the startling theological unity that unites Pentecostals around the world.[20] This is the legacy of Hollenweger's myth of the non-theological nature of the Pentecostal movement. Kärkkäinen pays homage to this oft-repeated and again uncritically accepted axiom when he states, "Pentecostalism was birthed out of dynamic experience rather than a theological discovery."[21] This statement is problematic at two levels. First, virtually any theological statement might be described in this way, that is, as first emerging as an experience. Secondly, the fact of the matter is that the Pentecostal movement actually was founded on a theological discovery. There is widespread agreement that the origins of the modern Pentecostal movement can be traced back to January 1, 1901 and a little Bible school in Topeka, Kansas.

17. Kalu, "Sankofa," 135–52 (quote from p. 147).

18. Kalu, "Sankofa," 149, citing Jenkins, *New Faces of Christianity*. Note also Mbiti, *Bible and Theology in African Christianity*.

19. Thus, as Kärkkäinen notes, contemporary mainline theologians are eager to relate pneumatology to politics, the environment, issues of equality, and other religions; but, I would add, less keen on highlighting the work of the Spirit in empowering proclamation of the apostolic message and enabling apostolic models of ministry, which include "signs and wonders."

20. It should be noted that Kärkkäinen actually acknowledges this unity, albeit a bit grudgingly, when he chides Pentecostals for being too heavily influenced by conservative theology.

21. Kärkkäinen, "Pneumatology of Religions," 160. In a footnote Kärkkäinen cites two of Hollenweger's writings to support this claim.

There, a clear connection was made between the experience of baptism in the Holy Spirit and speaking in tongues. This theological discovery—that the experience described in Acts should serve as a model for contemporary Christian experience, that the baptism in the Holy Spirit (Acts 2:4) is a post-conversion enabling for mission, and that speaking in tongues marks this experience—was transmitted to William Seymour, an earnest black preacher who brought the Pentecostal message to a small, makeshift mission in Southern California. Thus, the Azusa Street Revival (1906-9) was born. This became the catalyst for a movement that spread around the world. It is important to note that Seymour came to Los Angeles with a clear and distinctive message, one that flowed from Charles Parham and his students in Kansas. Of course many, especially the students and heirs of Hollenweger such as Allan Anderson, dispute the claim that the origins of the modern Pentecostal movement can be traced to the Azusa Street Revival. A parade of other revival movements from diverse locations around the world (India, Korea, and Wales, to name a few) is cited, all of which predate the Azusa Street Revival. Yet, the fact remains, none of these other revival movements produced a clear and distinctive theological message like that at Azusa Street. Only at Azusa Street was the connection made between baptism in the Spirit and speaking in tongues, which flowed from a particular understanding of the narrative in Acts. In short, the modern Pentecostal movement may not be able to point back to hundreds of years of tradition, but the movement possesses an important theological legacy nonetheless. The scope and unifying power of this theological heritage should not be missed or minimized.

Much is made of the theological diversity that marks the Pentecostal movement, but this is in reality a matter of semantics. Kärkkäinen writes that there are "several more or less distinct Pentecostalisms" and then he names them, classical Pentecostals, charismatics, and neo-charismatics.[22] If we can name them (as we can) and they have definable theological distinctives (as they do), then why not speak with a bit more precision? Generally, theologians like to speak with precision because it is helpful. So, rather than perpetuating the confusing and bewildering notion that there are many Pentecostalisms, let's simply define what we mean and use appropriate terms to designate the various groupings. I have provided this sort of sorely needed taxonomy in an Appendix below. When we do this, we find that the term, "Pentecostal," becomes meaningful and that it describes

22. Kärkkäinen, "Pneumatology of Religions," 161.

a significant and remarkably cohesive group of Christians and churches around the world.

BIBLICAL AUTHORITY AND THEOLOGICAL METHOD

Kärkkäinen's essay also points to an important question that his work and that of others like Amos Yong pose for Pentecostals. How shall we do theology? This might seem like a simple and straightforward question, but it is not. At first glance, we might assume that of course our theology must flow from careful study of the Bible. However, several signs suggest that Kärkkäinen and Yong are not satisfied with this simple approach or response. The first indication that this simple answer is insufficient for Kärkkäinen is his statement, "All theology is contextual and 'locational.'"[23] Of course, in a sense this statement is formally true. Every statement is made in a specific language and by a person located in a specific culture and time. Yet, it is also true that we would be wise to be wary of accepting this statement without qualification as definitive. Does this mean that we are unable to convey the essence of the gospel clearly across cultures? Does this mean that we are hopelessly trapped in our own cultural "ghetto," unable to communicate in a meaningful way with other Christians around the globe? I think not. In fact, as a missionary who has lived for over twenty-five years in China, I continue to be amazed at the similarities (rather than the differences) that link all human beings together—we share similar dreams, aspirations, weaknesses, and fears—and the power of the biblical message to communicate to people of diverse cultural settings. As we have noted, the biblical "map of the universe" resonates with people around the world and Pentecostals have been successful in their evangelistic and church-planting efforts precisely because we take this worldview seriously. The real question is then, how great is the cultural divide? The greater we see the divide, the more we feel the need to "translate" or reconstruct the message. Historically, this has led many mainline churches to depart from declaring the apostolic message and, in some cases, to abandon the very notion of sharing the gospel across cultural boundaries. A Pentecostal approach to the theological enterprise, I would suggest, sees the divide in very manageable terms. This is especially the case when we recall the promise of the Spirit's enabling (Acts 1:8). Our job is not to reconstruct the message, but rather to translate and apply it so that it can be clearly understood and appropriated. I would note that the

23. Kärkkäinen, "Pneumatology of Religions," 177.

issue of authority is central here, for the greater we see the divide, the more we will focus on analysis of contemporary culture rather than the biblical witness. There is little question that in many WCC circles that spoke of contextualization, the perceived needs or concerns of the contemporary culture quickly took precedent over the apostolic message.

Another indication that Kärkkäinen is dissatisfied with a simple focus on the Bible as the source of our theology is his call for Pentecostals to link our pneumatology more broadly to matters beyond personal piety and spirituality, such as politics, the environment, the struggle for equality, and, of course, other religions.[24] This challenge to think more broadly is also connected to his encouragement to engage mainline theologians, who have for some time been pursuing this course. Once again, however, I would note that this clearly has not been the Pentecostal posture. As Kärkkäinen notes, Pentecostals have focused their attention on proclaiming the gospel and not on political or social action. This is not to stay that Pentecostals have not had a significant social impact. Although it often goes unrecognized, Pentecostals around the globe are having a dramatic social impact. But they are doing so precisely because they are focused on a clear biblical message of repentance, forgiveness, and transformation. This message builds worshiping communities that embody and foster virtues that build families, empower women, nurture children, and enable the poor to prosper.[25] Pentecostals typically do what Graham Twelftree suggests was the practice of the early church: they preach and demonstrate with signs and wonders the gospel to those outside the church; and they apply social justice within the church.[26]

24. Note also that Kärkkäinen's proposed five-volume systematic theology, written under the series title, *Constructive Christian Theology for the Pluralistic World*, is extremely broad in its scope. He calls for "a robust and consistent dialogue with not only the historical and contemporary theological disciplines . . . but also the beliefs and insights of living faiths (in this case, Judaism, Islam, Hinduism, and Buddhism) as well as the natural (and, at times, behavioral and social) sciences" (Kärkkäinen, *Trinity and Revelation*, 2). Yong also affirms this broader understanding of the theological task and thus laments the fact that his view of the Holy Spirit's person and work as a young Pentecostal was "too individualistic, too spiritualistic, and too ecclesiocentric." He seeks an interpretation of Luke–Acts that sees the Spirit at work outside the church in and through the economic and political systems of society as well as wider cultural and religious realities (Yong, *Who is the Holy Spirit?*, x [previous quote, ix]).

25. For an objective but positive assessment, see Martin, *Pentecostalism: The World Their Parish*. This point is also acknowledged by Kärkkäinen, "Pneumatology of Religions," 166.

26. Twelftree, *People of the Spirit*, 203. Twelftree concludes, "Social action, in terms

PART IV: PENTECOSTAL THEOLOGY

This Pentecostal approach has the advantage of featuring a message that clearly centers on the word of God and that thus serves to unite the community of faith. The further afield the church moves into the realm of political or social action, the less it is able to speak with clarity about its suggested course of action. It is forced to draw upon resources and authorities other than the Bible in order to establish its sense of direction.[27] Should Christians support a welfare state as a compassionate choice for the poor? Or should they encourage less government intervention so that individuals and churches have more freedom and resources to minister to them? These are the kind of questions that individual Christians often consider. However, because these questions are not directly dealt with in the Scriptures, they normally generate conflicting responses. Pentecostals have, for the most part, avoided theological reflection and philosophical speculation that takes the church away from its apostolic foundations and its central truths. They show little interest in political theology or interfaith dialogue. Kärkkäinen and Yong appear impatient with this posture, but I believe history has shown that it is a great strength. One wonders why Pentecostals would want to travel down the well-worn path that the mainline churches have already trod? Given the powerful impact of Pentecostal churches and the relative impotence of our mainline counterparts, I find it difficult to understand why Kärkkäinen feels that we should follow in their footsteps.

OTHER RELIGIONS

Finally, we come to the question of a Pentecostal theology of religions. Kärkkäinen acknowledges that Pentecostals have shown little inclination to speak of the work of the Spirit in other religions:

> While Pentecostals have excelled in missionary activities with impressive results by any standards, their thinking about the ministry of the Spirit in the world lags behind. Not only that, but—aligning with the more conservative wing of the church—they have also been the first to raise doubts about any kind of saving role of the Spirit apart from the proclamation of the gospel. Most Pentecostals

---

of caring for the physical needs of the outsider, plays no part in Luke's view of mission" (p. 203). On the priority of proclamation over social action in Luke's view of mission, see also Menzies, "Complete Evangelism: A Review Essay," 133–42.

27. In his review of Moltmann's *Spirit of Life*, Kuzmic notes the lack of serious engagement with the Bible, "Here, as elsewhere in the book, his exegesis is poor and his selective use of Scriptures hermeneutically questionable" ("Croatian War-Time Reading," 21).

have succumbed to the standard conservative/fundamentalist view of limiting the Spirit's saving work to the church (except for the work of the Spirit preparing one to receive the gospel).[28]

Clearly, Kärkkäinen sees this Pentecostal tendency as a deficiency, an error to be corrected. And, of course, he doesn't need to look far to find a champion. His Fuller Theological Seminary colleague, Amos Yong, has been the leading voice in this field over the past decade. Yong's perspective is strikingly different than that of the typical Pentecostal. He views other religions quite positively, as "instruments of the Holy Spirit [who, through them, is] working out the divine purposes in the world." Yong also suggests that the Spirit might work in salvific ways in other religions. While he is quick to tie this salvation in some sense to Christ and the Spirit, he suggests that this salvation may be "mediated through the religious beliefs and practices available to them [this is, through the beliefs and practices of other religions]."[29] It is evident that Yong is an inclusivist—while all salvation comes from Christ, the saved may not necessarily know this—and that his position flows from the conviction that the Spirit is at work in saving ways in other religions, even if they do not name the name of Jesus.[30]

There are several important points to note at this juncture. First, it should be acknowledged that Yong's theology is not really Pentecostal but rather pneumatological. That is, Yong's conclusions and methods do not reflect what is normally meant by the term, Pentecostal.[31] This is not only true of his theology of religions, but also his broader theological perspective as reflected in *The Spirit Poured Out on All Flesh* and *Who Is the Holy Spirit?* Even if we adopt Kärkkäinen's rather vague definition of Pentecostal theology, one would be hard pressed to see Yong as supporting these convictions. Yong probably could be described as an ecumenical charismatic theologian, but the term Pentecostal seems misplaced.

Furthermore, when we describe Yong's theology as pneumatological, we highlight the fact that Yong's approach is rooted in an emphasis on the

---

28. Kärkkäinen, "Pneumatology of Religions," 170.

29. Kärkkäinen, "Pneumatology of Religions," 174, citing Yong, *Spirit Poured Out on All Flesh*, 235–36 (both quotes).

30. For a clear statement of Yong's approach, see Yong, *Beyond the Impasse*. For a good analysis and critique of the inclusivist position see Phillips, "Evangelicals and Pluralism," 229–44.

31. For a similar assessment see Anderson, "Review of *The Spirit Poured Out on All Flesh*," 160–61. Anderson writes, "Neither does Yong represent global Pentecostal theology in any 'traditional' or normative sense" (p. 160).

work of the Spirit. Indeed, it is precisely this emphasis on the Spirit rather than on Christ that enables Yong as a Christian to speak of God being at work in other religions.[32] This pneumatological orientation also enables Yong to see congruence between the Christian experience of the Holy Spirit and the spiritual experiences of those in other religions. This is, however, where we encounter problems.

The main difficulty that I have with Yong's proposal is that it is so out of step with the apostolic witness as recorded in the New Testament. It is difficult to imagine, for example, Paul dialoguing with his Jewish or Gentile audiences as merely an interested fellow learner, assuming that they all speak on an equal footing and that everyone has something significant to contribute. This is not Paul's posture. Rather he is compelled to speak, because the gospel revealed to him through his encounter with Christ is "the power of God for the salvation of everyone who believes" (Rom 1:16; cf. 2 Cor 5:14–15). Indeed, Paul is so gripped by the message of Jesus, that he is willing to "endure everything" so that he might proclaim it to "the elect, that they too may obtain the salvation that is in Christ Jesus, with eternal glory" (2 Tim 2:8–10). The same may be said of Luke and his vision of the church and its mission. The church, Luke reminds us, is nothing less than a community of prophets who have been called and empowered to proclaim the good news of Jesus to a lost and dying world (Acts 1:8; 2:17–21). Peter and John's bold declaration, "Salvation is found in no one else, for there is no other name under heaven given to men by which we must be saved" (Acts 4:12), and their Spirit-inspired compulsion to proclaim the message in spite of opposition ("we cannot help speaking about what we have seen and heard" [Acts 4:20]), are lifted up as models for Luke's readers. In other words, Yong's exhortations for us to sit down as fellow learners and discuss our mutual experiences of God with those religious others that we encounter, sounds more like a product of our contemporary Western and liberal culture rather than the apostolic mandate. The New Testament calls us to be prophets, not dialogue partners.

Certainly, Yong is well aware of these tensions and he should be commended for his attempt to communicate with a global and largely non-Christian audience. His *Beyond the Impasse* is a bold and, given its abstract and philosophical nature, amazingly clear call to formulate a theology of

---

32. So, for example, Yong declares, "Rejection of the *Filioque* may free up some room for a development of a pneumatology of religions as a distinct or at least related stream in the history of salvation" (*Beyond the Impasse*, 186).

religions and engage those of other religions in authentic dialogue. Nevertheless, as I read this book I kept thinking that the basic posture of humility (we have much to learn from other religions for, after all, God through his Spirit is at work in them too) that he advocates appears to miss the fact that in our experience of Christ through the Holy Spirit we have been uniquely gripped by the power of God. Our boldness should not be confused with selfish arrogance; rather, it is a reflection of God's great and glorious work in Christ. It is not the product of ignorance, but of a clear revelation.

I write this short chapter from Southwest China, where I have just returned after a short time back in the United States. Earlier today I ate a bowl of noodles in a small Muslim restaurant while conversing in Mandarin with the owner, Mr. Ma, who happened to be listening to Muslim instruction piped to him over the internet in his own Salar language from Qinghai Province.[33] I asked Mr. Ma what the message he was attentively listening to was about. He indicated that it centered on life after death and the fact that we should have an eternal perspective. Of course this was a perspective that I could affirm. We both agreed that this talk of eternity was quite different from the normal Marxist materialism that colors so much of public discourse in China. This encounter was the beginning of a conversation and a friendship that I pray will continue to develop. I do believe that this is the sort of dialogue that Amos Yong seeks to encourage (and appropriately so), although Yong's vision also includes more formal, academic dialogue as well. Yet I must admit that my posture in this dialogue is not what Yong appears to advocate. I unapologetically enter into this discussion convinced that I have a message of the utmost importance for Mr. Ma (not vice versa) and a burning desire to communicate this message about Jesus to him. I do want to learn more about Mr. Ma, his background, his people, their beliefs, and their history. And by listening, I hope to earn the right to speak. However, I do not view this "dialogue" as an opportunity to learn from Mr. Ma more about God's ways and purposes as expressed in Islam (although I gladly admit that Mr. Ma's baked bread is of divine origin). Nor am I very interested in attempting to discern how (if at all) the Spirit is at work in his life. I am already convinced that the Spirit is at work in Mr. Ma's life through me and our encounter. I want to be attentive to how I might bear witness for Jesus to this man who appears untouched by the gospel.[34]

---

33. This a different "Mr. Ma" than the one referenced previously in chapter 5. The Mr. Ma of chapter 5 is a member of the Hui minority group.

34. According to Hattaway, 87 percent of the Salar have never heard the gospel

I want to share the most precious, valuable gift that I have with my new friend. I believe that the love of Christ and the power of the Holy Spirit demand nothing less.

This leads me to another problem with Yong's proposal. Yong's biblical analysis appears to overemphasize the universal dimensions of the Spirit's work on the one hand, and downplay the particular, Christo-centric nature of the Spirit's salvific work on the other. Yong's reading of Acts 10:34 and 2:17 is a good example of both. Yong writes:

> The Christian belief that God is no respecter of persons (Acts 10:34)—regardless of race or ethnicity, gender, social standing, religious affiliation, or geographical location—and that the Holy Spirit is being poured out universally (Acts 2:17) means that whatever else we as human beings might be up to, we do not live apart from the Spirit of God nor can we escape the Spirit's presence and activity (cf. Ps 139:7–12).[35]

In spite of the eloquence of Yong's statement, I believe it misses the heart of Luke's message. Neither of these quotations from Peter—"I now realize how true it is that God does not show favoritism but accepts men from every nation who hear him and do what is right" (Acts 10:34–35) and "I will pour out my Spirit on all flesh" (Acts 2:17, quoting Joel 2:28)—refer to the work of the Spirit among people who are not followers of Jesus. In fact, the point is quite the opposite: faith in the message of Jesus enables people from every nation to enter the kingdom of God and to experience the Spirit's power, which marks them as members of Joel's end-time band of prophets.

One of the striking features of Luke's narrative in Acts is the conspicuous role played by speaking in tongues.[36] Speaking in tongues is associated with prophecy and presented as a significant sign in both of the passages noted above (Acts 2 and 10). The stage is set in Acts 2.

In Acts 2:17–18 (cf. Acts 2:4) speaking in tongues is specifically described as a fulfillment of Joel's prophecy that in the last days all of God's people will prophesy. The cacophony produced by the tongues-speech of Jesus' disciples is not the result of too much revelry; rather, Peter explains, it is the sound of inspired utterances issued by God's end-time prophets (Acts 2:13, 15–17). The meaning of the symbolism of the speaking "in other

(Hattaway, *Operation China*, 464).

35. Yong, *Beyond the Impasse*, 131. See also Yong, *Spirit Poured Out on All Flesh*, 195–202.

36. See Menzies, *Speaking in Tongues*, 15–41.

tongues," which enables "the Jews from every nation under heaven" to hear the message in their "own language" (Acts 2:5–6), is clearly explained. It marks this group as members of Joel's end-time prophetic band and indicates that the "last days" and the salvation associated with it have arrived. Thus, Luke narrates Peter's powerful declaration concerning Jesus, "Exalted to the right hand of God ... he [Jesus] has poured out *what you now see and hear*" (Acts 2:33). "Therefore," Peter declares, "let all Israel be assured of this: God has made this Jesus, whom you crucified, both Lord and Christ" (Acts 2:36). The logic of the narrative is transparent: Since the Spirit of prophecy is only given to the "servants" of God (Acts 2:18)—that is, the true people of God, the heirs of the promise God made to Israel (Joel 2:28–32)—and, since the disciples of Jesus are those who are now receiving this gift, it follows that Jesus is Lord (Acts 2:33) and that his disciples constitute the true people of God. In Acts 2 tongues speech (the audible and visible effect of the gift of the Spirit), then, serves as a sign that both validates the disciples' claim that Jesus is Lord and confirms their status as members of Joel's end-time prophetic band.

The association with prophecy is made again in Acts 10:42–48. While Peter was still preaching to Cornelius and his household, the Holy Spirit "came on all those who heard the message" (Acts 10:44). Peter's colleagues "were astonished that the gift of the Holy Spirit had been poured out even on the Gentiles, for they heard them speaking in tongues and praising God" (Acts 10:45–46). Notice how the Holy Spirit interrupts Peter just as he declares, "He [Jesus] commanded us to preach to the people and to testify that he is the one whom God appointed as judge of the living and the dead. *All the prophets testify about him* that everyone who believes in him receives forgiveness of sins through his name" (Acts 10:42–43). It can hardly be coincidental that the Holy Spirit breaks in and inspires glossolalia precisely at this point in Peter's sermon. Indeed, when Cornelius and his household burst forth in tongues, this act provides demonstrative proof that they too are in fact part of the end-time prophetic band of which Joel prophesied. They too are prophets that "testify" about Jesus. How, then, can Peter and the others withhold baptism from them?

All of this makes it abundantly clear that in these passages Luke does not refer to the work of the Spirit beyond the boundaries of a specific and particular group of people, the people of God. Rather, in these passages Luke redefines the concept, "the people of God." This group, the people of God, is no longer limited to Israel, but now includes those of every nation who believe in Jesus and receive "forgiveness of sins through his name" (Acts 10:43; Acts 10 makes explicit what Acts 2 anticipates).

In fact, throughout the New Testament the salvific work of the Spirit is associated with a special gift of the Spirit (as opposed to the general operation of the Spirit in creation that gives physical life) and is always related to the proclamation, imitation, or worship of Christ. The key point to note is that the measuring stick for determining whether an experience, action, or event is inspired by the Spirit is its relationship to Christ. This is true for Luke (Acts 1:8; 2:33), for Paul (1 Cor 12:3), and for John (John 3:5–8; 20:22). The New Testament presents a uniform witness: we know that something is of the Spirit if it exalts Christ. Apart from this Christological test, we have no way of knowing whether what is being evaluated is a work of the Spirit or not.[37] An act of kindness or generosity may be good and noble, but this is no assurance that it is a work of the Spirit (in the normal New Testament sense of the word). Only if this act is performed out of a desire to exalt Christ do we know that it is a manifestation of the kingdom of God. An appeal to the general work of the Spirit in creation offers no escape, for this dimension of the Spirit's activity is not viewed as salvific by the New Testament authors. Only the operation of the Spirit that is bestowed by Christ is salvific. Thus, the soteriological work of the Spirit in and among people is only recognizable by its Christological nature (i.e., empowering proclamation, enabling ethical transformation, and energizing worship). To speak, then, of the work of the Spirit in salvific ways in other religions is, at best, pure speculation.

I am here reminded of J. Rodman Williams' critique of Harvey Cox's book, *Fire from Heaven*.[38] Williams criticizes Cox, who was Amos Yong's mentor, for his "tendency to view Pentecostalism as basically a religious expression that belongs to human existence at large" and queries, "But is there not something distinctive about Pentecostal spirituality? Is it only

---

37. Kärkkäinen acknowledges this point in his article, "How to Speak of the Spirit Among Religions," 121–27, see especially p. 123. Yong too is very much aware of the problem (e.g., *Beyond the Impasse*, 169) and his entire program can be viewed as an attempt to deal with this issue while at the same time speaking to a larger, non-Christian audience. However, there does not seem to be much clarity (at least in Yong's writings) on the distinction between the work of the Spirit among all people (and beyond) in creation and the work of the Spirit as Christ's (and the Father's) gift that is only given in response to repentance and faith.

38. Cox, *Fire From Heaven*. See also Williams, "Harvey Cox and Pentecostalism."

a powerful breaking forth of what is latent anywhere and everywhere?"[39] Additionally, Williams notes, "What seems to be lacking in Cox's treatise is any focus on the idea of 'a special encounter'. For not only, I would say, did the Holy Spirit dwell in Jesus; He was also sent forth by Christ (see Acts 2:33). This seems lacking in Cox's book wherein the Spirit represents an immanent reality that may break forth at any time."[40]

Finally, Kärkkäinen insists that this endeavor championed by Yong "should be attempted without giving up the priority of evangelism on the one hand or, on the other hand, commitment to the authority of Scripture."[41] Yet history has demonstrated that this exhortation has little chance if any of being realized. Take a look at our mainline brothers and sisters. The evidence is clear and the logic difficult to refute. How can discussion of the saving work of the Holy Spirit in other religions not adversely impact our evangelistic and church-planting efforts? And given the seemingly apparent contradictions with apostolic practice as presented in the New Testament, this endeavor cannot help but raise questions about the authority of Scripture and its role in the theological enterprise.[42]

CONCLUSION

Kärkkäinen and Yong are without question brilliant thinkers and they will undoubtedly, at times, prod Pentecostals to think in fresh and positive ways. However, I believe that Pentecostals need to tread carefully here and must critically evaluate the writings produced by these fine scholars. Although Kärkkäinen and Yong hail from Pentecostal backgrounds, their theological orientation is probably better described as charismatic rather than Pentecostal. Their approach might be termed pneumatological rather than Pentecostal, and their methods have more in common with mainline or ecumenical theologians than their Evangelical or Pentecostal colleagues. More specifically, Kärkkäinen and Yong's call for Pentecostals to embrace a

---

39. Williams, "Harvey Cox and Pentecostalism," 3.

40. Williams, "Harvey Cox and Pentecostalism," 4.

41. Kärkkäinen, "Pneumatology of Religions," 174, who also cites Amos Yong, *Discerning the Spirit(s)*, 24-25. At the same time, Yong seems very much aware of the fact that he is in reality proposing a different approach to missions (see *Beyond the Impasse*, chapters 5 and 6).

42. There is a striking dearth of biblical references or analysis in Yong's article, "From Azusa Street to the Bo Tree and Back: Strange Babblings and Interreligious Interpretations in the Pentecostal Encounter with Buddhism," 203-26.

more inclusive theology of religions is fraught with perils. As Peter Kuzmic notes, "If we see in everything the work of the Spirit (or the spiritual) then we can never recognize or become the recipients and instruments of the Spirit of God."[43] I believe that Pentecostals will be better served, and thus serve better, by following more closely the apostolic model.

---

43. Kuzmic, "A Croatian War-Time Reading," 22.

CONCLUSION

I HAVE NO DOUBT that while the ink on these pages is still wet there will be those who will protest, "Pentecostals are not Evangelicals. Pentecostals and Evangelicals represent two very different ways of looking at the world, the Bible, and the church. They represent a cataclysmic clash of worldviews." This protest will be raised by some—indeed, a significant number—in the Pentecostal academy. They want to distance the noble mystics from the sterile rationalists. But this protest will also be heard in the halls of fundamentalist churches and whispered in their pews. Now, of course, the protest will contrast sober-minded Christians rooted in the solid precepts of the Bible with wild-eyed enthusiasts constantly caught up in the latest spiritual fad.

My only defense against such objections is to suggest that this notion—that a great gulf of different worldviews separates Evangelicals and Pentecostals—rests on a caricature of both movements. R. A. Torrey, in my mind, shows the fallacy of superficial judgments concerning Evangelicals in this regard. It should also be noted that one of the great metaphors of Evangelicalism is "the sawdust trail," a picture which captures the profoundly experiential nature of the movement.[1] Evangelicals may quibble and disagree over many things, but to suggest that they are sterile rationalists clearly misses the mark. And while Pentecostals highlight "encounter" with God, the remarkable similarity of experience and praxis that mark Pentecostal believers and churches around the globe bears witness to the fact that the biblical record is the impetus and measure of their faith. Additionally, I have argued that the word "encounter" alone does not take us to the heart of Pentecostal theology or practice. For Pentecostals, the divine

---

1. George, *Pilgrims on the Sawdust Trail: Evangelical Ecumenism and the Quest for Christian Identity*.

encounter produces a call. Thus, I have suggested that Pentecostals are not mystics, but rather prophets. Indeed, a key reason why I wrote this book is to highlight this important point.

Although, as I have stated, I am quite certain that many, especially those in the Pentecostal academy, will find fault with my thesis, I am equally confident that the vast majority of Pentecostal believers, pastors, and church leaders (and, perhaps most importantly, young students) will embrace and find encouragement in this perspective. I also believe it will help a sizeable number of non-Pentecostal Evangelicals better understand Pentecostals and perhaps their own faith as well. In short, I am confident that my perspective will resonate with the vast majority of Pentecostals in the pulpits and the pews, if not a select group in the academy. So, I would suggest that this is the real gulf in perception that exists—the one that separates the vast majority of Pentecostal believers from a select group in the academy. In view of this gulf in perception, I see a clash, a sort of fundamentalist-modernist controversy, albeit one centered on new issues (worldview, hermeneutics, and ultimately theology), coming. This is why I believe this discussion is important and unavoidable.

To those friends who disagree with my conclusions (and here I address my remarks primarily to my Pentecostal brothers and sisters), I want to raise one final question. The question flows out of my own personal experience and expresses a nagging fear. I am concerned about the next generation of Pentecostals, that we not lose our Evangelical moorings. The Methodist denomination of the late nineteenth and early twentieth century is a great example of how quickly a vital spiritual movement can lose its way. As I have stated in my other writings and affirm again in this one, Pentecostals have a unique contribution to make to the larger Evangelical family; but, if we abandon our Evangelical values, we will lose our way and God will raise up others to make this contribution.

My final question is embedded within a story. Recently I was privileged to visit a church near the city of Qujing in China's Yunnan Province. The church in the village of Zhan Yi was established by Pentecostal missionaries, Max and Emily Bernheim, in the 1930s. The Bernheims, along with one son, were murdered by bandits in 1940. This tragic event left the Bernheim's five remaining children orphans. Additionally, the location of the bodies of Max, Emily, and their son, David, remained a mystery for decades. However, late in 2015 members of the Zhan Yi church discovered the Bernheims' original burial site and moved their remains to the church's

CONCLUSION

current location the following year. In June of 2017 a Chinese Christian brother notified me of these more recent developments. He hoped that I might be able to notify the family of these recent events.

So, along with a group of friends, I visited the burial site and found a beautiful memorial stone marking the Bernheims' grave. More significantly, I found that the church in Zhan Yi they planted—there were about fifty believers in 1940—is vibrant and thriving. The local Chinese believers repeatedly expressed their thankfulness for the Bernheims' ministry and sacrifice. The church in Zhan Yi now numbers over seven hundred and the church leaders are deeply aware of their rich legacy. They noted with thankfulness the truth of Tertullian's words, "The blood of the martyrs is the seed of the church." These words are etched on the memorial stone that marks the Bernheims' grave, now located next to the church.

As I ponder the Bernheim family's story, a thought and a question race through my mind. The thought is simply this: While I am sure that back in 1940 many could not comprehend how Max and Emily Bernheim could take their six children into the chaos of war-torn Southwest China, I am convinced that only time and eternity will reveal the true significance of their obedience and their sacrifice. Already, we can catch a glimpse of the amazing impact the gospel they proclaimed is having upon the lives of the people of Southwest China.

My question touches upon the central purpose of this book. I have argued in successive chapters: that the modern Pentecostal movement, from the very beginning, was steeped in Evangelical doctrine and praxis; that Pentecostals have always been "people of the book" and rooted their belief and practice in a simple, straightforward reading of the Bible; that while Pentecostals celebrate the present-ness of the kingdom and live with an expectation that "signs and wonders" will mark the life of the church today, this expectation is tempered and guided by the biblical text; that Pentecostals are Christ-centered and highlight the importance of an intimate, personal relationship with God in Christ; that Pentecostals, with their narrative approach to Luke–Acts, have a distinctive missiological understanding of the Christian life that resonates well with related Evangelical emphases; and, finally, that in spite of calls to the contrary, Pentecostals must not forget their rich Evangelical heritage. So, my final question is this: if Pentecostal churches forget, reject, or consciously move away from the rich Evangelical heritage outlined in the pages of this book, will we continue to have the strength, the will, and the ability to send out missionaries like the Bernheims into the harvest field—a harvest field that is growing increasingly hostile and dangerous?

I believe the answer to this question is quite clear. Sadly, some appear to be calling us to do this very thing. The fact that more than a few conservative Evangelicals are unwilling to acknowledge our common roots and the theological unity that we share does not help in this regard.[2] This myopia only diminishes their ability to speak to and to be enriched by the Pentecostal movement. My hope is that this book might encourage both groups—Pentecostals, especially those in the academy who are tempted to reject core Evangelical values, and conservative Evangelicals who, espousing unexamined tropes, have rejected the Pentecostal movement—to consider once again the theological convictions that unite these two powerful and overlapping Christian movements.

I am also convinced that if we Pentecostals will remember and affirm the rich Evangelical heritage that is ours, then we will continue to enjoy the Lord's blessing and experience Pentecostal power. We will then continue to prayerfully and joyfully send out countless emissaries for Jesus like the Bernheims to difficult, dangerous, and needy points around the globe. And, along with our other Evangelical brothers and sisters, we will see the fulfillment of John's vision come to pass: a "great multitude" from every nation, tribe, and language, will together sing, "Salvation belongs to our God . . . and to the Lamb!" (Rev 7:9–10).

---

2. See, for example, the caricature of the Pentecostal movement and comments offered by John MacArthur in his book, *Strange Fire*.

APPENDIX

Defining the Term, "Pentecostal"

MANY TODAY APPEAR RELUCTANT to define the term, "Pentecostal," in a clear and precise way. One of the key reasons for this is the assumption that the Pentecostal movement does not possess a theological message. Supposedly it is a movement defined by experience, not doctrine. Clearly, Walter Hollenweger's shadow still looms large.[1]

This assumption has led many to define the term, Pentecostal, phenomenologically (that is, according to experience). A good example of this approach is found in the way that many sociologists describe the Chinese "house churches." Most scholars are reluctant to describe these churches as possessing a clear Pentecostal identity—one that is rooted in their reading of the Bible. A host of other factors are offered in an attempt to explain why Chinese Protestants have gravitated toward Pentecostal forms of belief and praxis. For example, Hunter and Chan point out that Pentecostal values resonate with important features of Chinese folk religion and thus meet the felt-needs of many Chinese believers.[2] Fenggang Yang argues that the vicissitudes in China created by the transition to a market economy have created a new kind of angst and the need for a new worldview "to bring sense and order" to peoples' lives.[3] He asserts that Pentecostal spirituality helps meet this need. Chen-Yang Kao argues that the Cultural Revolution (1966–76) paved the way for the emergence of "practice-led Pentecostalism" by

---

1. For example, Hollenweger describes the Pentecostal movement as "a movement whose main characteristic is not verbal agreement but correspondence of sentiments" (*Pentecostals*, xx). See also Kärkkäinen, "Pneumatology of Religions," 160, and Anderson, *Introduction*, 14.
2. Hunter and Chan, *Protestantism in Contemporary China*, 141–63.
3. Yang, "Lost in the Market, Saved at MacDonald's," 432.

stripping away various forms of ecclesiastical authority that, without the strident persecution that characterized this era, would have been present. Thus, "there was no Christian authority that was able to provide a doctrinal framework or institutional regulation for discouraging those ecstatic experiences and the exercise of charismatic power."[4]

While all of these explanations may help us in varying degrees understand more clearly why China, like so many places around the world, has been such fertile ground for Pentecostal church growth, they all fail to account for the central dynamic: the biblical record. Yes, the Pentecostal faith, with its openness to the supernatural, provides spiritual resources for significant felt needs. Yes, the Pentecostal message, centered as it is in faith in Christ, provides stability in the chaos of moral confusion. And certainly, Pentecostal faith thrives where there is limited ecclesiastical structure. But none of these explanations takes us to the heart of the matter. Pentecostal faith is rooted in the Bible and flows from the conviction that the stories in the book of Acts are our stories: stories that provide models for life and ministry. Is it not significant that the Pentecostal movement in China was given first breath through the printed page?[5] Why should we imagine that it is any different today? Indeed, even among largely illiterate Pentecostals, the stories of the Bible, passed on orally, serve as models for their faith and praxis.

Certainly, not every Chinese believer that prays for the sick, exorcises demons, or prophesies, would affirm a baptism in the Spirit distinct from conversion that is marked by speaking in tongues. Nevertheless, there are a significant number who do.[6] And their influence, as well as the clarity of their biblical convictions, should not be underestimated. The common thread that unites Pentecostals in China with other Pentecostals around the world is their sense of connection with the apostolic church as reflected in the book of Acts. Chinese Pentecostals pray for the sick, worship with joyful abandonment, speak in tongues, and seek the enabling of the Spirit for bold witness in the face of persecution because they find all of these experiences described in the New Testament. The message and methods of the early church are models for their lives and ministry. All of this suggests

---

4. Kao *Cultural Revolution and the Post-Missionary Transformation of Protestantism in China*, 102.

5. See Menzies, "Pentecostals in China," 70–71.

6. Menzies, "Pentecostals in China," 74–90.

DEFINING THE TERM, "PENTECOSTAL"

that Simon Chan is right when he declares, "an adequate definition of Pentecostalism cannot be restricted to phenomenological description."[7]

As I have outlined in this book, the Pentecostal movement has a clear history, rooted in a particular understanding of the New Testament and especially the book of Acts. Thus, it has an important theological message. Furthermore, it is a message that can be clearly defined. Much is made of the theological diversity that marks the Pentecostal movement; but, as I have pointed out, this is in reality a matter of semantics. The terms, Pentecostal, neo-Pentecostal, and charismatic, become meaningful when we give them specific definition and use them in precise ways. When we do not, the result is confusion: a vague, blurry picture of an amorphous movement emerges. Or worse, this lack of precision can result in distortion. It encourages and enables the sort of caricature of the Pentecostal movement recently produced by John MacArthur. In his book, *Strange Fire*, MacArthur paints the entire movement with broad brushstrokes and in this way suggests that all Pentecostals think and act like Benny Hinn or Jan Crouch. Good theologians speak with precision and that is what is needed when discussing the Pentecostal movement.

With this in mind, I would like to suggest the following taxonomy for describing renewalist churches:

- *Pentecostal*: a Christian who believes (or a church which affirms) that the book of Acts provides a model for the contemporary church and, on this basis, encourages every believer to experience a baptism in the Spirit (Acts 2:4), understood as an empowering for mission distinct from regeneration that is marked by speaking in tongues, and who affirms that "signs and wonders," including all of the gifts listed in 1 Corinthians 12:8–10, are to characterize the life of the church today.

- *Neo-Pentecostal*: a Christian who agrees and acts in accordance with all of the Pentecostal tenets listed above except the affirmation that speaking in tongues serves as a normative sign for Spirit baptism.

- *Charismatic*: a Christian who believes that all of the gifts listed in 1 Corinthians 12:8–10, including prophecy, tongues, and healing, are available for the church today; but, rejects the affirmation that baptism in the Spirit (Acts 2:4) is an empowering for mission distinct from regeneration.

---

7. Chan, "Wither Pentecostalism?," 578.

- *Non-Charismatic*: a Christian who rejects the affirmation that baptism in the Spirit (Acts 2:4) is an empowering for mission distinct from regeneration and who also rejects the validity of at least one or more of the gifts of the Spirit listed in 1 Corinthians 12:8–10 for the church today.

All of the categories listed above are compatible with the term, Evangelical. In this book, I have argued that the term, Pentecostal, is not only compatible with the adjective, Evangelical, but incomprehensible apart from it. Thus, to be Pentecostal is, by definition, to be Evangelical.[8] I define "Evangelical" in this way:

- *Evangelical*: a Christian who (or a church that) affirms: the authority of the Bible; the importance of a personal relationship with Christ, who is understood to be the Lord and unique Savior of the world; and that sharing the "good news" of Jesus with non-Christians (evangelism) is a central aspect of the Christian life.

I would also note that the general categories (Pentecostal, neo-Pentecostal, charismatic, non-charismatic) listed above might be qualified by a host of other descriptive terms that offer more precision:

- Theological Orientation: "Evangelical," "ecumenical," "liberal" (e.g., an ecumenical charismatic).
- Denominational Affiliation: "independent," "mainline," "denominational" (e.g., an independent neo-Pentecostal).
- Approach to the Bible: "Evangelical" and the contrasting term, "Spirit-centered." The latter term might be used to describe Christians or churches that feature extra-biblical experiences such as "glory manifestations" (gold dust, angel feathers, etc.). For example, we could speak of a Spirit-centered charismatic church.
- Theological Emphases: "word faith" and "prosperity" would describe those who feature these respective emphases; "third wave" might designate an Evangelical group that emphasizes "signs and wonders" (e.g., third wave charismatics).

Finally, I would suggest that the terms "renewalist" or "continuationist" (as the counterpoint to "cessationist") are particularly useful and

---

8. The one possible exception would be non-trinitarian "Oneness Pentecostals."

appropriate when one wishes to speak more broadly of the Pentecostal and charismatic movements collectively.

A more nuanced approach to the study and discussion of renewalist churches is, I believe, in everyone's best interest. It will help us communicate with one another more effectively. Hopefully, this in turn will enable us to understand and encourage one another as we seek "to speak the truth in love" and together grow into maturity as the body of Christ (Eph 4:15–16).

BIBLIOGRAPHY

Anderson, Allan H. *An Introduction to Pentecostalism: Global Charismatic Christianity.* Cambridge: Cambridge University Press, 2004.

———. "Review of *The Spirit Poured Out on All Flesh: Pentecostalism and the Possibility of Global Theology*." *International Bulletin of Missionary Research* 30 (2006) 160–61.

Archer, Kenneth J. "The Making of an Academic Tradition: The Cleveland School." Presented at the 45th Annual Society for Pentecostal Studies Meeting, San Dimas, CA, Life Pacific College (March 10-12, 2016).

———. *A Pentecostal Hermeneutic for the Twenty-First Century: Spirit, Scripture and Community.* Journal of Pentecostal Theology Supplement Series 28. London: T. & T. Clark International, 2004.

Bailey, Kenneth E. *Jesus Through Middle Eastern Eyes: Cultural Studies in the Gospels.* Downers Grove, IL: IVP Academic, 2008.

Barclay, William. *The Gospel of Luke. The Daily Study Bible Series.* Rev. ed. Philadelphia: Westminster, 1975.

Barratt, David B., and Todd M. Johnson. "Annual Statistical Table on Global Mission: 2001." *International Bulletin of Missionary Research* 25 (2001) 24–25.

Bartleman, Frank. *Azusa Street.* 1925. Reprint, Plainfield, NJ: Logos International, 1980.

Bauckham, Richard J. *Jude, 2 Peter.* Word Biblical Commentary 50. Waco: Word, 1983.

Bebbington, David. *Evangelicalism in Modern Britain: A History from the 1730s to the 1980s.* Grand Rapids: Baker, 1989.

Best, E. "Spirit-Baptism." *Novum Testamentum* 4 (1960) 236–43.

Bock, Darrell L. *Acts.* Baker Exegetical Commentary on the New Testament. Grand Rapids: Baker, 2007.

———. *Luke.* The IVP Commentary Series. Downers Grove: InterVarsity, 1994.

———. *Luke 9.51—24.53.* Baker Exegetical Commentary of the New Testament. Grand Rapids: Baker Academic, 1996.

Brumback, Carl. *What Meaneth This?* Springfield, MO: GPH, 1947.

Bruner, Frederick Dale. *Theology of the Holy Spirit: The Pentecostal Experience and the New Testament Witness.* Grand Rapids: Eerdmans, 1970.

Castelo, Daniel. *Pentecostalism as a Christian Mystical Tradition.* Grand Rapids: Eerdmans, 2017.

Chai, Teresa, ed. *A Theology of the Spirit in Doctrine and Demonstration: Essays in Honor of Wonsuk and Julie Ma.* APTS Press Monographic Series. Baguio City: APTS, 2014.

BIBLIOGRAPHY

Chan, Simon. "Wither Pentecostalism?" In *Asian and Pentecostal: The Charismatic Face of Christianity in Asia*, edited by Allan Anderson and Edmond Tang, 575–86. Costa Mesa: Regnum, 2005.

Cho, Youngmo. *Spirit and Kingdom in the Writings of Luke and Paul: An Attempt to Reconcile these Concepts*. Paternoster Biblical Monographs. Milton Keynes: Paternoster, 2005.

Cox, Harvey. *Fire From Heaven: The Rise of Pentecostal Spirituality and the Reshaping of Religion in the Twenty-first Century*. Reading, PA: Addison-Wesley, 1995.

Cullmann, O. *Christ and Time*. Philadelphia: Westminster, 1964.

Cunningham, Scott. *"Through Many Tribulations:" The Theology of Persecution in Luke-Acts*. Journal for the Study of the New Testament Supplement Series 142. Sheffield: Sheffield Academic Press, 1997.

Dayton, Donald W. "The Doctrine of the Baptism of the Holy Spirit: It's Emergence and Significance." *Wesleyan Theological Journal* 13 (1978) 114–26.

———. *Theological Roots of Pentecostalism*. Metuchen, NJ: Scarecrow, 1987.

Dunn, James D. G. *Baptism in the Holy Spirit*. London: SCM, 1970.

———. "Baptism in the Spirit: A Response to Pentecostal Scholarship." *Journal of Pentecostal Theology* 3 (1993) 3–27.

———. *Jesus and the Spirit: A Study of the Religious and Charismatic Experience of Jesus and the First Christians as Reflected in the New Testament*. London: SCM, 1975.

Ellis, E. Earle. *The Gospel of Luke*. New Century Bible Commentary. Rev. ed. Grand Rapids: Eerdmans, 1974.

Evans, Craig. *Luke*. New International Biblical Commentary. Peabody: Hendrickson, 1990.

Fea, John. "Power from on High in an Age of Ecclesiastical Impotence: The 'Enduement of the Holy Spirit' in American Fundamentalist Thought, 1880–1936." *Fides et Historia* 26 (1994) 23–35.

Fee, Gordon D. *The First Epistle to the Corinthians*. New International Commentary on the New Testament. Grand Rapids: Eerdmans, 1987.

———. *God's Empowering Presence: The Holy Spirit in the Letters of Paul*. Peabody: Hendrickson, 1994.

Findlay, James F., Jr. *Dwight L. Moody: American Evangelist 1837–1899*. Chicago: The University of Chicago Press, 1969.

Frodsham, Stanley H. "Disfellowshiped!." *The Pentecostal Evangel* (August 18, 1928) 7.

———. "Why We Know the Present Pentecostal Movement Is of God: An Answer to a Tract, *Is the Present Tongues Movement of God?*" *The Christian Evangel* (August 9, 1919) 4–5.

Gee, Donald. *All with One Accord*. Springfield, MO: GPH, 1961.

———. *Concerning Spiritual Gifts*. Springfield, MO: GPH, 1972.

———. *Is It God?* Springfield, MO: GPH, 1972.

———. *The Pentecostal Movement, Including the Story of the War Years (1940–1947)*. Rev. ed. London: Elim, 1949.

———. *Why Pentecost?* London: Victory, 1944.

George, Timothy, ed. *Pilgrims on the Sawdust Trail: Evangelical Ecumenism and the Quest for Christian Identity*. Grand Rapids: Baker Academic, 2004.

Gilbertson, Richard. *The Baptism of the Holy Spirit: The Views of A.B. Simpson and His Contemporaries*. Camp Hill, PA: Christian Publications, 1993.

Gloege, Timothy E. W. "A Gilded Age Modernist: Reuben A. Torrey and the Roots of Contemporary Conservative Evangelicalism." In *American Evangelicalism: George*

Marsden and the State of American Religious History, edited by Darren Dochuk et al., 199–229. Notre Dame: University of Notre Dame Press, 2014.

———. *Guaranteed Pure: The Moody Bible Institute, Business, and the Making of Modern Evangelicalism*. Chapel Hill, NC: The University of North Carolina Press, 2015.

Graves, Robert, ed. *Strangers to Fire: When Tradition Trumps Scripture*. Tulsa: Empowered Life, 2014.

Green, Gene L. *Jude and 2 Peter*. Baker Exegetical Commentary on the New Testament. Grand Rapids: Baker Academic, 2008.

Green, Joel B. "Learning Theological Interpretation from Luke." In *Reading Luke: Interpretation, Reflection, Formation*, edited by Craig G. Bartholomew et al., 55–78. Scripture and Hermeneutics Series 6. Grand Rapids: Zondervan, 2005.

———. *The Gospel of Luke*. New International Commentary on the New Testament. Grand Rapids: Eerdmans, 1997.

Gresham, John L. *Charles G. Finney's Doctrine of the Baptism of the Holy Spirit*. Peabody: Hendrickson, 1987.

Hacking, Keith J. *Signs and Wonders, Then and Now: Miracle-working, commissioning and discipleship*. Nottingham: Apollos/IVP, 2006.

Harkness, Robert. *Reuben Archer Torrey: The Man and His Message*. Chicago: The Bible Institute Colportage Association, 1929.

Harvey, Robert, and Philip H. Towner. *2 Peter and Jude*. IVP New Testament Commentary Series 18. Downers Grove, IL: InterVarsity, 2009.

Hattaway, Paul. *Operation China: Introducing All the People of China*. Carlisle, UK: Piquant, 2000.

Hollenweger, Walter J. *The Pentecostals*. Peabody: Hendrickson, 1988.

Horton, Stanley M. *Reflections of An Early American Pentecostal*. Pentecostalism, Around the World. Baguio City: APTS, 2001.

———. "Review of R. A. Torrey, *The Person and Work of the Holy Spirit*." *Paraclete* 3 (1969) 29–30.

Hunter, Alan, and Kim-Kwong Chan. *Protestantism in Contemporary China*. Cambridge: Cambridge University Press, 1993.

Isgrigg, Daniel. "The Pentecostal Evangelical Church: The Theological Self-Identity of the Assemblies of God as Evangelical 'Plus.'" A paper presented at the 46th Meeting of the Society for Pentecostal Studies, March 2017.

Jellicoe, Sidney. "St Luke and the 'Seventy(-Two).'" *New Testament Studies* 6 (1960) 319–21.

Jenkins, Philip. *The New Faces of Christianity: Believing the Bible in the Global South*. New York: Oxford University Press, 2006.

———. *The Next Christendom: The Coming of Global Christianity*. Oxford: Oxford University Press, 2002.

Kalu, Ogbu U. "Sankofa: Pentecostalism and African Cultural Heritage." In *The Spirit in the World: Emerging Pentecostal Theologies in Global Contexts*, edited by Veli-Matti Kärkkäinen, 135–52. Grand Rapids: Eerdmans, 2009.

Kao, Chen-Yang. "The Cultural Revolution and the Post-Missionary Transformation of Protestantism in China." PhD thesis, University of Lancaster, 2009.

Kärkkäinen, Veli-Matti. "How to Speak of the Spirit Among Religions: Trinitarian 'Rules' for a Pneumatological Theology of Religions." *International Bulletin of Missionary Research* 30 (2006) 121–27.

———. "Pentecostal Pneumatology of Religions: The Contribution of Pentecostalism to Our Understanding of the Work of God's Spirit in the World." In *The Spirit in the World: Emerging Pentecostal Theologies in Global Contexts*, edited by Veli-Matti Kärkkäinen, 155-80. Grand Rapids: Eerdmans, 2009.

———. "Theology of the Cross: A Stumbling Block to Pentecostal/Charismatic Spirituality?" In *The Spirit and Spirituality: Essays in Honour of Russell P. Spittler*, edited by Wonsuk Ma and Robert Menzies, 150-63. Journal of Pentecostal Theology Supplement Series 24. London: T&T Clark International, 2004.

———. *Trinity and Revelation*. Vol. 2, *Constructive Christian Theology for the Pluralistic World*. Grand Rapids: Eerdmans, 2014.

Kärkkäinen, Veli-Matti, ed. *The Spirit in the World: Emerging Pentecostal Theologies in Global Contexts*. Grand Rapids: Eerdmans, 2009.

Karris, Robert J. "Missionary Communities: A New Paradigm for the Study of Luke-Acts." *Catholic Biblical Quarterly* 41 (1979) 80-97.

Käsemann, Ernst. *Commentary on Romans*. Grand Rapids: Eerdmans, 1980.

———. *Perspectives on Paul*. Philadelphia: Fortress, 1971.

Keener, Craig S. *Spirit Hermeneutics: Reading Scripture in Light of Pentecost*. Grand Rapids: Eerdmans, 2016.

King, Gerald W. *Disfellowshiped: Pentecostal Responses to Fundamentalism in the United States, 1906-1943*. Eugene, OR: Pickwick, 2011.

Kummel, W. G. *Promise and Fulfillment*. London: SCM, 1957.

Kuzmic, Peter. "A Croatian War-Time Reading." *Journal of Pentecostal Theology* 4 (1994) 17-24.

Ladd, G. E. "The Kingdom of God—Reign or Realm?" *Journal of Biblical Literature* 81 (1962) 230-38.

———. *The Presence of the Future*. Grand Rapids: Eerdmans, 1974.

———. *A Theology of the New Testament*. Revised version edited by Donald A. Hagner. Grand Rapids: Eerdmans, 1993.

Lee, Chang-Soung. "In the Beginning There Was a Theology: The Precedence of Theology over Experience in the Pentecostal Movement." https://pentecost.asia/articles/in-the-beginning-there-was-a-theology-the-precedence-of-theology-over-experience-in-the-pentecostal-movement/.

Luz, Ulrich. "Paul as Mystic." In *The Holy Spirit and Christian Origins: Essays in Honor of James D. G. Dunn*, edited by Graham N. Stanton et al., 131-43. Grand Rapids: Eerdmans, 2004.

Ma, Wonsuk, and Robert Menzies, eds. *The Spirit and Spirituality: Essays in Honour of Russell P. Spittler*. Journal of Pentecostal Theology Supplement Series 24. London: T. & T. Clark International, 2004.

MacArthur, John. *Strange Fire: The Danger of Offending the Holy Spirit with Counterfeit Worship*. Nashville: Nelson, 2013.

Macchia, Frank D. "Sighs Too Deep for Words: Toward a Theology of Glossolalia." *Journal of Pentecostal Theology* 1 (1992) 47-73.

Maddox, Robert. *The Purpose of Luke-Acts*. Edinburgh: T. & T. Clark, 1982.

Marsden, George M. *Fundamentalism and American Culture*. 2nd ed. Oxford: Oxford University Press, 2006.

Marshall, I. Howard. *The Gospel of Luke: A Commentary on the Greek Text*. New International Greek Testament Commentary. Grand Rapids: Eerdmans, 1978.

Martin, David. *Pentecostalism: The World Their Parish*. Oxford: Blackwell, 2002.

Martin, Roger. *R. A. Torrey: Apostle of Certainty*. Murfreesboro, TN: Sword of the Lord, 1976.

Matson, David. *Household Conversion Narratives in Acts: Pattern and Interpretation.* The Library of New Testament Studies 123. Sheffield: Sheffield Academic Press, 1996.
Maynard-Reid, Pedrito U. *Complete Evangelism: The Luke-Acts Model.* Scottdale, PA: Herald, 1997.
Mbiti, J. S. *Bible and Theology in African Christianity.* Nairobi: Oxford University Press, 1986.
McLoughlin, William G., Jr. *Modern Revivalism.* New York: Ronald, 1959.
Menzies, Robert P. "Acts 2:17-21: A Paradigm for Pentecostal Mission." *Journal of Pentecostal Theology* 17 (2008) 200-218.
———. "Complete Evangelism: A Review Essay." *Journal of Pentecostal Theology* 13 (1998) 133-42.
———. *Empowered for Witness: The Spirit in Luke-Acts.* Journal of Pentecostal Theology Supplement Series 6. Sheffield: Sheffield Academic Press, 1994.
———. *The Language of the Spirit: Interpreting and Translating Charismatic Terms.* Cleveland, TN: Centre for Pentecostal Theology, 2010.
———. "The Nature of Pentecostal Theology: A Response to Kärkkäinen and Yong." *Journal of Pentecostal Theology* 26 (2017) 196-213.
———. *Pentecost: This Story is Our Story.* Springfield, MO: GPH, 2013.
———. "Pentecostals in China." In *Global Renewal Christianity: Spirit-Empowered Movements Past, Present, and Future: Asia and Oceania,* edited by Vinson Synan and Amos Yong, 1:67-90. Lake Mary, FL: Charisma House, 2015.
———. "The Persecuted Prophets: A Mirror-Image of Luke's Spirit-Inspired Church." In *The Spirit and Christ in the New Testament & Christian Theology,* edited by I. Howard Marshall et al., 52-70. Grand Rapids: Eerdmans, 2012.
———. "A Review of Darrell Bock's *Acts.*" *Pneuma* 30 (2008) 349-50.
———. "A Review of Keith J. Hacking's *Signs and Wonders, Then and Now: Miracle-working, commissioning and discipleship.*" *Evangelical Quarterly* 79 (2007) 261-65.
———. "The Sending of the Seventy and Luke's Purpose." In *Trajectories in the Book of Acts: Essays in Honor of John Wesley Wykoff,* edited by Paul Alexander et al., 87-113. Eugene, OR: Wipf & Stock, 2010.
———. *Speaking in Tongues: Jesus and the Apostolic Church as Models for the Church Today.* Cleveland, TN: Centre for Pentecostal Theology, 2016.
———. "Subsequence in the Pauline Epistles." *Pneuma* 39 (2017) 342-63.
Menzies, W. William, and Robert P. Menzies. *Spirit and Power: Foundations of Pentecostal Experience.* Grand Rapids: Zondervan, 2000.
Merk, Otto. "Das Reich Gottes in den lukanischen Schriften." In *Wissenschaftgeschichte und Exegese: Gesammelte Aufsätze zum 65. Geburstag,* edited by Martin Karrer and Martin Meiser, 272-91. Beihefte zur Zeitschrift für die Neutestamentliche Wissensch. Berlin: De Gruyter, 1998.
Metaxas, Eric. *Martin Luther: The Man Who Rediscovered God and Changed the World.* New York: Viking, 2017.
Metzger, Bruce. "Seventy or Seventy-Two Disciples?" *New Testament Studies* 5 (1959) 299-306.
Mittelstadt, Martin W. *Reading Luke-Acts in the Pentecostal Tradition.* Cleveland, TN: Centre for Pentecostal Theology, 2010.
———. *The Spirit and Suffering in Luke-Acts: Implications for a Pentecostal Pneumatology.* Journal of Pentecostal Theology Supplement Series 26. London: T. & T. Clark International, 2004.

BIBLIOGRAPHY

Moody, D. L. "Question Drawer." In *College Students at Northfield*, edited by T. J. Shanks, 204–5. New York: Revell, 1888.

Nickle, Keith F. *Preaching the Gospel of Luke: Proclaiming God's Royal Rule*. Louisville: Westminster John Knox, 2000.

Nienkirchen, Charles. "A. B. Simpson: Forerunner and Critic of the Pentecostal Movement." In *The Birth of A Vision*, edited by David F. Hartzfeld and Charles Nienkirchen, 125–64. Beaverlodge, Canada: Buena, 1986.

Noll, Mark A. *The Scandal of the Evangelical Mind*. Grand Rapids: Eerdmans, 1994.

Nolland, J. *Luke 9.21—18.34*. Word Biblical Commentary 35B. Dallas: Word, 1993.

Phillips, Gary W. "Evangelicals and Pluralism: Current Options." *Evangelical Quarterly* 64 (1992) 229–44.

Poirier, John C. *The Tongues of Angels: The Concept of Angelic Languages in Classical Jewish and Christian Texts*. Wissenschaftliche Untersuchungen zum Neuen Testament 2/287. Tübingen: Mohr Siebeck, 2010.

Poloma, Margaret M., and John C. Green. *The Assemblies of God: Godly Love and the Revitalization of American Pentecostalism*. New York: New York University Press, 2010.

Ridderbos, H. N. *The Coming of the Kingdom*. Philadelphia: Reformed and Presbyterian, 1962.

Schnackenburg, R. *God's Rule and Kingdom*. Montreal: Palm, 1963.

Smeeton, Donald D. "The Charismatic Theology of R.A. Torrey." *Paraclete* 14 (1980) 20–23.

Smith, James K. A. "The Closing of the Book: Pentecostals, Evangelicals, and the Sacred Writings." *Journal of Pentecostal Theology* 11 (1997) 49–71.

Spittler, Russell P. "Review of John C. Poirier's *The Tongues of Angels*." *Journal of Biblical and Pneumatological Research* 3 (2011) 146–52.

Stibbe, Mark. *Know Your Spiritual Gifts: Practising the Presents of God*. London: Marshall Pickering, 1997.

Stronstad, Roger. *The Prophethood of All Believers: A Study in Luke's Charismatic Theology*. Journal of Pentecostal Theology Supplement Series 16. Sheffield: Sheffield Academic Press, 1999.

Sweet, J. P. M. "A Sign for Unbelievers: Paul's Attitude to Glossolalia." In *Speaking in Tongues: A Guide to Research on Glossolalia*, edited by Watson E. Mills, 141–64. Grand Rapids: Eerdmans, 1986.

Synan, Vinson. *An Eyewitness Remembers the Century of the Holy Spirit*. Grand Rapids: Chosen, 2010.

———. *The Century of the Holy Spirit: 100 Years of Pentecostal and Charismatic Renewal*. Nashville: Nelson, 2001.

Tannehill, Robert C. *The Narrative Unity of Luke-Acts: A Literary Interpretation*. Vol. 1, *The Gospel According to Luke*. Philadelphia: Fortress, 1986.

Tennent, Timothy C. *Theology in the Context of World Christianity*. Grand Rapids: Zondervan, 2007.

Thiselton, Anthony C. *The Holy Spirit: In Biblical Teaching, through the Centuries, and Today*. Grand Rapids: Eerdmans, 2013.

Tiede, D. L. "The Exaltation of Jesus and the Restoration of Israel in Acts 1." *Harvard Theological Review* 79 (1986) 278–86.

Timenia, Lora Angeline Embudo. "Understanding 'Toronto Blessing' Revivalism's Signs and Wonders Theology in the Filipino Context: with Critical Evaluation from a

Classical Pentecostal Perspective." MTh Thesis, Asia Pacific Theological Seminary, Submitted November, 2019 (soon to be published by APTS Press).

Torrey, R. A. *The Baptism with the Holy Spirit*. Minneapolis: Bethany Fellowship, 1972.

———. *Divine Healing: Does God Perform Miracles Today?* N.p.: Pantianos Classics, 2017.

———. *Great Pulpit Masters: A Book of Sermons*. New York: Revell, 1950.

———. *The Holy Spirit: Who He Is, and What He Does*. New York: Revell, 1927.

———. *The Person and Work of the Holy Spirit*. Rev. ed. Grand Rapids: Zondervan, 1974.

———. *What the Bible Teaches*. New Kensington, PA: Whitaker, 1996.

———. *Why God Used D. L. Moody*. In *How to Pray and Why God Used D. L. Moody*, loc. 1041–520. N.p.: Christian Classics Treasury, 2011. Kindle edition.

Turner, Max. "Does Luke Believe Reception of the 'Spirit of Prophecy' Makes All 'Prophets'? Inviting Dialogue with Roger Stronstad." *Journal of the European Pentecostal Theological Association* 20 (2000) 3–24.

———. "Every Believer as a Witness in Acts?—in Dialogue with John Michael Penney." *Ashland Theological Journal* 30 (1998) 57–71.

———. *The Holy Spirit and Spiritual Gifts Then and Now*. Carlisle: Paternoster, 1996.

———. *Power from on High*. Sheffield: Sheffield Academic Press, 1996.

———. "The Spirit and Salvation in Luke-Acts." In *The Holy Spirit and Christian Origins: Essays in Honor of James D. G. Dunn*, edited by Graham Stanton et al., 103–16. Grand Rapids: Eerdmans, 2004.

Twelftree, Graham H. *People of the Spirit: Exploring Luke's View of the Church*. Grand Rapids: Baker, 2009.

Wacker, Grant. *Heaven Below: Early Pentecostals and American Culture*. Cambridge: Harvard University Press, 2001.

———. "The Holy Spirit and the Spirit of the Age in American Protestantism, 1880–1910." *The Journal of American History* 72 (1985) 45–62.

———. "Travail of a Broken Family: Evangelical Responses to Pentecostalism in America, 1906–1916." *Journal of Ecclesiastical History* 47 (1996) 505–27.

Waldvogel, Edith L. "The 'Overcoming' Life: A Study in the Reformed Evangelical Contribution to Pentecostalism." *Pneuma* 1 (1979) 7–19.

Ward, Horace S., Jr. "The Anti-Pentecostal Argument." In *Aspects of Pentecostal-Charismatic Origins*, edited by Vinson Synan, 99–122. Plainfield, NJ: Logos International, 1975.

Warrington, Keith. *Pentecostal Theology: A Theology of Encounter*. London: T. & T. Clark, 2008.

Wedderburn, A. J. M. "Romans 8.26—Towards a Theology of Glossolalia." *Scottish Journal of Theology* 28 (1975) 369–77.

Williams, J. Rodman. ""Harvey Cox and Pentecostalism: A Review of *Fire From Heaven*." Paper read at the Azua Lectures, Regent University, April 1995. https://aps-journal.com/index.php/APS/article/download/48/45?inline=1.

Wimber, John, and Kevin Springer. *Power Evangelism*. San Francisco: Harper & Row, 1991.

Witherington, Ben, III. *The Acts of the Apostles: A Socio-Rhetorical Commentary*. Grand Rapids: Eerdmans, 1998.

Wright, N. T. *Surprised by Hope: Rethinking Heaven, the Resurrection, and the Mission of the Church*. New York: HarperOne, 2008.

Yang, Fenggang. "Lost in the Market, Saved at MacDonald's: Conversion to Christianity in Urban China." *Journal for the Scientific Study of Religion* 44 (2005) 423–41.

Yong, Amos. *Beyond the Impasse: Toward a Pneumatological Theology of Religions*. Grand Rapids: Baker Academic, 2003.

———. *Discerning the Spirit(s): A Pentecostal-Charismatic Contribution to Christian Theology of Religions*. Journal of Pentecostal Theology Supplement Series 20. Sheffield: Sheffield Academic Press, 2000.

———. "From Azusa Street to the Bo Tree and Back: Strange Babblings and Interreligious Interpretations in the Pentecostal Encounter with Buddhism." In *The Spirit in the World: Emerging Pentecostal Theologies in Global Contexts*, edited by Veli-Matti Kärkkäinen, 203–26. Grand Rapids: Eerdmans, 2009.

———. *Spirit of Love: A Trinitarian Theology of Grace*. Baylor: Baylor University Press, 2012.

———. *The Spirit Poured Out on All Flesh: Pentecostalism and the Possibility of Global Theology*. Grand Rapids: Baker Academic, 2005.

———. *Who Is the Holy Spirit? A Walk with the Apostles*. Brewster, MA: Paraclete, 2011.

INDEX OF NAMES

Abrams, Minnie, 31n133
Ananias, 116
Anderson, Allan H., 104, 127, 131n31
Archer, Kenneth J., 12n40, 16, 34n147, 39n150
Aristotle, 97

Bailey, Kenneth E., 94, 95n7
Barclay, William, 74
Barnabas, 48
Barratt, David B., 50n21
Bartleman, Frank, 26nn110–11, 32
Bauckham, Richard J., 62n21
Bebbington, David, xvin3, xvn3
Bediako, Kwame, 126
Bell, E. N., 31n133
Bernheim, David, 140
Bernheim, Max and Emily, 140–41, 142
Best, E., 44n8
Bock, Darrell L., 45n11, 45n12, 82, 109n10
Boddy, A., 31n133
Brumback, Carl, 31, 31n134
Bruner, Frederick Dale, 31n137, 32
Burgess, Marie, 32

Calvin, John, 12, 106
Castelo, Daniel, xviiin9, xviin9, 35n148
Chan, Kim-Kwong, 143
Chan, Simon, 145
Cho, David Yonggi, 112n16
Cho, Youngmo, 77n15
Cornelius, 46, 135
Cox, Harvey, 136–37
Crouch, Jan, 145

Cullmann, O., 75n8
Cunningham, Scott, 110n13

Dayton, Donald W., 7–8, 9n28, 12
Dowie, John Alexander, 29–30, 34
Dunn, James D. G., 42n2, 43, 59, 63, 64n25, 66–67, 69nn36–37, 70n38, 109n11
Durham, William, 20n81, 32

Eldad, 46
Ellis, E. Earle, 83n26
Evans, Craig, 45n11

Fea, John, 3n1
Fee, Gordon D., 57, 66n28
Findlay, James F., Jr., 30n129
Finney, Charles G., 5, 8, 9, 32
Fletcher, John, 7, 8, 12
Frodsham, Stanley H., 22–24

Gang, Yi Zhi, 39n149
Gee, Donald, 31, 86
George, Timothy, 139n1
Gilbertson, Richard, 9n26, 9n27, 11n35, 12n38, 32n143
Gloege, Timothy E. W., 16n59, 17n61, 18n73, 24, 25n104, 27, 28–29, 29nn124–25, 30nn129–31, 32n139, 32n142, 33nn144–45
Gordon, A. J., 4, 8, 9
Gortner, J. Narver, 31n133
Graves, Robert, xvn1
Gray, James M., 30, 33
Green, Gene L., 60n16

INDEX OF NAMES

Green, Joel B., 45n11, 111n15
Green, John C., 35n148
Gresham, John L., 9n27

Hacking, Keith J., 109n10
Harvey, Robert, 60
Hattaway, Paul, 133n34–134n34
Hinn, Benny, 145
Hollenweger, Walter J., 31n132, 126, 127, 143
Holsinger, Calvin, 96n8
Horton, Stanley M., 18n73, 19n75, 32
Hunter, Alan, 143
Hus, Jan, 98

Isgrigg, Daniel, xvn2, xviin7, xviiin10

Jacob, 49
James, 60
Jellicoe, Sidney, 45n10
Jenkins, Philip, 4n2, 24n101, 126
Jesus Christ, xviii, xix, xx, 7, 14, 14n47, 17, 23, 41, 42n3, 44, 45, 46, 48, 49, 49n20, 50, 51, 53, 55, 57, 60, 61, 62, 63, 67, 74, 75, 75n10, 76, 77, 78, 79, 80, 81, 82, 83, 84, 85, 87, 88, 92, 93, 94, 95, 96, 98, 99, 101, 101n16, 103, 105, 108, 110, 111, 113, 114, 116, 117, 132, 134, 135, 136, 137, 142
Joel, 80, 111, 112, 113, 116, 134, 135
John, xix–xx, 41, 102, 114–15, 116, 132, 136, 142
John the Baptist, 43, 44, 82, 83
Johnson, Todd M., 50n21
Joshua, 46
Jude, 60

Kalu, Obu U., 125–26
Kant, Immanuel, 39n150
Kao, Chen-Yang, 143, 144n4
Kärkkäinen, Veli-Matti, 85n28, 121–31, 136n37, 137, 143n1
Karris, Robert J., 110n14, 115n20
Käsemann, Ernst, 66n28, 68n31, 70
Keener, Craig S., xixn11, 39n150
King, Gerald W., 22n90, 27n112, 28n120, 31n135, 33n146

Kummel, W. G., 75n8, 76n12
Kuzmic, Peter, 122n3, 130n27, 138

Ladd, George, 75
Lee, Chang-Soung, xviiin10
Leigh, David, 31n133
Luke, 12, 13, 41, 42, 42n3, 43, 44, 45, 46, 47, 47n16, 48, 49n20, 50, 52, 78, 79, 80, 81, 83, 84, 87, 88, 100, 101, 101n16, 102, 105, 106, 106n6, 107, 109, 110, 111, 112, 112n17, 113, 114, 116, 117, 132, 134, 135, 136
Lupton, 22n90
Luther, Martin, xx, 12, 85, 96, 97, 97n9, 98, 99, 100, 102, 103, 106
Luz, Ulrich, 58, 59n13, 73

Ma, Mr. (#1), 91
Ma, Mr. (#2), 132, 132n33
Ma, Wonsuk, 121n1
MacArthur, John, xv, 99n14, 142n2, 145
Macchia, Frank D., 66n27
Maddox, Robert, 110n12
Marsden, George M., 5, 15, 16n57, 25n106, 26nn108–109, 27n115, 31n132, 61n20
Marshall, I. Howard, 45n11, 81, 87n32
Martin, David, 129n25
Martin, Roger, 4n3, 9n29, 11n37, 17n64, 20nn77–80, 25
Matson, David, 116n22
Maynard-Reid, Pedrito U., 79
Mbiti, John, 126
McLoughlin, William G., Jr., 15, 25
McPherson, Aimee Semple, 33
Medad, 46
Menzies, Robert P., xixn12, 13n41, 13n42, 14n50, 15n53, 18n71, 19n75, 22n89, 39n150, 44n9, 46n13, 47n16, 51n1, 52nn2–3, 56n8, 68nn33–34, 80n18, 105n4, 106n5, 107n8, 108n9, 109n10, 110n14, 121n1, 130n26, 134n36, 144nn5–6
Menzies, W. William, xixn12, 13n41, 39n150, 80n18, 106n5, 107n8

INDEX OF NAMES

Merk, Otto, 76n12
Metaxas, Eric, 97nn9-11, 98n12
Metzger, Bruce, 45
Mittelstadt, Martin W.,
    xixn13, 85n28, 110n13
Moltmann, Jürgen, 122n3, 130n27
Moody, D. L., 5, 7, 8, 10n34, 11, 13n43,
    18, 19-20, 30, 32n143, 61n20
Moses, 20, 45, 46, 47, 48, 114

Nickle, Keith F., 46n14
Nienkirchen, Charles, 32n143
Nolland, John, 45n11

Olazbal, Francisco, 32

Parham, Charles, 17, 20, 20n81,
    22n90, 32, 38, 127
Paul, xx, 9-10, 12, 13, 21, 41, 42n3, 48,
    50, 51-72, 78, 85, 86, 93, 95, 99,
    101, 102, 106, 106n6, 107, 108,
    110, 116, 117, 132, 136
Peter, 14, 41, 49n20, 78, 80, 109, 110,
    111, 114-15, 116, 132, 134, 135
Peterson, Eugene, 75n7
Philip, 48, 110, 117
Phillips, Gary W., 131n30
Phillips, J. B., 74
Poirier, John C., 92n2, 94n5
Poloma, Margaret M., 35n148

Ridderbos, H. N., 75n8

Schleiermacher, Friedrich, 39n150
Schnackenburg, R., 75n8
Seymour, William, 17, 26,
    38, 39, 86, 127
Simeon, 44
Simpson, A. B., 4, 8, 9, 12n38, 32n143
Smeeton, Donald D.,
    19n75, 31n134, 32n141
Smith, James K. A., 34n147, 35n147
Spittler, Russell P., 94n5, 121
Springer, Kevin, 107n7

Stephen, 41, 110, 115, 116, 117
Stibbe, Mark, 53n6
Stronstad, Roger, 116n21
Sweet, J. P. M., 62n22, 68n32
Synan, Vinson, 17nn62-63,
    43n4, 73n2, 74n3

Tannehill, Robert C., 45n11, 84n27
Tennent, Timothy C., 100n15
Tertullian, 141
Thiselton, Anthony C., 106n6
Tiede, D. L., 48n18
Timenia, Lora Ange-
    line Embudo, 86n29
Torrey, Blanche, 29
Torrey, Edith, 33
Torrey, Elizabeth, 29, 29n127
Torrey, Mrs., 33
Torrey, R. A., 3-35, 42, 49, 61n20, 139
Towner, Philip H., 60
Turner, Max, 42n2, 46n15, 47n15,
    47n17, 49n20, 55n7
Twelftree, Graham H., 129

Wacker, Grant, 15, 20n82, 21nn87-88,
    25n105, 27n116, 50n22, 104n1
Waldvogel, Edith L., 15n54, 33n146
Ward, Horace S., Jr., 31, 32n138
Warrington, Keith, 105n3
Wedderburn, A. J. M., 69n35
Wesley, John, 8, 12, 32
Williams, J. Rodman, 136-37
Wimber, John, 107n7
Witherington, Ben, III, 109n10, 109n11
Woodworth-Etter, Maria, 22n90
Wright, N. T., 83n25
Wycliffe, John, 98

Yang, Fenggang, 143
Yong, Amos, 39n150, 121, 122, 124,
    128, 129n24, 130, 131-34,
    136, 136n37, 137

Zheng, Uncle, xxin14

INDEX OF ANCIENT DOCUMENTS

OLD TESTAMENT

Genesis

35:23–26	45

Exodus

13:9–10, 16	92n1

Numbers

11	46
11:24–30	45
11:25	46
11:29	46, 79, 114
15:38–40	92n1

Deuteronomy

6:8	92n1
11:18	92n1

Joshua

1:2	20

Psalms

115:5	52
139:7–12	134

Isaiah

4:4	43
11:2–4	44
11:4	44
32:15	49n20
49:6	46, 48, 48n19, 49, 49n20, 114
53	48
61:1	14
61:1–2	111

Jeremiah

31:31–34	12n38

Ezekiel

36:25–28	12n38

Joel

	113
2:28	114
2:28–32	111, 112, 134, 135
2:30	80
2:30–31	79

DEUTEROCANONICAL BOOKS

1 Enoch

49:3	43
62:2	43, 44n7

Psalms of Solomon

17–18	82
17:26–37	44
17:37	44

DEAD SEA SCROLLS
1QSb

5:24–25	44n7

NEW TESTAMENT
Matthew

6:9	95
6:9–13	93
17:9	113n18
28:18–20	107

Mark

	66n29, 111
5:5	67
9:26	67
14:35–36	93
14:36	93, 94
16	23
16:9–20	52
16:17	66n29

Luke

	16, 19, 76, 77, 111, 114
1:35	49n20
1:69, 71, 77	76, 76n11
1:77	76n11
2:27	62n21
2:30	76, 76n11
2:32	48n19
2:34	44
3:3	76n11
3:6	76n11
3:16	43, 83
3:16–17	43
3:17	44, 83
3:21–22	14
4	111
4:1	62n21
4:1, 14, 18	14
4:16–21	14
4:16–30	111
4:18	76n11
4:18–19	114
4:21	75
6:9	76n11
6:22–23	115n20
7:21–23	79, 82
7:23	82
7:28	75n10
7:48	78
7:50	76, 76n11, 78
8:12, 36, 48	76n11
8:12, 50	76
9:1–2	79
9:24	76n11
9:26	83
9:27	83
9:39	67
9:57–62	78
10:1	45, 46, 47, 49
10:1–16	44–47, 47n16
10:4	47n16
10:9	47, 79
10:16	45
10:18	75
10:21	xx
11:1	93
11:1–4	93, 101n16, 102
11:1–13	xx
11:2	83, 85
11:2–4	93
11:3	83
11:9–13	18n71
11:13	42n3, 49n20, 71, 101n16
11:13, 20	83
11:20	75, 79, 82
12:8	115n20
12:11–12	107, 114
12:37–46	83
13:23	76n11
13:28	75n10
13:28–29	75
13:29	78

INDEX OF ANCIENT DOCUMENTS

14:14	77, 78
14:16–24	78
14:26–35	78
14:47–48	48
15:11–32	95
16:16	75, 75n10, 83
16:19–31	83
17:18	76
17:19	76, 76n11
17:20–21	74, 82, 87, 88
17:21	74, 75, 81, 87
17:22–37	83
17:23	83
18:24	75n10
18:26	76n11
18:42	76
19:7–9	79
19:9	76n11
19:10	xviii, 76n11
19:11	75
20:35	77
22:27–30	78
22:29	75
22:36	47n16
24:5–7	47
24:25–26	48
24:27	48
24:44	48
24:45	48
24:45–49	47–49
24:46	48
24:47	48, 49, 76n11
24:47–49	49n20
24:48	49
24:49	5, 15, 15n51, 49n20
49:6	49n20

John

1:12	xix–xx
3:5–8	136
3:16	102
20:22	136

Acts

xix, xx, 7, 8, 16, 19, 34, 41, 46, 48, 51, 66n29, 76, 77, 78, 79, 80, 105, 106, 107, 108, 116, 117, 123, 144, 145

1–2	108, 109n10
1:4–5	15, 43, 44
1:4–8	46, 49n20
1:5	5, 7, 43, 47, 50
1:5, 8	9
1:6	49
1:8	31, 42, 48, 49, 49n20, 50, 105, 107, 108, 123, 132, 136
2	16, 23, 42, 46, 53n5, 100, 134, 135, 136
2 and 10	134
2:4	xvi, 5, 9, 100, 101, 106, 127, 134, 145, 146
2:4–11	66n29
2:5	100
2:5–6	135
2:6	100
2:7–8	100
2:11	61, 63n23, 100
2:13, 15–17	134
2:14–41	111
2:16–18	62
2:16–21	14
2:17	111, 113, 114, 134
2:17–18	42n3, 46, 49, 49n20, 134
2:17–21	111–16, 132
2:17–22	15
2:18	112, 114, 135
2:19	80, 84, 88, 107, 112, 113
2:19, 22, 43	80n17
2:19–20	80, 113
2:19–22	82
2:20	112
2:21	112
2:21, 40, 47	76n13
2:22	80, 84, 88, 113
2:32	77
2:33	79, 101, 135, 136, 137
2:36	135
2:38	76n13
2:39	14
2:43	82, 113
2:47	76, 78
3:15	115
4	115
4:2	77

Acts (continued)

Reference	Pages
4:8	115
4:9, 12	76n13
4:9, 33	77
4:12	76, 76n13, 132
4:19–20	115
4:20	132
4:29–30	84
4:30	80n17
4:31	46, 80, 107
4:31, 33	9, 42n3
5	115
5:12	80, 80n17
5:28	115
5:29–32	115
5:31	76n13, 78
5:41–42	115
6:8	80, 80n17
6:10	115
7	115
7:25	76n13
7:31	113n18
7:36	80n17
7:51–52	115
7:55	115
7:55–56	115n20
8:12	47, 76, 77
8:12–16	7
8:12–17	15, 15n51
8:14–17	46
8:34	48
8:35	48
9:10, 12	113n18
9:10–12	113n19
9:16	116
10	136
10:2–6	5
10:3, 17, 19	113n18, 113n19
10:34	134
10:34–35	134
10:38	14
10:42–43	135
10:42–48	135
10:43	76n14, 78, 136
10:43–46	62, 76n13
10:44	5
10:44–48	46, 135
10:45	5
10:45–46	135
10:46	63n23, 66n29
11:5	113n18, 113n19
11:6	5
11:14	76, 76n13
11:16	43
12:9	113n18
13:26, 47	76n13
13:38	76n13
13:38–39	76n14
13:47	48
14:3	80, 80n17
14:9	76n13, 76n14
14:22	75n10, 77
15:1, 11	76n13
15:11	76
15:12	80n17
16:7	77
16:9–10	112n7, 113n18, 113n19
16:17	76n13
16:30–31	76n13, 76n14
16:31	76
17:24–31	53
18:9	113n18
18:9–10	113n19
19:1–6	15, 15n51
19:1–7	18n71, 46
19:6	63n23, 66n29
19:8	77
19:21	62n21
20:25	77
24:15, 21	77
26:18	76n13, 76n14, 78
26:23	48n19, 77
27:20, 31	76n13
27:34	76n13
28:23, 31	77
28:28	76n13
28:31	76, 116

Romans

Reference	Pages
	106
1:16	132
1:16–17	96
6:1	69n37
6:4–5	70n38

INDEX OF ANCIENT DOCUMENTS

7–8	12n38	12:8–10	xvi, 145, 146
8	64, 68	12:10	53
8:2	9	12:10, 30	53, 69
8:9–13	65	12:13	13, 42
8:14–17	65	12–14	21, 51, 52, 53, 54, 55, 56, 57–58, 66n29, 72, 86, 107, 108
8:15	66, 67, 93, 101		
8:15–16	xx, 61, 93, 99, 99n13	12:30	10, 19, 19n75, 21, 53n4, 68n33
8:15–16, 26–27	66n29		
8:15–17	95	12:31	72
8:16	61, 65, 67, 99	13:1	xx, 53, 53n4, 55
8:16, 23	65	14	66n29, 71
8:17	67	14:2	53, 54, 56, 57
8:18	65	14:2, 4, 6, 13, 18, 23, 27, 39	53n4
8:18–27	67	14:2, 14–17	61
8:22	65, 67	14:2, 16	58
8:23	65, 67	14:4	54, 56
8:23, 39	65	14:5	55, 56
8:26	64, 65, 66, 66n27, 67, 68, 69, 69n36, 70, 71	14:5, 18, 39	68n33
		14:6–19, 28	53
8:26–27	61, 65	14:9	54
8:27	66	14:14	53, 59
12	69	14:14–15	57, 59
12:6–8	69	14:14–17	57, 59, 63, 99n13
13:13	69n37	14:15	57n11, 60, 63, 64
14:1—15:6	69, 69n37	14:15–16	60
16:17–18	69n37	14:15–17	62, 71
16:17–20	69	14:16	59n14
		14:16–17	59, 61, 63
		14:17	59, 71
		14:18	56

1 Corinthians

	56, 66n29, 71
1–4	69n37
1:4–7	55
5–6	69n37
8	69n37
8:26	69
10:23–33	69n37
11:17–22	69n37
12	9, 13
12:2	52
12:2–3	59, 63, 99n13
12:3	53, 57, 61, 62n21, 136
12:4	53
12:4, 8–11	10
12:4–6	54
12:4–11	21
12:7	54
12:7–11	58

14:20	54
14:23–25	54, 71
14:27	54
14:39	56, 62
15:12	70

2 Corinthians

5:1–4	68
5:4	66n29
5:14–15	132

Galatians

	106
3:2, 14	12n38
4:6	61, 66, 67, 93, 99, 99n13, 101
4:6–7	xx, 93

Galatians *(continued)*

5:22–23	107

Ephesians

2:19	95
3:6	56
4:11–16	95
4:15–16	147
5:18	63, 64, 99n13
5:18–20	62
5:18–21	63, 64
5:19	63, 66n29, 71, 71n40
5:19b	63
5:21	63
6:17	59
6:18	59, 60, 62, 63, 66n29, 99n13

Colossians

3:16	63, 64, 66n29, 71, 71n40, 99n13

1 Thessalonians

5:16–18	62
5:16–22	62
5:19	62, 63, 66n29, 71, 99n13
5:19–20	62
5:19–22	62

2 Timothy

2:8–10	132

Jude

	60
8	60n17, 112
19	60
20	63, 66n29, 71, 99n13

Revelation

7:9–10	101, 142

www.ingramcontent.com/pod-product-compliance
Lightning Source LLC
Chambersburg PA
CBHW020849160426
43192CB00007B/847